HANDCRAFTED SHELVES & CABINETS

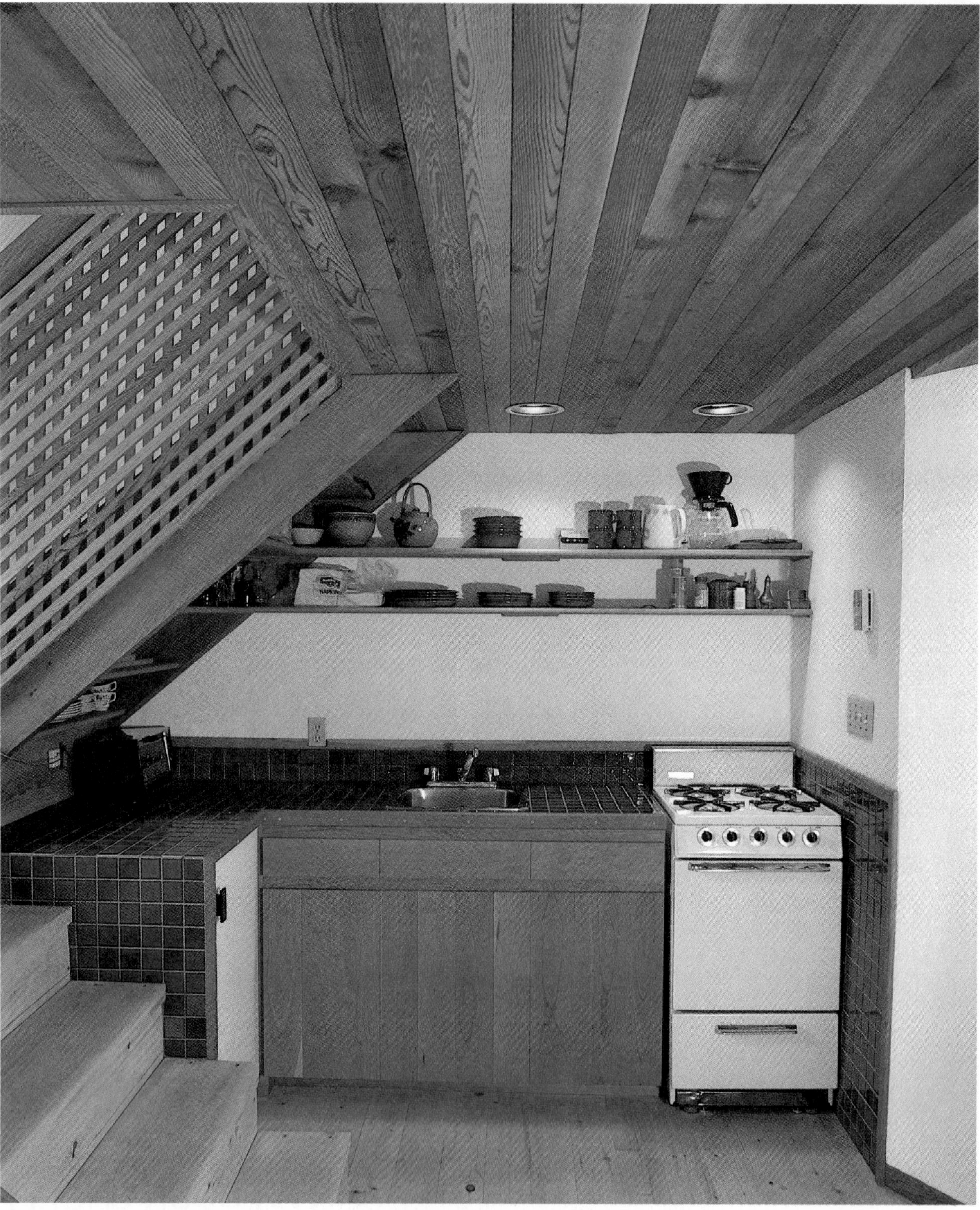

HANDCRAFTED SHELVES & CABINETS

by

William H. Hylton
Marilyn Hodges and Roger B. Yepsen, Jr.

Michael Kanouff and Mitch Mandel photographs
Barbara Field illustrations
Amy Zaffarano Rowland and William H. Hylton editors

Rodale Press, Emmaus, Pennsylvania

Printed in the United States of America

Book and cover design by Barbara Field
Page layout by Anita Noble

Library of Congress Cataloging in Publication Data

Hylton, William H.
Handcrafted shelves & cabinets.

Bibliography: p.
Includes index.
1. Cabinet-work. 2. Shelving (Furniture) I. Hodges, Marilyn. II. Yepsen, Roger B. III. Rowland, Amy Zaffarano. IV. Title. V. Title: Handcrafted shelves and cabinets.
TT197.H95 1984 684.1'6 84-6816

ISBN 0-87857-481-6 hardcover
ISBN 0-87857-482-4 paperback

4 6 8 10 9 7 5 hardcover
4 6 8 10 9 7 5 3 paperback

CONTENTS

ACKNOWLEDGMENTS

Just as a lot more is involved in crafting a cabinet than meets the eye, so too with a book, particularly a book like this one. *Handcrafted Shelves and Cabinets* is the work of many hands and heads.

Amy Zaffarano Rowland did the initial shaping of the book. The author of *Handcrafted Doors and Windows,* she shaped this book by establishing the structure, selecting the projects and craftsmen for "A Gallery of Shelves and Cabinets," assigning photographs, doing research and conducting interviews, and writing the Appendices.

Barbara Field, like Amy, holds a tenured position on the team. She developed the basic design for this book when she designed *Handcrafted Doors and Windows.* With Amy, she spent weeks making the initial Gallery and photo selections and creating basic layouts. Equally as important, she stepped in as illustrator, penciling the drawings that are so important to an understanding of *how* pieces of wood are assembled to make shelves and cabinets.

Although the work of a dozen or more photographers is displayed in this book, Mitch Mandel and Michael Kanouff earned top billing by taking between them about 60 percent of the photos used. Mitch, a staff photographer, roamed the East and Midwest, while Michael, a freelancer, covered the West Coast.

Marilyn Hodges and Roger Yepsen wrote the Gallery section. Through interviews, each mastered the construction details of particular projects, then tried—and succeeded, I think—to convey in words a picture of each craftsman who made an item, as well as explaining how it was built.

In addition, Marilyn served informally as *my* editor as I wrote the text of "The Making of Shelves and Cabinets." She and other people on the staff played a part in selecting photos for inclusion, but the final choice had to be mine.

The finishing touches were applied by copyeditor Tina Negron and designer Anita Noble. The work they did has a lot in common with hand sanding and hand rubbing the almost-finished cabinet. It is laborious and thankless, yet without it, the work that has gone before is wasted.

The work of these editorial and visual artists wouldn't have meant much without the works of and cooperation and information from dozens of craftsmen; these artists made the cabinets you see in these pages and were willing to talk to us about why and how they did what they did. A number of them—Ellis Walentine, Steve Ripper, Larry Golden, Jack Larimore, Phil Gehret, and Fred Matlack—submitted to extended interviews that served as the basis for the text of "The Making of Shelves and Cabinets." Then, on short notice they read and commented on the final manuscript. For all this, I am particularly appreciative.

There are literally hundreds of others who made small but important contributions: a name or telephone number, a bit of cabinetmaking advice, a word of encouragement. We thank them all.

William H. Hylton

INTRODUCTION

What this book is about is designing and building custom cabinetry. It is an appreciation of woodworking as manifested in shelves, dressers and chests, kitchen cabinets, bathroom vanities, armoires, little cupboards and all other sorts of cabinetry.

It is a picture book—a book to *look* at—first. (Whether it is that foremost must be decided by you.) The photographs show the work of better than half-a-hundred woodworkers, some of them amateurs, but most of them professionals. All kinds, designs and styles of cabinets are shown. The idea is to give you a look at a variety of custom cabinets, including photo studies of some of the details—the wood and its figure, inlays, the fit of mating pieces and the tightness of joints, the purely functional and decoratively useful hardware, the finishes.

You may draw from the photos what you will: inspira-

Cabinetmaker Alex MacLean converted "one of those big wasted space closets" into a child's study nook. The tall cabinet houses clothes that ordinarily would be hung in a closet, the desk provides a workplace, and the shelves display stuffed animals, books and other possessions.

tion, ideas, encouragement, fair warning.

Handcrafted Shelves and Cabinets is a book of verbal information second. Rather than recite dull facts found in almost *all* books about woodworking, we chose instead to make an effort to convey the woodworking sensibilities of the individuals behind the cabinets being shown.

Sure, the cabinets are wood and glue and fasteners. Their bits and pieces are united through exactly the sorts of joints shown in *every* woodworking book (including this one). So technique is important.

And yes, the cabinets are functional first, serving as the repositories of dishes and cans and jars and clothing, even unmentionables, and books and games and papers and files and junk. But they are creative works, too. They are cultural artifacts; perhaps some are even artworks. They are pleasant to look at, and by all accounts, wonderful to live with.

Moreover, they are, for the most part, exquisitely made. Perfectly square cases, sound, well-hung doors, smoothly opening drawers. Tight glue lines. Smooth, flawless surfaces. To be sure, there are a couple of deceptive pieces herein, the kind that look great but have blobs of glue and a bent nail or two hidden in a dark inside corner or at the back of a drawer. But I'd bet you won't be able to identify them.

The cabinets, in other words, are products of hard-and-fast technique, but more than that, they are extensions of the personalities of their makers. That's why it seems so appropriate to focus on the cabinetmakers as much as their cabinets, and on *why* they do what they do.

I wanted to go beyond recitations of what joints were used where, and get into *why* the joints were used. I wanted to get into *why* a particular material was used. Or *why* a particular work sequence was followed. Or *why* a certain finish or bit of hardware was chosen.

These cabinets, made by Gary Church for a California kitchen, are out of the ordinary only in appearance. Their carcasses are made of high-grade plywood. The joinery is not unusual. But two native California woods are used where appearance counts: tan oak for the various frames, sycamore for the panels, including the exposed cabinet end panels. The black accent stripes are ebony.

As an amateur woodworker—particularly as one who struggles to avoid being amateurish—I already know there is more than one acceptable solution to every woodworking problem. But I have had the sense that there is a *best* solution, and I often believe it's beyond my grasp, either because I haven't the proper tool, or the material is too expensive, or the technique is one I haven't mastered, or—let's be honest—I haven't the patience for it. So ofttimes when I settle on a solution I can deal with, I end up harboring a feeling of dissatisfaction: there is a better solution, but I'm not woodworker enough to make it work.

If you are like me, you should take heart. I have. Page through this book. Study the photos. Read the text. It encouraged *me* to be involved in this book's creation. It created a broad perspective for me to work in. Knowing *why* is as important as knowing *how.* And so is knowing that *every* solution is a compromise.

Even the most dogmatic woodworker, I discovered, makes compromises. Some woodworkers portray their craft as a procession of compromises. They talk in terms of appropriate choices, for example. Others, those dogmatic ones, come across as less flexible, but even they weigh their decisions. The craft is a succession of individual choices.

So in interviewing men who are woodworkers for their livelihood, I found myself drawn simultaneously to very different individuals. I could applaud a dedication to craft at the same time I could join in a sneer at its pretenses. There are guys here who have a touch of the poseur in their finishes, posturing either as uncompromising artists or as men who brook no such nonsense. And I liked both types and learned from both types.

What I learned, along with what Roger, Marilyn and Amy learned, we have tried to pass along. We've tried to give some whys along with the hows. We've tried to create a context; if you don't like Clye Cabinetmaker's work, you probably won't want to take his advice. But at least you'll have a picture of who is giving the advice, and you'll be able to appreciate why he gives it.

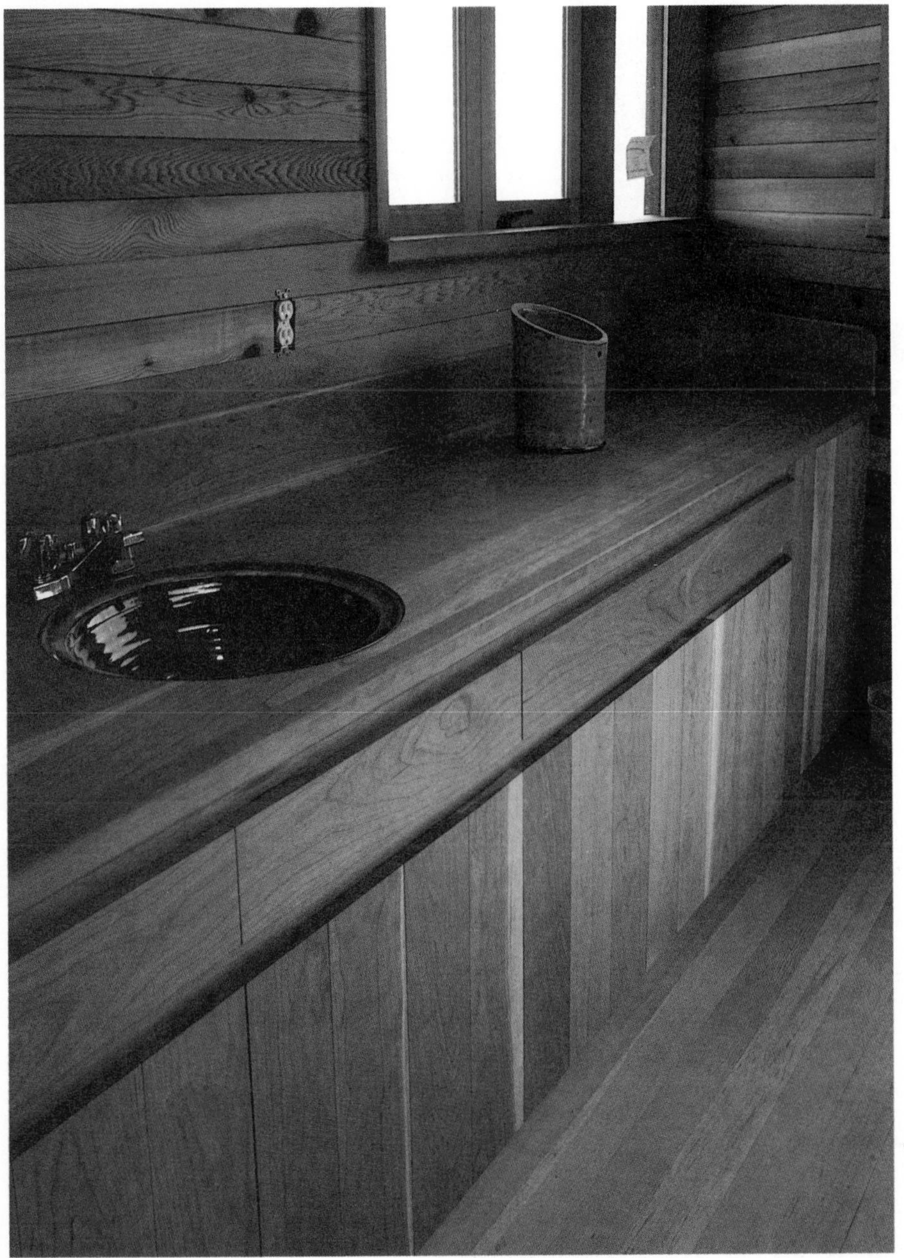

There are situations that de-mand *handcrafted cabinetry. This bathroom in a custom-built house in British Columbia had to have a vanity custom-made to fit the angle at which the walls converge, but also to complement the character of the room, with its warm, native wood paneling.*

THE MAKING OF SHELVES AND CABINETS

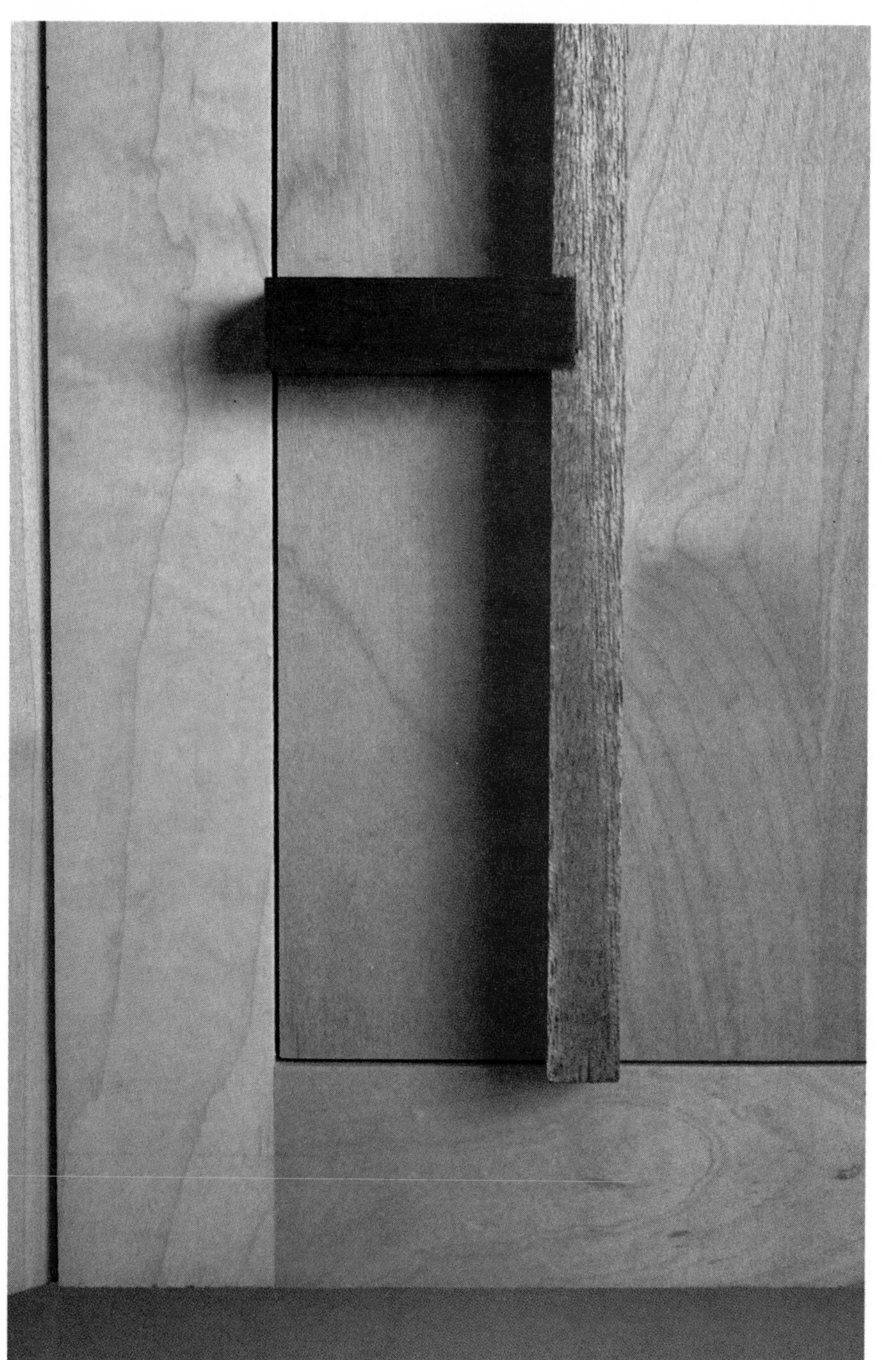

CABINETS AND THEIR MAKERS

The cabinets and shelves you see in this book were made by people who, at one time, knew nothing about wood or tools or cabinetmaking. Each was, at one time, a rank novice.

I bring this up now so that, if you are like me, you will bear in mind that these craftsmen didn't spring from a knothole fully realized. They floundered along for a time, too.

None of them are novices any longer. A few are amateurs — but that's no liability. Some are hungry professionals — capable, imaginative, but chronically short of paying work. Others are productively busy. All are craftsmen.

The work of all of them seems in one way or another remarkable. That is instantly apparent. Even in photographs. The goal of these craftsmen was uniform: To make a utilitarian object that was beautiful. Yet because they are all individuals, with unique visions, perspectives and skills, each came up with a different way of achieving this goal.

Ellis Walentine, who designed and, with his brother Craig, crafted the built-in on the front cover, has been making custom furniture and cabinets as a professional for ten years, learning on the job. It takes a certain chutzpah to turn pro on the basis of a single commission, but, according to Walentine, that's basically what he did. After college, he worked here and there in construction, then tried his hand at making a table. The interior designer who became his first customer saw it, liked it, and asked Walentine to make one for a customer. That first commission led to others. Ellis has learned a great deal since then, but has no apologies for shortcomings his early creations might have. "Anything I make is a statement of my level of skill at the time," he explains.

Walentine's work, what I've seen of it, tends to be along traditional lines, meaning he designs variations on classical themes. It's conservative good taste.

His personal design style is an amalgam of influences: "Greene and Greene, Japanese architecture and the whole functional-naturalistic philosophy behind it, art deco masterpieces in their distinctiveness and choice of elegant materials, and the 'workman's aesthetic,' which arises from experience in building something," he says. Of these, he is somewhat wary of the workman's aesthetic. "The workman's aesthetic reflects past experience," he explains, "the way you're accustomed to doing things. As such, it is self-limiting and can be prejudicial to the design problem at hand."

Greene and Greene, by way of elaboration, are Charles and Henry Greene, turn-of-the-century architects who not only designed a structure but also all of its furniture. The brothers grew up in St. Louis, where their education included daily stints in the workshop. After studying architecture at the Massachusetts Institute of Technology, they traveled to California, where they set up a shop and a practice. The Greenes too were influenced by Japanese art and design, but also by the Arts and Crafts movement and English country architecture. Their furniture designs were simple, elegant and thoughtfully detailed. They would not embellish a piece to mask its construction, but rather would highlight the joinery with plugs and pins of contrasting woods, frequently ebony. The plugs would conceal screws, the pins would lock joints. If there are dominating characteristics of their work, they are attention to detail and superb craftsmanship.

And if there is a dominating characteristic to Walentine's work, it too is exquisite craftsmanship. "Top work in this field [custom woodworking] is never cheap, because the most humble piece must be executed to a standard that is uncompromising—extensive hand craftsmanship to assure perfect fits, much hand scraping and sanding, and a finish that is hand-rubbed to an unmistakable luster," he says. "What sets our work apart is the attention to detail that occurs during the finishing process. The end result is always determined with the same care and attention."

Walentine's shop is not particularly big, but it is very well equipped, both with industrial woodworking machines and with hand

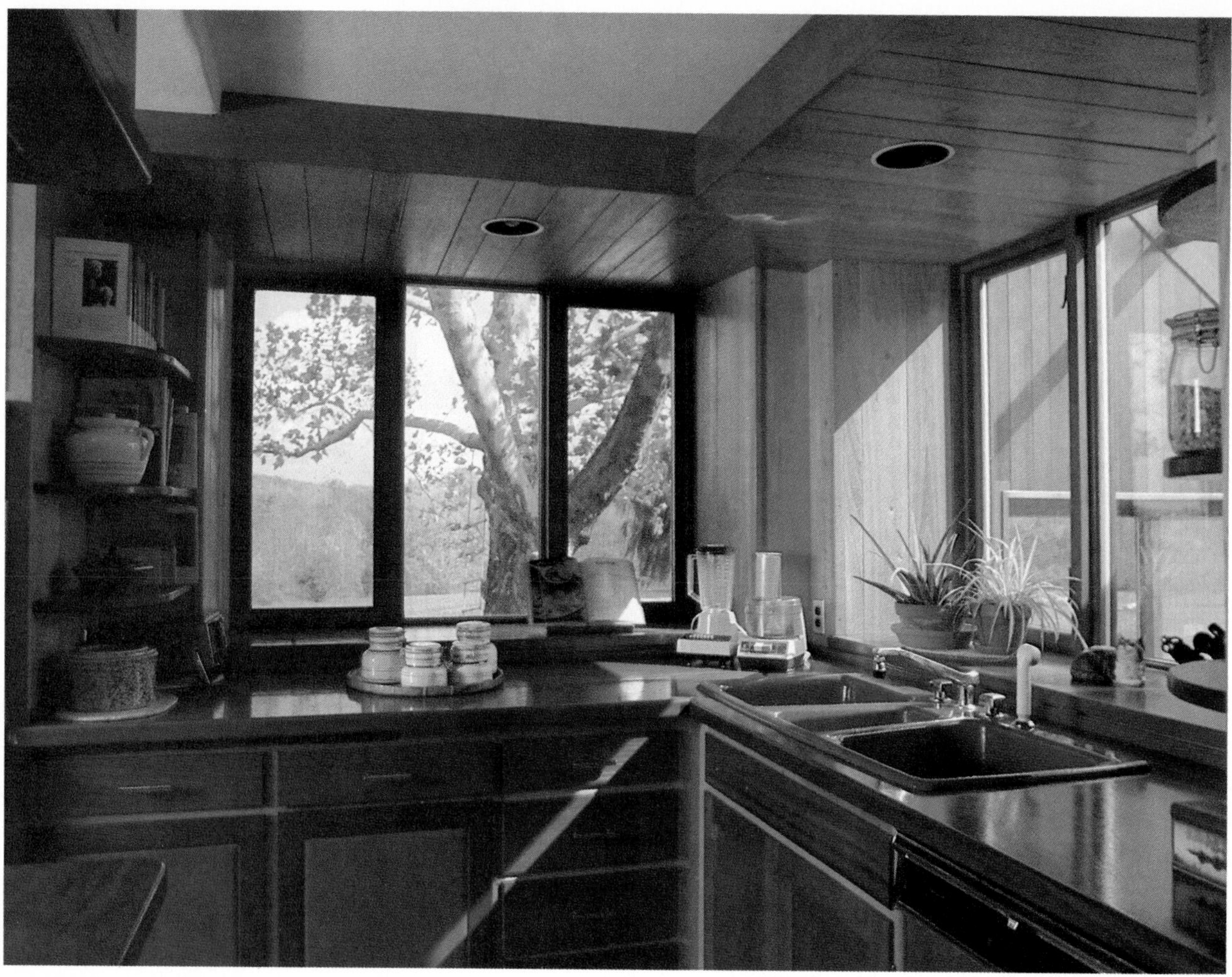

The two woods that dominate this kitchen—it's a part of Walentine's opus magnum*—are Brazilian mahogany, selected for its durability, its remarkable stability once kiln-dried, and its color, and cypress, which has good figure and a color to complement the mahogany.*

tools. While a great deal of work is done on the machines, hand tools are used extensively throughout each project. Boards are hand-planed after they've been milled on the thickness planer. Mortises and tenons are pared with chisels to their final fits. And, of course, the final surface is established through hand scraping.

All of this hand crafting takes time and runs into money, but Walentine always has work. "It's the people who can afford the best who buy our work," he says. "It's people who understand what the best is who buy it."

A hallmark of the best work is attention to detail. Walentine is adamant about detailing. Given the appropriate budget on a commission he'll make the entire piece of solid woods, eschewing plywood completely. The typical customer may never discern the presence of plywood in a cabinet, but Walentine would. Besides, designing and working solid wood in a way that compensates for wood's instability is a craftsman's challenge that Walentine seems to relish.

Moreover, Walentine will plane everything, and apply finish everywhere, not just to the obviously visible surfaces. Drawers, for example, are finished "quite thoroughly" because, he explains, "they are made to be seen and felt on virtually all surfaces." But he tries not to get carried away. "Built-ins need never be finished on the sides that are concealed."

While he likes the subtle surprise, such as pulling a drawer all the way out and discovering that the back is as nice as the front, he isn't taken with that inlaid maple leaf lurking on the drawer's side. That's decadent.

"Decadence is an elusive term—very relative and subjective," he explains. "I usually think of it as pertaining to a piece or style with a superfluity of ornament, where its essential nature is obscured by or subordinated to decorative elements. It's hard to draw the line, to say where good taste ends and decadence begins."

The piece shown on the front cover is a small part of Walentine's biggest single project, the re-creation of a huge sandstone farmhouse in Pennsylvania's Bucks County. He started with a shell and designed the kind of interior and exterior alterations that completely change the character of a building. All the doors and interior trim were handcrafted, as were the kitchen cabinets (see pages 4 and 5), and the extensive built-ins, such as those in the ham radio and sewing rooms (see page 186). There was so much woodworking to be done that Walentine subcontracted elements to other craftsmen. Even then more than two years were consumed in completing the job. It cost the kind of money most of us only dream of having. But it was the kind of project that Walentine loves: not a ditty, not a tone poem, not even a concerto, but a whole symphony. He wrote the music, he orchestrated it, and he conducted it. Then he played parts of it, too.

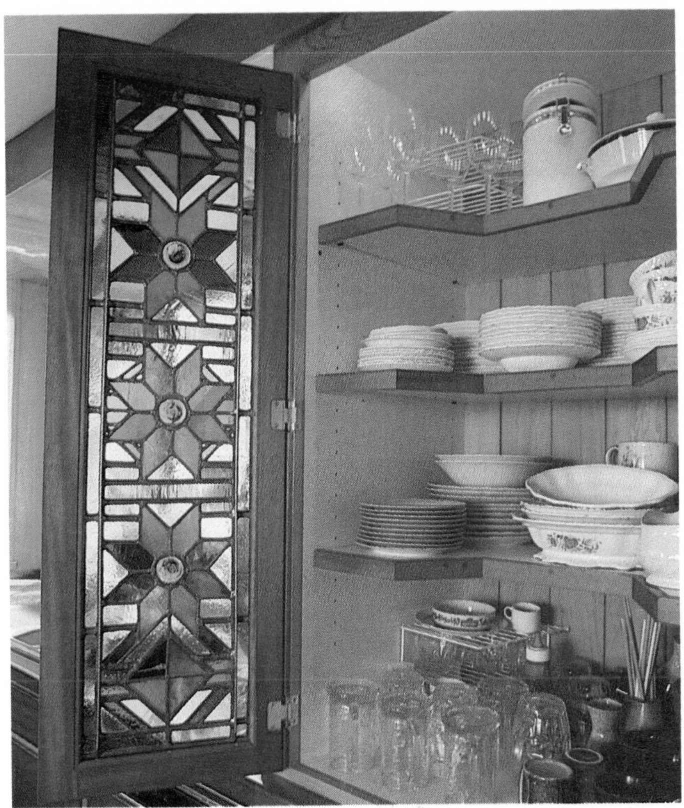

A stained glass artist was commissioned to create the panels for this china cupboard. Inside the cabinet is a light fixture to illuminate the contents, but also to show off the stained glass. The shelf cut-outs improve access to items on the shelves and provide a corridor for the light.

Steve Ripper, Walentine's friend, seems more content to refine the less ostentatious forms of cabinetmaking. The walnut bookcase—he is offended by comparisons of it to the work of George Nakashima—and the small cedar and chestnut wall cabinet are in his own home. The dressing stand was made on speculation to sell through the Guild Ten gallery, which Ripper maintains in conjunction with his home and shop in Applebachsville, Pennsylvania.

Ripper's work is marked by the same exquisite workmanship as Walentine's, but where Walentine specializes in architectural detailing—and the scale of projects thus entailed—Ripper favors discrete pieces. His is the craft as an end in itself. Where Walentine will take 10,000

Pillow doors, so called "simply because they give you a soft pillow effect, rather unlike wood," are used throughout the house. This one is on the sewing cabinet (see page 186). All were cut in Walentine's shop using a shaper cutter custom-made for the job.

board feet of cherry and do over the interior of a house, Ripper will take a half dozen scraps of chestnut and red cedar and create a wall cabinet to grace just one corner of a room.

As do most woodworker-craftsmen, Ripper seems to be in woodworking as much for the satisfaction as for the remuneration. The craft ethic is particularly strong in him. On the occasions I visited his shop, it was his work that dominated the Guild's gallery, all pieces that had been made because Ripper wanted to make them and not because a buyer was waiting for them.

Guild Ten is an association of fine woodworkers—more than the ten who originally formed it—in the upper Bucks County area. Ripper is the current president; he and Walentine are founding members. It functions like the craft guilds of old, providing a medium for members to get together and talk shop and philosophy and thus to learn from each other. It does provide some marketing help, too: The gallery is available to all members, and Walentine is trying to stir interest in a catalog of members' work. But the interaction of the membership seems closer to Ripper's interests.

To grow as a woodworker, a person must seek judgment of his work, says Ripper. "Seek opinions of people and friends. Get honest and valid opinions." When working alone, as the majority of woodworkers do, you lose perspective. "You get cabin fever. You get tunnel vision. One of the functions of the Guild is to critique, to exchange ideas."

A graduate of the Philadelphia College of Art, Ripper has spent many years teaching and learning. He's traveled, always seeking out woodworkers with whom to talk and from whom to learn. He taught college-level woodworking courses himself, organized many woodworking seminars, and even now talks of using the Guild as a medium for organizing more.

As much as the product, he is enthralled by the process. He did, after all, teach the process for nearly ten years, beginning always in the classroom with lectures on wood and it's nature, on tools and how you use them, then moving into the shop for exercises with

Ripper made this chestnut and cedar wall cabinet for his own home. The chestnut was taken from a section of an old telephone pole. "The size of the cabinet and so forth was dictated by the amount of material I had," Ripper says. "I just wanted to use that wood and make something useful out of it. A home project."

hand tools: planing a rough-sawn board square and true; crafting one joint after another, until a very basic understanding of wood, tools and techniques was established. And even today he is teaching: "People come and work for me for no pay, for experience." He is, in fact, a mother lode of information—useful how-to tips, or, as Larry Golden, another woodworker, puts it, "the small things that only the one who's messed it up five times knows."

But that he's also a demanding teacher seems apparent. He demands a lot of his students, of himself, *and* of his craft. He's uncomfortable with a lot of contemporary work—"It's either overbuilt and underdesigned or overdesigned and underbuilt"—and he tries, it seems, through his own woodworking and through his Guild and teaching activities to spread his view of how it should be.

He's a traditionalist. "What tradition means to me is that there's been no better way to do it. The furniture has to hold up and endure and stand the tests of time. Then it can become tradition."

Though Ripper says he didn't fuss over this shelving unit—it was an exercise in "composing the rectilinear form using the flitch-cut pieces in a pleasing way"—he made it of walnut using sliding dovetail joints.

As a consequence of this attitude, his work is always well crafted. It's that traditional craft ethic. He considers himself an artist, but his conversation suggests he'd sacrifice art for craft. "Woodworkers today aren't satisfied being craftsmen. They are trying to be artists. Not every piece I make is a work of art. But they are all well crafted."

The same philosophy shapes his aesthetic preferences. He likes clean shapes, quiet colors, and harmony. He likes pieces of refined good taste, of decorous excitement. "I've developed this theme, this concoction of influences," he tries to explain. Oriental designs and Mission furniture are in the concoction. "It's very clean and simple. It's straightforward, harmonious, and quietly exciting. When I do my own personal work, work of my choice, this is the style I use."

The dressing stand is particularly representative of his work. "There are no frills, but the structure's there," he says. "It has a strong utility, a purposeful design."

Ripper points out that he is "not trying to go for trendy, popular" effects in the piece. He didn't "exaggerate the proportions to excite the eye" or use sharply contrasting woods. His ideal is woodworking as a humble craft, not one of notoriety. And, of course, Ripper's work reflects his ideals.

Larry Golden is a definite counterpoint. "The craft ethic is not my number one concern," he says. "My intent is to do the best that I can, but my concern is, 'I want it to look a certain way.' "

His work, too, is an intriguing counterpoint. Although he doesn't consider himself a cabinetmaker—as in the comment, "For me it's a special effort to make drawers; I'm not a cabinetmaker"—he's made shelves, kitchen cabinets, bathroom vanities and similar pieces, all with a Golden flair and sculptural touch. His work is characterized by:

- Imaginative use of materials: the shelves shown on page 46 are made of naked particle board edged with redwood strips.
- Color: "I like *color.* I use a variety of woods; basically it gives you color." Hence he combines walnut, oak, padauk, birch and oak plywood in the dresser shown in the Gallery section (see page 134).
- Relatively simple joinery: "I don't practice doing dovetail joints. I'd just as soon do a box joint, 'cause then I can use the table saw."
- An occasional touch of whimsy: the open mouth that gives access to a hidden waste basket is a droll motif for a dentist's office (see page 16).

As might be expected of such a woodworker, Golden's work hasn't been defined or confined by any formal training. He studied art and sculpture in college and worked, in those days, primarily with clay. But as his artistic vision expanded, he came to see wood as the best medium for the structures he wanted to create.

After college, he did residential construction work, ranch maintenance work, and sculptural work. Always the iconoclast, he discovered that he liked to create "funny doors and funny windows, funny in the sense that they weren't square." If he has a specialty, making one-of-a-kind doors and windows is it. But he sees himself in general as "an explorer in wood, an experimenter."

Golden continues, "I'm not a person who's interested in finish. I'm a structuralist. I'm a sculptor first. I'm interested in shapes. Whether it's wonderful to the touch or shiny doesn't interest me. I get real bored sanding." This doesn't mean Golden is unversed in technique.

He never uses construction drawings. Instead, he pictures what he wants in his mind, figures out the most simple way to make it, and gets to work. "I had a couple of sticks of this, a couple of sticks of that," he'll say. "I threw them together, and it came out." When pressed for details of the joinery, he'll draw a blank. "You know," he'll say, genuinely chagrined, "I don't remember. I really don't remember."

In person, of course, Golden isn't at all as cavalier as his bare words might make him seem. He speaks out of modesty, not with a lack of concern. If the final luster of a piece isn't important, neither is it neglected. If the specific joinery isn't memorable, neither is it ill considered. Larry Golden is a consummate craftsman; his designs demand quality workmanship. His mastery of the techniques he uses is as sure as that of any old-world, tradition-bound joiner. Simply, he seldom uses the old-world joints and the old-world techniques. "I'll tell you what it is," he'll say, "it's high tech."

Larry Golden didn't come into woodworking with a conscientious desire to master joinery and to make shelves and cabinets and chairs and tables. He didn't methodically learn about wood, then about tools, then about joinery.

Great effort went into the design and construction of this black walnut dressing stand. Ripper fussed over the details of the design, eliminating hardware and flashy detailing. "To me," he says, "the jazziest effects are the ebony and rosewood pegs." Particular boards were chosen for subtleties of figure and color. The marble top was selected to harmonize rather than contrast with the wood. "I was thinking of a totally integrated design. It's actually a very complicated piece."

Ripper's work is full of details that are not flashy but clearly are a lot of extra work. In building this walnut wall cabinet, for example, he handcrafted the catch. He turned the knob from a scrap of walnut, then made it into a turnbutton using walnut scraps and a miniature mortise-and-tenon joint.

Few woodworkers do. He learned along the way the knowledge and techniques he needed in order to create the shapes he wanted to create. If the shapes were functional, so much the better. So he's learned, for example, to avoid combining woods of dissimilar densities in one piece. He has become dexterous enough to make tightly fitted joints. He has discovered ways of finishing a piece attractively and durably without hours of hand sanding and hand rubbing.

He once, he says, spent several hours in a Midwestern gallery studying the work of a respected craftsman. Classical motifs, traditional joinery, lots of hand work. "You know what I thought?" he asks. "It was dull. The dovetails were marvelous. The finish was immaculate. But it was dull.

"If I spend the next five years practicing dovetail joints, I could do work that good. But that's not what I'm doing. I'm coming to woodworking as a sculptor who likes to put parts together. Yes, I like beautiful wood. But that's enhancement. That's not the issue."

Jack Larimore is a cabinetmaker who shares the concerns that drive Ripper and Walentine as well as those that propel Golden. He has an appreciation for the craft ethic, and his designs are out of the ordinary. Is the erotic ornamentation on the shelving he built (see page 117) decadent? It certainly is whimsical, even appropriate. Is his bathroom shelf (see page 112) humble? With its bright colors, it's not exactly quiet. It may not be haughty, but it is proud; not arrogant, but certainly assertive.

Larry Golden likes contrasts and unusual shapes, and this bathroom cabinet reflects that. He used mahogany plywood for the exposed parts of the case and particle board for the hidden parts. Black plastic laminate was applied to the drawer fronts. The drawer pulls were sculpted from laminated pieces of mahogany and padauk and a thread of padauk was inlaid in the mahogany countertop edge.

Both pieces, and all of Larimore's work are well crafted. "It's foolish not to make things well crafted," he says. "The negative message you send by not caring about craftsmanship far outweighs the positive one, because it is more obvious. If we're to participate in society, that's the one thing we're offering—a well-built object that has care in it."

But craftsmanship isn't an end in itself. "It is for some people. That's the only reason they're in it—to elevate their own craftsmanship. For me," says Larimore, "craftsmanship is an important means of communicating certain ideas. Craftsmanship is an element of the things I design."

Larimore's formal education focused on design. He studied landscape architecture at Michigan State, but his post-graduation experience in the field was unsettling. Consequently, when he took a leave of absence to renovate

The Shelf as Sculpture

"People always ask, 'Will you build me shelves?' " Larry Golden explains. "Everybody always wants shelves. We are a nation of collectors. People always need shelves."

What he is explaining is his series of shelf-sculptures, of which *Marriage*, shown above, is a part. Golden's intent in doing the series was to create shelves that would be difficult to use as shelves, and by doing so to challenge preconceptions and assumptions about shelves. It was his artistic reaction to "Will you build me shelves?"

Golden is a sculptor-woodworker who persistently challenges convention. You can see that in his other work, shown on the neighboring pages and in the Gallery section. He made 14 pieces for the series, working off and on over a two to three year period. *Marriage* was the eighth or ninth.

To create *Marriage*, Golden used particle board, birch and mahogany plywoods, redwood, padauk, pine, Plexiglas, plastic laminate, glue, the tine from a farm cultivator and a bird's nest, plus his considerable skill as a woodworker. The finished piece can be displayed on the floor or hung on a wall. The diamond-shaped enclosure houses the bird's nest. The cultivator tine rests on the shelf.

The nest is a key part of the piece for Golden. A nest, he says, "hangs on a branch kind of like a shelf on a wall. I'm extending the idea of a branch, which is usually a horizontal projection." Golden also sees a nest as "something to hold something, repeating the theme of a shelf." And finally, he notes that "birds are not bad builders. I think of nests as really beautiful structures."

Why the title *Marriage*? "Everything needs a title," Golden responds. "If I call it this, it should give clues to what the piece is about."

Ultimately, Golden is enigmatic about the piece. As an artist, he explains, "you do the piece and give some hints. The viewer should try to make the rest of the connections."

his house, the leave got longer and longer. During the three years the project took, he got to know "that part of me that likes to design and *build,* to realize the design right away."

After his house was completed, he was asked to design and build an addition for someone else, which led him into contracting work. "Because I liked more refined work," he continues, "I was steered in that direction by friends and clients, so I got into cabinetry, then furniture." He now has a shop in the Fishtown section of Philadelphia and three craftsmen (David Page, Jeff Day and John Howard) working for him, making him—more than a mere artist and craftsman—a small businessman.

The business aspect must be dealt with, but Larimore clearly has little taste for it. There's the shop to maintain, equipment to be kept in good repair, insurance to be considered, and, of course, the employees to manage. "It's pretty good if you can figure out how to be in business as a woodworker. I admire people who can do that," he says.

His approach has been to follow the lead of other craftsmen in his area who work cooperatively. Hence, he shares his shop with another woodworker, Bob Ingram, so there are two businesses paying for the space, utilities and maintenance costs instead of one. When it comes time to order materials, Larimore will not infrequently pool his order with those of other woodworkers, so they all get the discounts none would get ordering individually.

Lining up paying customers, often the biggest woe for the small businessman, doesn't seem to be a problem for Larimore. Past customers are pleased with his work, so word-of-mouth is good. He works with architects. He does discrete pieces and built-ins. "Right now," he reveals, "I have lots of commissions as well as a lot of work I'm preparing on speculation for shows. I feel that the spec work is important in that it expands my concepts of what furniture is or can be. And it also expands my market."

High school shop aside, Larimore's only formal woodworking training came *after* he'd been working for more than a year as a cabinetmaker. He was working, but it was slow and painful and frustrating; he didn't have a sure enough grasp of procedures. "I could eventually get things made," he says, "but I had to backtrack and repair mistakes." He signed up for an evening woodworking course at the Philadelphia College of Art. "When you are trying to make a living, you have to limit the margin of error as much as you can." Taking the course served him so well that he took it a second time.

His high school shop experience, by contrast, had been a bust. "I can't remember anything I learned there," he says. "It doesn't work the way it's supposed to. I think they're too busy teaching people about the standard array of things to do, rather than 'this is why you do it.' It is taught as if 'you ought to know this because you're a male,' rather than a more spiritual approach. I think that's why a lot of kids don't get anything out of it."

The spiritual approach is important to Larimore. "It has mostly to do with people," he explains. "I think the key thing is that craftsmen as a group are oriented that way. Most are oriented toward the spiritual aspects of the work and the fulfillment it gives." In landscape architecture he sensed it was missing. In high school shop it had been missing. But in woodworking, it has to be there. "If you're doing commissioned work, you have to be very connected to people." You have to care.

The first time he sensed this in a woodworker, he was quite young. "There was a friend of my father's, Claude Evett, who gave me a nice set of carving tools. I must have been 12 years old or so. Under his direction, I carved a duck, and some decoys. He had more to do with my interest in woodworking than shop. You could tell that he was someone who understood and loved wood." He cared.

Caring is the whole point of craftsmanship. "You can certainly say that craftsmen are people who make objects," Larimore says, "but also craftsmen are people whose main priority is caring about what they're doing. Craftsmen put that care into their work.

"By and large, you don't make your decisions as a small businessman. You make them as a craftsman, in the interest of quality rather than cost—although they are not always at odds with each other." He continues: "In a business sense, in that arena, we as craftsmen can't really compete on the grounds of price, availability, distribution. People have to wait a long time. It is usually more expensive. One thing we *can* offer is quality. The care."

That's what Larimore does. It hasn't made him rich, but it has made him fulfilled. "As a

The oriental style of this Larry Golden-designed cabinet is derived solely from the drawer pulls. Otherwise, the cabinet is straightforward. Although Golden is hazy about the details, such as what prompted him to design the pulls the way he did, he does recall that he built the unit on the worksite using a saber saw and a "very poor" table saw as his only power tools. The case is plywood, the solid wood elements pine.

Golden's whimsical side is revealed clearly in this cabinet made for a dentist's office. The open mouth provides access to a wastebasket. He made the case and doors of particle board and covered the latter with plastic laminate. The trim is mahogany with walnut accent stripes.

male, I had certain expectations about prosperity in business, that whole kind of bundle of live wires. It's a constant struggle. You feel you should be making money, but you are so fulfilled that you can hardly work yourself into a depression because you aren't making money. There are so many people making a lot of money who don't have the joy I have."

Phil Gehret is another cabinetmaker who plies his craft for fulfillment more than money. He presents several new aspects to the handcrafted picture, the most interesting being his attitude toward the work he does. Although he has a great deal of experience, a well-equipped shop, and a hands-on interest in history that blends well with his woodworking capabilities, he doesn't necessarily extend himself on everything he makes. In the context of a gathering of craftsmen single-mindedly devoted to Quality, that's a pretty horrifying thing to say.

But Gehret is a practical man. "The quality of it is dependent upon its use," he explains. "If you want to pass it along to your children, then the quality you put in should be the best you can afford." He is unmoved by handcraftedness per se. "I have seen handcrafted, quote unquote, kitchen cabinets that I wouldn't put in my pigpen. And I *have* a pigpen."

The word "afford" is key. Time is money, and the best work is time-consuming. High-quality materials are expensive. So top quality translates into a lot of money. For a man of no apparent artistic pretensions, for a man working two jobs, affordability is important.

Gehret is, first of all, a busy man with a diversity of interests. Woodworking is only one of them. He works full time in the wood shop of Rodale Press's Design Center. The shop is run "along the lines of a model shop," says one of Gehret's fellow workers. "We build anything." "Anything" ranges from all the woodwork in the center's offices to solar collectors. A majority of the work is creating prototypes for build-it-yourself plans published in the company's magazines and books.

Gehret lives on a 250-acre farm and considers himself a full-time farmer. He has 150 sheep, a few Angus cattle, usually 15 to 20 hogs. He brings in enough hay to be able to sell some each year as a cash crop. But he concedes that his employment at Rodale is his "livelihood" and that he farms "for fun."

On the side, he is an active member of

the Goschenhoppen Historical Society. The most visible society activity is its annual festival, in which old ways of doing things are demonstrated. Gehret chairs the festival and participates by demonstrating early 19th century woodworking techniques.

As you might expect, Gehret's particular cabinetmaking interest is the reproduction of historical pieces, such as the chest-on-chest that graces his bedroom. In preparing to make such a piece, Gehret will pore over photographs and drawings of cabinets or dressers that are representative of what he wants to make. He won't reproduce exactly any single piece, but will create a new piece that echoes their collective style. The goal is "to come close to an original." It is likely that any piece he makes will "reflect the Pennsylvania design. I'm into the Pennsylvania German tradition."

In his shop, located in the barn on his farm, Gehret will "combine modern technology with traditional design. I don't expect to plane all the moldings by hand. I'll run them through a shaper and make them that way. If the moldings are different from having been done on a shaper rather than by hand, they'll be a little different. But it'll be a close facsimile." In addition, he'll use some modern materials. He'll use plywood for the back, for drawer bottoms. He'll use "modern glues rather than the hot hide glues, which are difficult to find and miserable to use." But the cherry or walnut stock he uses for the principal parts of the case and drawers and doors will probably be drawn from his "private stock," boards sawn from trees he's cut on his farm and carefully stacked in the barn to cure. The joinery will be traditional, so hand-cut dovetails will be used in the drawer construction.

The use of the plywood is based in practicality, and as Gehret likes to say, "You never do anything without a reason for doing it." In those spots where he expects to use plywood, it is because it will solve the woodworker's age-old engineering problem: the materials instability. Solid wood is not stable, plywood is. Solid wood will change dimension with changes in humidity, plywood will not. If it is not authentic, Gehret is unconcerned. "I have no good reason to sell this as an antique. It's being made as a reproduction."

The truth of the matter is that a Gehret reproduction, by virtue in part of its maker's reasoned substitution of modern materials, may be a longer-lasting, better quality piece than the ones it honors. It certainly has equivalent workmanship, for Gehret's reproductions are done for love, not money.

Gehret has been working wood for money most of his adult life. After high school, he served a four-year apprenticeship, learning carpentry from two old craftsmen who were very particular about their work but not about their teaching. "They wouldn't show you what to do until you thought you had it figured out for yourself," Gehret says. When the two discovered he was working on his own time, they fired him. On and off over the next 30 years or so, Gehret worked as a self-employed contractor and, as a part of the work, built a lot of kitchen, bathroom and rec room cabinets. The cabinets were "down to earth, basic, but good construction. They'll be around after I'm gone." But the hassle of collecting money from customers eventually got to him, and he took the job at Rodale.

The farming came into his life about 20 years ago, and the historical interests shortly thereafter. Gehret's first chore after moving his family, those 20 years ago, was to spruce up the house. No sooner was the work completed than someone connected with the historical society visited. "We were informed we had a rather unique old farmhouse." It had been built in the mid-18th century and still had, under its new face, much of the original woodwork. "The evidence was there and we didn't see it."

Restoration work started shortly thereafter and is still going on. Phil's initial "sprucing up" is being undone. He has uncovered fireplaces, returned rooms to their original layouts, restored trim and paneling where it existed and replaced it where it was gone. "It made me more aware of authentic details," he says. "I have come to be able to distinguish the time periods of moldings." The work prompted him to collect many 18th and 19th century hand tools and figure out how to use them. And, "because I'm crazy," he does use them. He'll use them "for fun or self-fulfillment or as a demonstration." But, turning practical again, he'll say, "I'm crazy but I'm not stupid. When something is a production job, production meaning it has to get done, I'm more likely to use power tools."

Those production jobs, outside of Gehret's routine work week, are fewer and fewer these days. The pieces he makes are personal. Another chest-on-chest is in the works, a wedding present for a daughter. It will be of the best quality.

The truly curious element in Phil Gehret's situation is that after 30 years of experience, after acquiring all the tools, after achieving proficiency with modern power tools and manmade materials as well as with old-world

Architectural Woodworking

Cabinetmaking, as generally portrayed in this book, may come across as the domain of cloistered artisans. The craftsman creates a design, then executes it. But such is not always the case.

Paul Moser, for example, heads a substantial woodworking business. He is the third generation of Mosers to run Moser Brothers, a millwork shop in Bridgeport, a gritty burg just west of Philadelphia. In business since 1915, a member of the Architectural Woodwork Institute since 1970, the firm is a big operation, doing major projects—all the counters and cabinets and doors and architectural trimmings for an entire hospital floor, for example (other, similar firms are doing the other five floors).

"We work for and through architects," explains Moser. "We don't necessarily design work ourselves. Generally, we just make shop drawings for what they're asking for. We want direction from the architect."

Ninety percent of the time, the architect's directive is to follow the AWI guidelines. The Architectural Woodwork Institute is a 600-member national trade association dedicated to insuring that its members use uniform, high-quality methods. To become a member, a firm must specialize in architectural woodworking, be recommended by architects, and have its work and its operation evaluated and approved by the group.

AWI guidelines cover every conceivable material, technique and situation. Moser is enthusiastic about the organization. "They are really our teachers. They've got the whole country contributing on techniques and how-to-do-it," he says.

Even beyond the AWI, firms like Moser's routinely interact, he says. "Woodworkers work together often. We share trade secrets, educate each other, let each other do the piecework." Moser Brothers, for example, picked up the hospital job to help another firm, then farmed out the milling of 3,000 to 5,000 feet of molding needed to still another outfit that had more efficient equipment for that particular job.

The scale of the hospital job makes it clear, if it wasn't already, that there's a vast difference between Moser's shop and that of the typical individual craftsman.

Nevertheless, Moser Brothers still does modest projects. The firm crafted the period-piece built-ins, right, designed for a residence near Philadelphia by architect Gary Michael Jones. (Although the firm got its start crafting wooden covers for powder cans, its present reputation is for the excellence of its historical reproduction work.) Individual woodworkers will drop in for the milling of rough-sawn hardwoods and for advice.

And Moser himself looks at cabinets in much the same way that an artist-craftsman does. "First is what you see, then how it actually feels, and then how it is put together. Is it functional or just beautiful to look at?"

This chest-on-chest is typical of the pieces that Phil Gehret labors over most intensively. It was made from walnut boards cut from a tree felled on his own farm. A reproduction of a style, rather than a particular item, it incorporates traditional design and joinery, but was made using some modern materials and many modern tools. Gehret views it as a family heirloom.

A closeup of Gehret's chest-on-chest reveals the level of workmanship that went into the piece. The natural beauty of the walnut has been enhanced by Gehret's finish, which characteristically blends old-world multistep methods with modern-day materials.

technology, he's finally attained . . . amateur standing. His finest work is done, not for money, but for love.

Of course, we have here another slur. For everyone knows that the dictionary definition of amateur is: "A person who does something more or less unskillfully." In the minds of many, the cabinet with loose joints, scarred and wavy surfaces, an uneven finish is not afflicted with bad workmanship, but rather with amateurishness.

But get that dictionary out again. The amateur as "a person who does something more or less unskillfully" is the second definition. The first is reflective of the word's derivation. The derivation is the Latin *amator,* meaning lover. The definition is: "A person who does something for the pleasure of it rather than for money."

And at least one person believes amateur standing is no slur. He is David Pye. An Englishman, Pye was formerly a professor of furniture design at the Royal College of Art in London. He has thought long about design and workmanship. He set some of his thoughts on paper in 1968 in a short book titled *The Nature and Art of Workmanship.* It's still available in paperback.

"One of the best professional cabinetmakers in Britain, Ernest Joyce, started as an amateur and learnt his job at first from books," writes Pye. " 'Amateur', after all, means by derivation a man who does a job for the love of it rather than for money, and that happens also to be the definition, or at least the prerequisite, of a good workman." (Ernest Joyce, to jog memories, is the author of *The Encyclopedia of Furnituremaking,* found in the books section of every mail-order tool catalog.)

The thrust of Pye's thinking is that workmanship has as much or more to do with the aesthetic qualities of an object—like a cabinet—than design. At the time he wrote the book, he felt that workmanship was deteriorating and that, as a consequence, "our environment will lose much of the quality it still retains." Amateurs were among those he looked to as conservators of good workmanship.

He explains: "It is time we separated the idea of the true amateur—that is to say the part-time professional—from the idea of 'do-it-yourself' (at its worse end) and all that is

Limited Production Shelves and Cabinets

Between the handcrafted, one-of-a-kind shelf or cabinet and the issue of a furniture-industry factory lies the unit that can be called, for want of a better term, the limited production item. Usually, it incorporates an all-but-unique design, carefully selected woods, lots of hand fitting in the construction, a hand-rubbed finish *and* a price somewhere between that of the handcrafted unit and the manufactured unit.

There are many ways to go about limited production. Some craftsmen increase their output by hiring skilled cabinetmakers to execute their designs under their supervision. Thomas Moser of New Gloucester, Maine, has a mail-order catalog from which a customer may choose. Each piece is made-to-order by one of Moser's employees.

Dean Santner of Emeryville, California, generates his limited production pieces in another way. He has a small-scale production line manned by a small group of experienced and skilled woodworkers. Rather than produce items one-by-one as demand arises, Santner makes many at one time, stockpiling them against future demand.

The modular shelf unit shown above is an example of the operation's work. Santner cautions that the design, though it looks simple, has subtleties that make it difficult to duplicate outside of the production shop environment.

He points out, for example, that the dimensions of the slots and the measurements between them are critical. By using templates and techniques that have evolved over the course of several production runs, Santner and his workers are able to ensure a uniformity of the various parts.

High-cost equipment also enters in. Santner says he has $40,000 invested in specialized industrial woodworking machinery that allows his workers to produce parts more quickly, more uniformly, more safely than would be possible using the typical woodworker's tools and equipment.

The upshot of all of this, for Santner, is an attractive blend of good design, quality construction, relative uniqueness and reasonable price.

amateurish. The continuance of our culture is going to depend more and more on the true amateur, for he alone will be proof against amateurishness. What matters in workmanship is not long experience, but to have one's heart in the job and to insist on the extreme of professionalism."

Clearly, in Pye's vision, the true amateurs are the Phil Gehrets, who do livelihood work by day and, for the love of it, do their very best work at night and on weekends. As an avocation.

What of the pure amateur? The person who works wood strictly for the love of it, for the satisfaction, and never, ever for money. One such amateur is Mitch Mandel.

Mandel started in woodworking—at this writing—about a year ago. He started at the do-it-yourself end, but he has pursued the craft with dedication. If his workmanship has been deficient, it's not been because of attitude. Attitude, in Pye's book, has a lot to do with craftsmanship.

"Workmanship of the better sort is called, in an honorific way, craftsmanship," Pye wrote. "Craftsmanship. . .means simply workmanship using any kind of technique or apparatus, in which the quality of the result is not predetermined, but depends on the judgement, dexterity and care which the maker exercises as he works. . .It may be mentioned in passing that in workmanship, the care counts for more than the judgement and dexterity; though care may well become habitual and unconscious."

Or as Jack Larimore puts it, "Within any field, you can approach it with a caring, or you can approach it as a job."

For Mandel, the judgment and dexterity have been coming with experience. The care has always been there. If he approached woodworking tentatively, it was because he was experiencing some trepidation. It's a feeling familiar to any rank novice. It is certainly a feeling familiar to me.

"I realize I wouldn't be doing this if I didn't have a house," he says. "The house probably started me on this. I needed a shelf for the kitchen, things like that. I didn't build any of my [kitchen] cabinets, but now I probably would."

"My first project was a shelf. We took all the plaster off a wall and exposed the brick. I talked to a guy at Dries [a local building supply], and he told me how to do it. I mean, I didn't know the first thing. But that was the first thing I ever did, and it gave me the inspiration, the confidence to carry on."

Carrying on, Mandel has since made a dozen or more pieces of furniture, including a cedar-lined, dovetailed blanket chest and an oak, four-drawer file cabinet of frame-and-panel construction. But it was getting a shelf hung on the kitchen wall that got him started. The experience is a common one. I can relate to it, since hanging shelves, now that I think about it, was probably my first significant woodworking experience, too.

It is a case of one thing leading to another.

You have a house. And you have excess possessions loitering in corners, hanging inconveniently about. You decide to do something about it. You "build" a shelf, perhaps in the basement so that, if you booger the job, it won't be on display for comment. It looks okay, so you build several more, then case in

Filing cabinet plans Mitch Mandel bought were so obviously flawed he didn't use them. Rather, he pulled together what he'd learned to create his own plans. Then for the first time, he built a piece of his own design.

several shelves to make a bookcase. You add doors to make a cabinet. Next, you hanker for a better appearance, so you try a different stain. Or you notice that the doors you made warped funny after a few months and you want to try a different design so you can correct that. After all, the doors on the cabinets you bought didn't warp, so why should the ones you make?

One thing leads to another.

You start looking at cabinets and dressers and bookcases with a new interest. You study the woods they're made of. You pull drawers all the way out and turn them over and over in your hands, evaluating joinery, craftsmanship, materials. You run a hand over the surfaces. You peer closely at joints, trying to determine what technique is on display there. You pull freestanding pieces away from the wall to examine the backs.

As a photographer, Mandel has gotten to study the work of a lot of cabinetmakers, including a number of the pieces shown in this book. "In the beginning," he reports, "I was saying, 'Gee, this guy is tremendous.' Lately, I've been less in awe."

That's because he understands through experience what went into a cabinet. "You keep going through stages of demystification," he explains. "Each piece I've made has been more complicated. Each piece has been more involved, more challenging." Consequently, he knows when to applaud a masterful construction, when to nod approvingly at a workmanlike job, and when to pass without remark on something that's just thrown together. Admiration he has. Only occasionally awe.

Mandel's break into woodworking came when he got the chance to buy a used Shopsmith, a five-in-one machine that can be converted from table saw to drill press to horizontal boring machine to disc sander to lathe. "For a relatively inexpensive price," Mandel says, "I got a shop, essentially, which enabled me to get into it. It was a good first investment. Since then, I've spent hundreds more on tools." The additional tools he has acquired include a used radial arm saw, a stationary disc/belt sander, a router, a saber saw, portable sanders and hand tools.

His first major purchase of hardwood lumber was similarly fortuitous. He ran across

Dovetails are not easy to make, especially not the first time around. If Mandel's most recent hand-cut dovetails aren't up to the standards of a practiced, old-world workman, they are far superior to the first ones he made.

an ad in the local newspaper listing a remarkably low price for kiln-dried oak. He threw his lot in with a fellow worker who owned a pickup, and together they bought almost 500 board feet. The supplier, it turned out, owned a small kiln in which he dried lumber purchased from local sawmills. Another neighbor owned a thickness planer and, for a price, would dress the lumber. The upshot was that for about $1.35 a board foot ("That's about half the price you'd get it at a lumber store"), Mandel got a stickered stack of hardwood with which to practice his woodworking.

And practice he has. With enthusiasm, with his heart in it.

"I really love it," he says. "I get a lot of satisfaction out of it. Of all the crafts I've dabbled in, woodworking is the most appealing and engaging."

His story thus seems proof of David Pye's contention: "Two minutes experience teach an eager man more than two weeks teach an indifferent one."

"Dovetails were intimidating at first," Mandel says. But an early project, a lap desk being made for a friend, called for dovetails, so Mandel tried them. Subsequent projects also called for dovetails, and with the additional practice, his workmanship has improved. "Now I look at the dovetails in Suzanne's lap desk, and they're terrible. I mean, they're *terrible.*" The lap desk is, to echo Ellis Walentine, a statement of Mandel's skill level at the time he made it. And the cedar chest, though its dovetails aren't flawless, states that Mandel has come a long way in just a short time.

Mandel's heart is still in the work, for practical reasons and for spiritual reasons. The practical: "I'm gradually replacing all my furniture. In the first place, you couldn't buy these things. And if you could, you couldn't afford them." The spiritual: "It's a very satisfying way to furnish your house. It's provided me with the satisfaction of knowing how they're made and that they are well made."

There's still a lot he wants to learn about wood, about tools, about techniques. He knows more than a rank novice, less than a workman who has matured in his craft. But he's encouraged by what he's been able to do so far. He's seen many of the remarkable cabinets pictured here, but has felt no awe. Instead, he's been challenged.

"I think the most exciting thing right now is looking forward to all the things I can do, the things I can make, the woods I want to try," he says. "I've lost the tentativeness. I'm looking forward to working with other woods. In the beginning, I bought oak because it was cheap, knowing that if I screwed up, it wouldn't matter. Now I know I can work the wood and not screw it up."

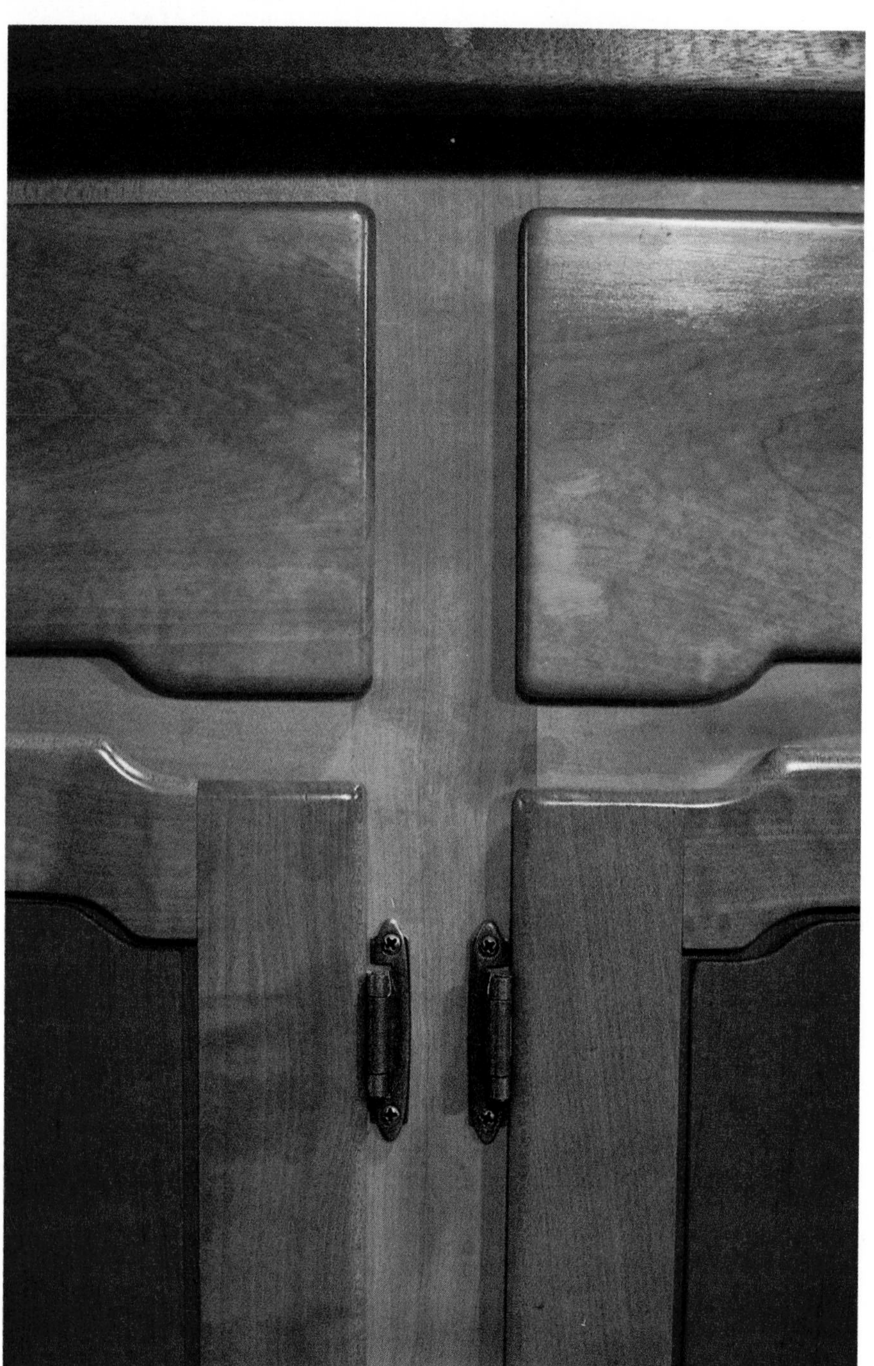

GETTING STARTED

The one best way to get into cabinetmaking probably doesn't exist. After you've seen what *can* be done, and after you've absorbed some book learning, there's still the matter of taking tool in hand and actually *working* wood, of actually generating some sawdust and wood scraps on the one hand and a bookcase or a drawer or a door on the other.

Most woodworkers you talk to will direct you down several paths simultaneously: a course, a formal or informal apprenticeship, reading and experimentation, hanging around a woodworker's shop. They are not mutually exclusive. The first step is commitment. You have to want to do it enough to pay tuition, to buy wood, to finance tools. You have to want to do it enough to learn the fundamentals, to practice and, ultimately, to do careful work, all time-consuming endeavors.

"I think the only way to get into it is to get into it,"

Lip drawers are clean and simple. Of all the kinds of drawers that are *made, these require the least expertise to make well. The rounded edge is quickly cut with a router, the lip hides less-than-perfect fits. With care, anyone can make drawers as elegant as these.*

Larry Golden says. If you are reluctant to make a substantial financial commitment, he suggests looking into a course somewhere. He also suggests trying to befriend someone with a shop and skill, developing "an exchange," wherein you offer your labor on whatever menial chores need to be done against the use of tools and whatever guidance the craftsman can offer. It's going "back to the old kind of apprenticeship system in some way or another."

The commitment here, of course, is that of time. You have to be willing to yield your time to sweep up, stack and restack lumber, sand, feed boards into a planer. This is drudge work, especially if you are working for someone else. And if your *real* commitment is to learning how to work wood, you soon may chafe at *always* cleaning up wood scraps instead of getting experience at cleaning up a roughed-out tenon.

Ideally, the commitment of time is mutual. In an informal apprenticeship, the commitment is a barter arrangement. You get some free lessons, the master gets some free labor. In a formal apprenticeship, you agree to work for starvation wages, the master agrees to give you training and increasingly challenging work.

"Apprentices really deserve and require a lot of time," Jack Larimore explains. "In exchange for paying them little money, you give them experience and knowledge and so forth." Just as the apprentice chafes, so too may the master. He yearns for more time for his woodworking or for *skilled* help. He finds he's a better cabinetmaker than a teacher.

Despite the drawbacks, the apprenticeship system is still widely regarded as a good way to learn. Through it alone, Golden points out, can you learn "the small things that only the one who's messed it up five times knows."

But Golden also perceives alternative means: "Buy a tool and see what you can do with it. Then buy another tool and see what you can do with *it.* Then buy another tool and another."

A great deal of self-education is possible. "You have to be willing to read some books," Larimore says. "All the information is there. It is useful to go through and follow someone else's instructions."

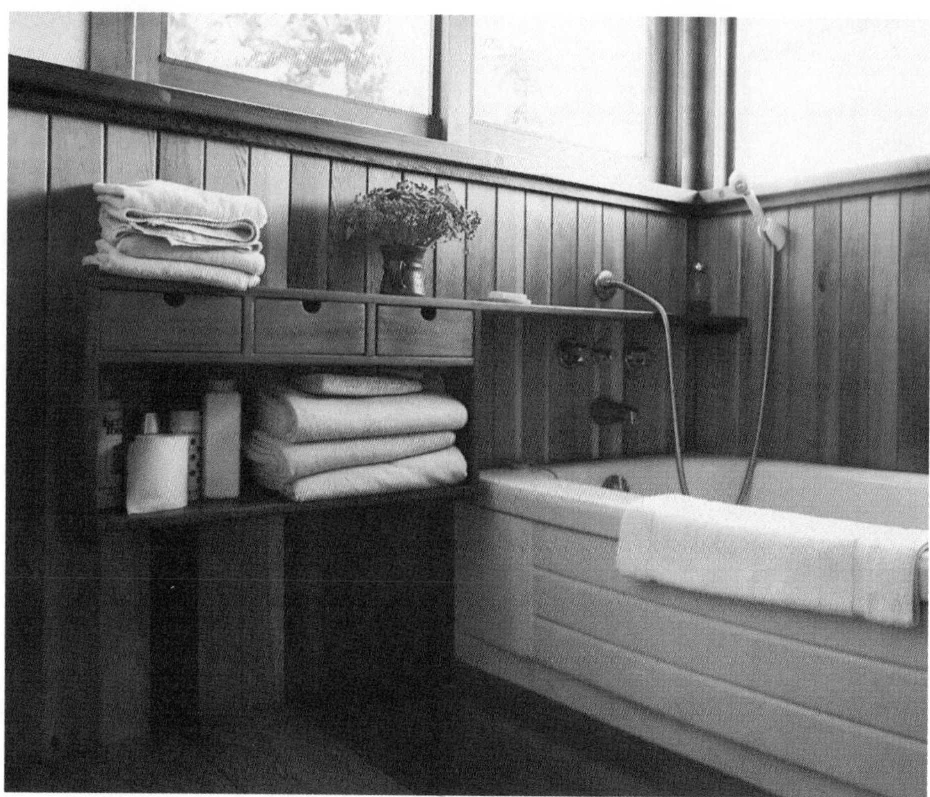

Here's a useful tub-side cabinet for towels and soap and other bathing necessaries. Designed and built by British Columbia cabinetmaker Tom Larsen, the unit is a handsome complement to the bathroom. It demonstrates that a piece need not be elaborate or difficult to make to succeed.

Following "someone else's instructions" can also mean that, from time to time, you need to at least *watch* a seasoned craftsman work. Better still if you can ask questions. This is where the course and the informal apprenticeship come in. You have to see it being done.

"Once you see it being done, it eliminates the mystique," Mitch Mandel says. "You can relate to it, approach it." You may recall that Mandel, an amateur, first got interested in woodworking through his work as a photographer. Working on one book, he was assigned to shoot a variety of staged woodworking photos, including those of a whole kitchenful of custom-made cabinets. Working on a subsequent book, he had to shoot hundreds of photos depicting how, step-by-step, to construct nearly a dozen woodworking projects. "Taking the photos for the book was like taking an individualized woodworking course," he says.

Of course, not everyone has an opportunity—or the desire—to record every detail of handcrafting a cedar-lined mahogany blanket chest, as did Mandel. But you can take that course.

In most courses, whether conducted at a YMCA, a vocational-technical school, a fine arts college or a private woodworking studio, you'll have a chance to learn the fundamentals. You'll have a chance to hold the wood, study it and work it. You'll manipulate the tools. You may even make something, like a small bookcase.

But most important of all, you'll get some hands-on experience under the tutelage of someone who knows woodworking. "There's no substitute for experience," Ellis Walentine says.

Walentine himself never took a formal course. He learned woodworking through experience, starting shortly after he graduated from college (as a psychology major). He would spend several weeks working in his Bucks County, Pennsylvania, shop, then travel to Rochester, New York, where he'd grill friends associated with the Rochester Institute of Technology's

Even handcrafted cabinets are sometimes painted. In making his own kitchen cabinets, Douglas Pinney chose paint for its durability: it is easier than any natural finish to maintain and redo. Having chosen paint, he was then able to use less costly materials. The cabinets are made of pine, the doors and drawer fronts of poplar. The only departure is the use of teak as an edging for the countertop.

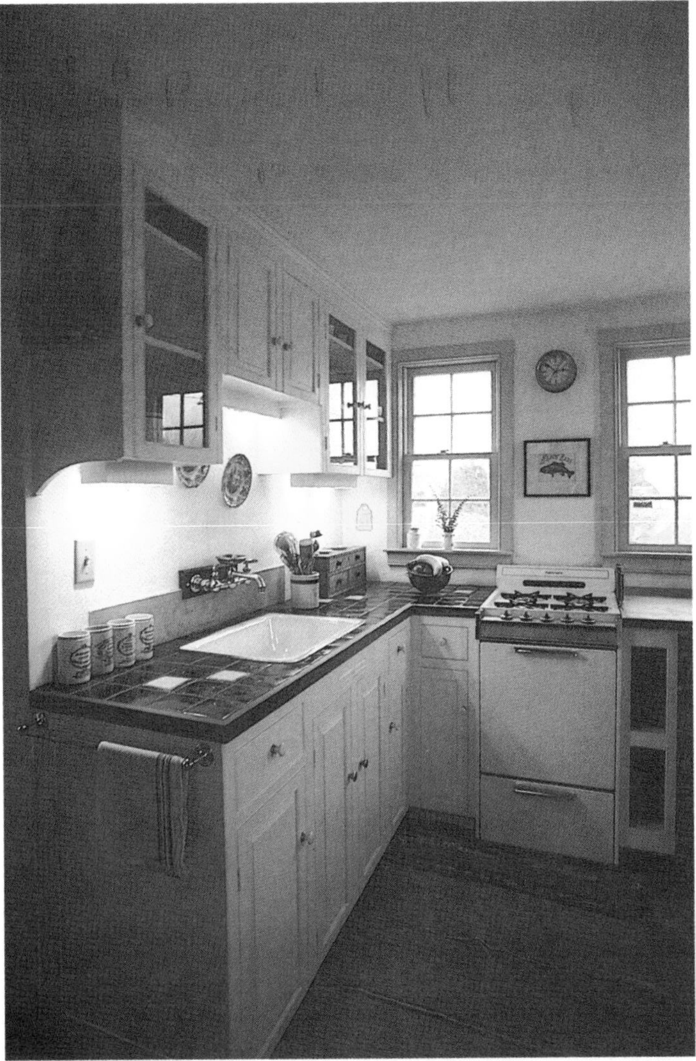

These kitchen cabinets, designed and built by British Columbia cabinetmaker Ed Colin, are completely without frills or excess. The design is clean, yet clearly well thought out. The filler beside the microwave oven echoes the motif of the doors. The pulls cut into the doors echo the drawer knobs.

School for American Craftsmen about situations he'd faced. The informal apprenticeship.

With each piece he'd make, he'd confront new woods, new joints, new problems. He'd ask questions of experienced woodworkers, and he'd seek critiques of his solutions to design and construction problems. As he gained experience, he won more and better commissions.

But he's still learning. And each new piece reflects the current state of his art.

Walentine isn't the only woodworker who has learned through experience. Skim through this book and look for notations of formal training (a course taken or an apprenticeship served). A few of the woodworkers represented here have formal training in related fields, architecture and fine arts and sculpture among them. But only Steve Ripper and Jack Larimore have had any formal training in woodworking, and Larimore's, you'll recall, he got *after* he'd started working wood professionally.

Al Garvey pursued woodworking under the guidance of a retired cabinetmaker who lived in the neighborhood, this while still in high school. In college, Garvey studied design, and through subsequent work drifted back into woodworking. He wanted to make what he was designing.

Larry Golden, as we learned in the first chapter, studied sculpture and fine arts in college. He started making "assembled things" out of wood simply because they couldn't be made of clay. Techniques he now uses were derived from construction experience. Others are his own inventions or adaptations.

Intensity has been a key element in the development of every one of these woodworkers. "You have to realize the level of interest with which you must pursue something like this," Steve Ripper says. He is a former teacher who now does custom woodworking full time. According to Ripper, he and Walentine and all the other woodworkers who meet his definition of *craftsmen* are mastering their craft in the shop. "You gain all this through experience and by making sure that all the work you do is your very best," he explains, adding, "Skill comes with practice."

Cabinetmakers frequently work with architects and interior designers, sometimes working to their specific plans, other times working more or less independently. This huge armoire was the result of such a collaboration. Interior designer Barbara Boughton sketched the rough outlines of the piece, then let craftsman David Goldfarb resolve the details and actually build it.

This is not to say you should resign yourself to a long apprenticeship before you'll be capable of good work. You *should* be capable of making useful objects almost from the start.

"Yes, a novice can make well-crafted cabinets," Larimore says. "You have to be willing to redo things if you make mistakes. That prevents a lot of people from getting off the ground."

Ripper concurs: "I've seen a lot of really intriguing work done by people who are novices and amateurs. I don't think beginning people should be discouraged because they don't think they have enough skill or enough talent."

It's all a matter of how you apply what you *do* know, and whether you challenge yourself. That's what Walentine and Golden and all the others continue to do.

Start with a course. But be aware that there are courses and there are courses. "Access to Machines" would have been an apt title for a cabinetmaking course I took at a vocational-technical school—one evening a week for three or four months. Formal instruction was not in the curriculum. All but two or three enrollees were there simply to use woodworking equipment that was beyond their means: a 24-inch planer, an 8-inch jointer with a 6-foot bed, a 20-inch band saw, a pin router, a 12-inch table saw, a 16-inch radial arm saw, a stroke sander, a drill press, dozens and dozens of bar clamps, hundreds of hand screws. The motley assortment of hand tools didn't move them; they weren't interested in hand tools. The instructor

When Bruce McQuilkin made a rich and exquisitely detailed room-divider cabinet (see page 74), he selected an elegant brass pull for the doors. The pull fits the design perfectly. A similar design fit is in the kitchen cabinets made by Gary Church (see page x). The rubber-covered metal pulls echo ebony accents, including strips that retain glass panes in the doors.

worked his way around the shop, setting up one machine after another, but offering little advice that would be germane outside of this well-equipped shop.

In Steve Ripper's woodworking courses at Bucks County Community College, quite a different atmosphere exists. The first hours are spent in a classroom. Ripper introduces the students, regardless of experience, to wood, then to hand tools. "Then I get into very simple things of doing joints," Ripper explains. As a practical exercise, he has each student make joints. Only manual hand tools are used. Two scraps of wood are joined in a butt joint. Two more in a dado joint. A mortise-and-tenon joint. Dovetails. He has each student plane a block of wood square and true.

Uniformly, the students find it, in Ripper's words, "profoundly eye-opening to work with hand tools for a period of weeks."

Eventually, of course, Ripper's students move beyond the solo exercise stage and begin pulling techniques together, producing practical, encouraging, even pleasing pieces. First duets, then trios and quartets. Eventually, the most gifted and intense workers create entire orchestrations of planing and jointing, ripping and plowing, of mortises and tenons, raised panels, hand-scraped surfaces and hand-rubbed finishes.

The transition from exercise to project is a tricky one. Fred Matlack, a woodworker in Rodale Press's Design Center, is a former vo-tech teacher. He believes the beginner needs "a combination of exercises and projects. It's nice if the exercises can be something functional, something leading up to a project."

Some cabinetmakers favor details that telegraph the joinery or reflect the woodworking skill they put into their work. Others, like John Vugrin, like visual surprises. Vugrin inlaid this maple leaf on the side of a drawer. You have to pull the drawer almost all the way out to see it.

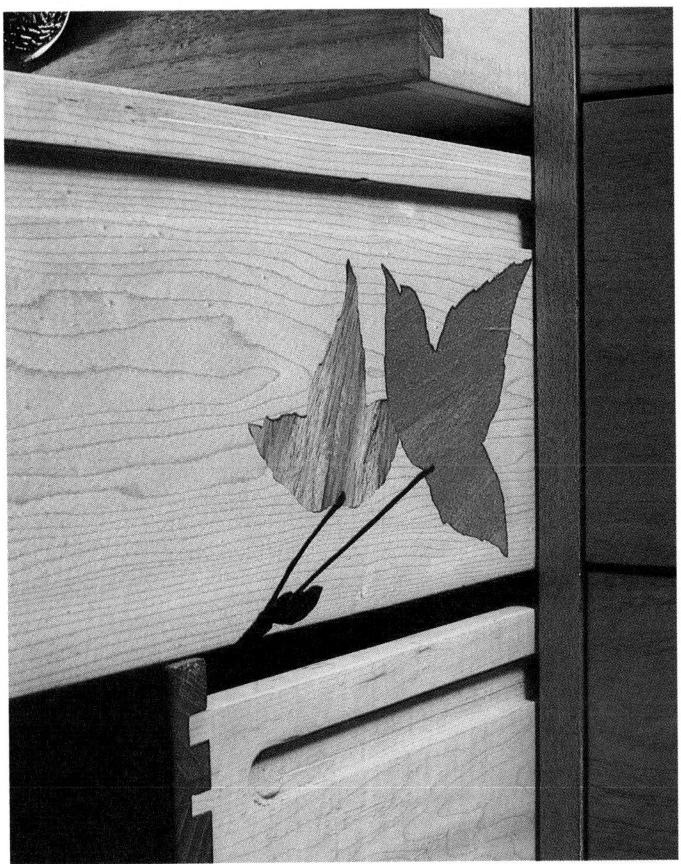

He continues: "I'm a big believer in trial setups. I do it all the time, even if it's something I've done a hundred times. I'd call that an exercise, but it's an exercise leading up to a project."

How does a beginner select a first project? Pick something you need, suggests Phil Gehret. "I am very much opposed to making projects just for the sake of making projects. If you're going to make something, make something that's functional and usable," he says.

Pick something you can cope with, recommends Matlack. "Simplicity is a virtue," he explains, "especially for the novice. Try building a bookcase. Something you can complete in one session. If you get bored with it, *then* do something more complicated."

The danger is that a too complicated project may bog you down. Matlack saw a lot of that in his teaching days. "You'd see projects sitting around for months and months because the kids got tired of them because they were too much for them to handle."

It's a good idea to find and follow plans for the first few projects you make. "You are better off not doing your own designs at the beginning," Larimore explains. "It adds quite a burden you needn't be encumbered by. The design aspect of it can be such a stumbling block that you don't enjoy the making."

Furthermore, he adds, "it's probably more informative to build someone else's design, because you are not clouding the information with ideas about the way it should look."

Speaking from his own experience, Mitch Mandel agrees. To make his first pieces, Mandel followed plans published in *Woodsmith,* a periodical, and *Make It! Don't Buy It,* a book for which he took the photographs. "I didn't have to worry about the design," he says. "I just had to worry about the technique."

It's not enough to practice and study and work. You have to be judgmental. You should *improve.* If your joints are gappy and your cases are slightly askew, there are specific techniques you must strive harder to master. If your dado joints are tight and your plywood cases are always square, evaluate your repertoire of techniques and decide whether you should expand it. Don't keep on doing only the same few joints.

Although this wall cabinet was made just as it would have been made 100 years ago and has the look of an old, old piece, its owner and builder, Douglas Pinney, doesn't consider it a reproduction. He designed it according to his own taste and crafted it of Cuban mahogany. He made everything but the lock assembly and its escutcheon. All the moldings were cut with hand planes. The finished piece was stained with an alcohol stain, then finished with a linseed-oil varnish.

This wall cabinet echoes the look of Douglas Pinney's other kitchen cabinets (see page 29) by using the same cornice molding and decorative beading. The shelf keeps the cat off the counters and its food away from the dogs.

Critique your designs, your engineering, your procedures.

Seek out the judgment of others. Guild Ten, the organization of professional woodworkers that Ripper and Walentine belong to, provides a formal way for them to grow as woodworkers. They get to see the work of others, they get to study and pick at each other's designs and craftsmanship, perhaps even to goad and be goaded by peers. Seeking this kind of judgment is, according to Walentine, "a continuing process, even on our level."

Walentine's level clearly is high. And his confidence level, too, must be high for him to seek out judgment fearlessly. The worker new to the medium may be more chary. If you are like me, you already know the failings of a piece you've made, and showing it to others for their critique can be devastating.

Even a professional like Jack Larimore is sensitive to the problem. "If I show my work, people can pick up on my mistakes more quickly than they pick up on the craftsmanship. They can articulate the mistakes."

The weight of judgment thus may be too much for the weak and the inexperienced. Larimore sees it keeping some of them out of just the situations they need: those in which their work is critiqued. "A lot of people are afraid of the exposure that comes when you take a course." But he points out that "the other option is to be frustrated out of woodworking."

What's a beginner to do?

Do what Larry Golden suggests: Plunge in. You'll never have to worry about criticism if you never give it a go. And the only way to get into woodworking is to get into it.

But dovetail the plunge with a Larimore suggestion: "Go somewhere where there is a proper setup and test your talents with a full deck. People getting into woodworking as an avocation can't afford to commit much time or money to set up. And that's a real key to success, being properly set up. [Not being properly set up] is the kind of risk you shouldn't take."

So take a course. Or find a mentor. Or spend some big money for tools and books and wood and plans. But get into it. Get started.

WOOD AND TOOLS

"I'd say getting started involves research," says Ellis Walentine. "Very little of it is intuitive."

Walentine believes the beginner should start his or her researches with the material. After something has been learned about wood, the beginner should research tools, then joinery.

Yet few fledgling woodworkers address their interest in so organized a fashion. The thing that got Mitch Mandel into woodworking wasn't that first shelf so much as the opportunity to buy a used Shopsmith. *His* researches began on several fronts simultaneously: he was learning about tools and wood at the same time he was trying out individual joints.

This is a pretty typical experience, I think. There is no truly logical starting point. You have to know a little about a lot to get even a simple bookcase made, and to progress to more sophisticated projects you must learn a lot about everything: about wood, tools, joinery, finishing, hardware, design, even about yourself. But the material is a good jumping off point.

WOOD

" 'Good material' is a myth," David Pye writes in *The Nature and Art of Workmanship.* "We talk as though good material were found instead of being made. It is good only because workmanship has made it so. . . .Some materials promise far more than others but only the workman can bring out what they promise."

Walnut is just a pretty-colored wood. In the hands of a woodbutcher, it is little better than a scrappy grade of pine. But in the hands of a craftsman like Steve Ripper, even relatively low-grade walnut boards can be the makings of a distinctive shelving unit. All the marvelous aesthetic qualities of the wood are brought out in Ripper's piece—the shapes of the logs, the unique figures of each board, the rich color. The promise is realized.

Flashy or exotic wood isn't a prerequisite for a distinctive project. Many cabinetmakers choose to work with woods that are freely and inexpensively available locally. Furnituremaker Steven Heckeroth built this hutch for his own home using madrone and tan oak, two woods native to California and quite popular with woodworkers there.

Making good material of wood is a difficult proposition. There are so many facets to cope with that not all can be easily mastered at one time. The more functional aspects tend to be dealt with and mastered first. After the practicalities become second nature, when you no longer have to plot out each step in crafting a mortise-and-tenon joint, then you can study the subtleties of how the aesthetic character of the particular boards you have at your disposal can complement the practicalities of what you are trying to construct.

"Wood," Jack Larimore points out, "is a difficult medium because there's so much variety in it. You have to be able to recognize, when you see it in the rough, whether you can work it

The wood used in a cabinet can enhance it visually. The wood's figure, which many people call grain, can complement a piece. Spectacular figure has been carefully bookmatched in a glued-up dresser side, left, *and in a panel for kitchen cabinet doors,* left center. *What might have been ordinary slabs of wood are far from that. Too, a board's figure can contribute to the unity of a piece by tying individual elements together, such as side-by-side drawer fronts cut from a single board,* right center. *The figure flows across the front of the cabinet, subtly enhancing the unity of the piece. Finally, old wood,* right, *has a character of its own that can be of value.*

or not. It is not manufactured, so there's no uniformity to it."

The way building materials are processed and marketed may lead the beginner, the do-it-yourselfer, to believe there *is* uniformity. The local home improvement center has all those nicely surfaced pine 1 × 6s and 1 × 8s and 1 × 10s. There's a system of sizing, a system of grading; there are even brand names stamped on some boards. But as he picks through the stack, even the most obtuse do-it-yourselfer will see there's no true uniformity. Some boards are straight and true, but all too many are cupped or twisted or bowed or knotty. The figure of one board is beautiful, another bland.

But the wood that Jack Larimore is talking about is not the stuff of home improvement centers. He's talking about hardwoods.

Hardwoods typically are sold in a rough-sawn state, in random widths and lengths. In sawing logs into boards, the sawyer's goal is to maximize the yield, so individual boards won't be trimmed to arbitrarily uniform widths or lengths. The only uniformity is the measure of the thickness—and that measure is commonly couched in terms of quarter inches; thus a 1-inch-thick board is a 4/4 board, a 2-inch-thick

board is an 8/4 board. According to Ripper, cabinetmakers primarily use 5/4 and 6/4 stock, along with some 8/4, 10/4 and 12/4.

A full-service lumberyard will stock some hardwood, and it usually will have the facilities necessary to dress the stock to your specifications.

Just how a craftsman shops in such a place depends both (or either) on the craftsman and the lumberyard. Just how far through a stack you can pick in search of the perfect board for your cabinet is something you learn only by experience. Woodworking experience will help you choose boards; shopping experience will help you pick suppliers.

A key point to remember is that no matter how carefully you shop, and how carefully you try to select individual boards, dressing the wood uncovers surprises. One surprise may be a defect, another an unexpectedly attractive figure or color.

So you pick and choose based on whim initially, based on experience later. But there's still the matter of finding a stack of boards from which to choose.

Beyond full-service lumberyards, there are specialty lumberyards. Larry Golden drives more than 50 miles from his rural Wisconsin shop to Minneapolis to buy at Youngblood Lumber Company. Youngblood, he says, has only hardwoods, domestic and exotic, and specialty plywoods. No construction lumber, no paint, no cement, no roofing materials. What he likes about the firm, in addition to the selection of woods, is the atmosphere. "It's a nice feeling," he says. "They trust you."

According to Golden, the craftsman is free to browse through the huge selection of woods, taking as much time as he wants to evaluate individual boards. Neither clerk nor yardman follows him around, monitoring his movements, urging him to take the first board off the pile, pressing him to complete the transaction.

Golden's trips for lumber are usually prompted by a commission. "My operation is so small I can't afford to go and get it whenever I want to," he explains. But when he *does,* he makes it a point to buy extra. "And that's part of my private stash."

Some woodworkers venture farther for wood. Jack Larimore, who lives and works in Philadelphia, shops in New York State and Massachusetts for much of his material. He shops by mail, so a different sort of trust comes into play.

The supplier, Larimore reports, sends him a sample of wood, guaranteeing that the sample is representative of the lot. Larimore has to trust that when the truck carrying his lumber arrives, the lot will in fact be like the sample. He's not picking and choosing, he's taking material sight unseen. On faith.

The trade-on is that he's getting stock not available to him in Philadelphia. Curiously, I know woodworkers who travel, in the manner of Larry Golden, 50 to 70 miles *to* Philadelphia to buy lumber. Larimore is *there,* but he shops 200 to 300 miles away.

This must all be a part of the materials mystique. *Traveling* to obscure locations is a piece of the mystique. Having a "stash" of special wood for special projects is another. And buying directly from a sawmill is still another.

Phil Gehret talks of his "private stock" in his barn. The boards were sawn from logs felled on his own farm. He uses them only for his reproductions, pieces he will, most likely, keep in his family. Can there be a more pure manifestation of mystique?

Larry Golden, too, has a private stash. Much of his, he says, comes from a friend who owns and operates a small sawmill. The friend, says Golden, is a gifted sawyer. He seems to have a special sense for the way to saw a log to enhance the aesthetic value of the lumber it yields. In characteristic fashion, Golden calls this "being able to run a saw better than other people." He clearly appreciates his friend's talent, for it is from this man's saw that Golden's most valued material comes. "He calls when something is good, and that's where another part of my private stash comes from."

The private stash can be a burden. Steve Ripper's wood shop is flanked by stickered stacks of wood. Its attic is full of wood stacks. His garage is full of wood. Periodically, he says, he tears down a stack, sorts through the boards, and restacks them. Setting up a stickered stack is a lot of physical labor. Tearing one down, then building it back up again is even more.

Therein lies Ripper's burden. Keeping an inventory of what you have, even when your private stash is small, is nearly impossible. The characteristics of individual boards can't be quantified. Finding material good for a particular project entails examining many candidates. Unstacking and restacking. If you are driven, as Ripper is, then you work hard at rotating your stock, at selecting boards with the best potential for the cabinet or bookcase to be made next. The mystique is a physical as well as a psychic burden.

Old wood is something both Gehret and Ripper have in their private stashes. Ever practical, Gehret says of this aspect of his stash, "I recycle a lot of stuff." If wood is sound, he'll use it regardless of age or previous uses.

Ripper is more effusive. "Old wood! You buy some wood 50 or 60 years old—it's a dream to work. It seems to get mellow with age. Under a hand plane, it planes like a dream."

Where does this old wood come from? A lot of it is what's left of the private stashes of woodworkers who have moved on to that great shop in the sky. Country auctions in my area—Eastern Pennsylvania—occasionally feature 100 to 500 board-foot lots of cherry or walnut that someone stashed in the barn "before the war,"

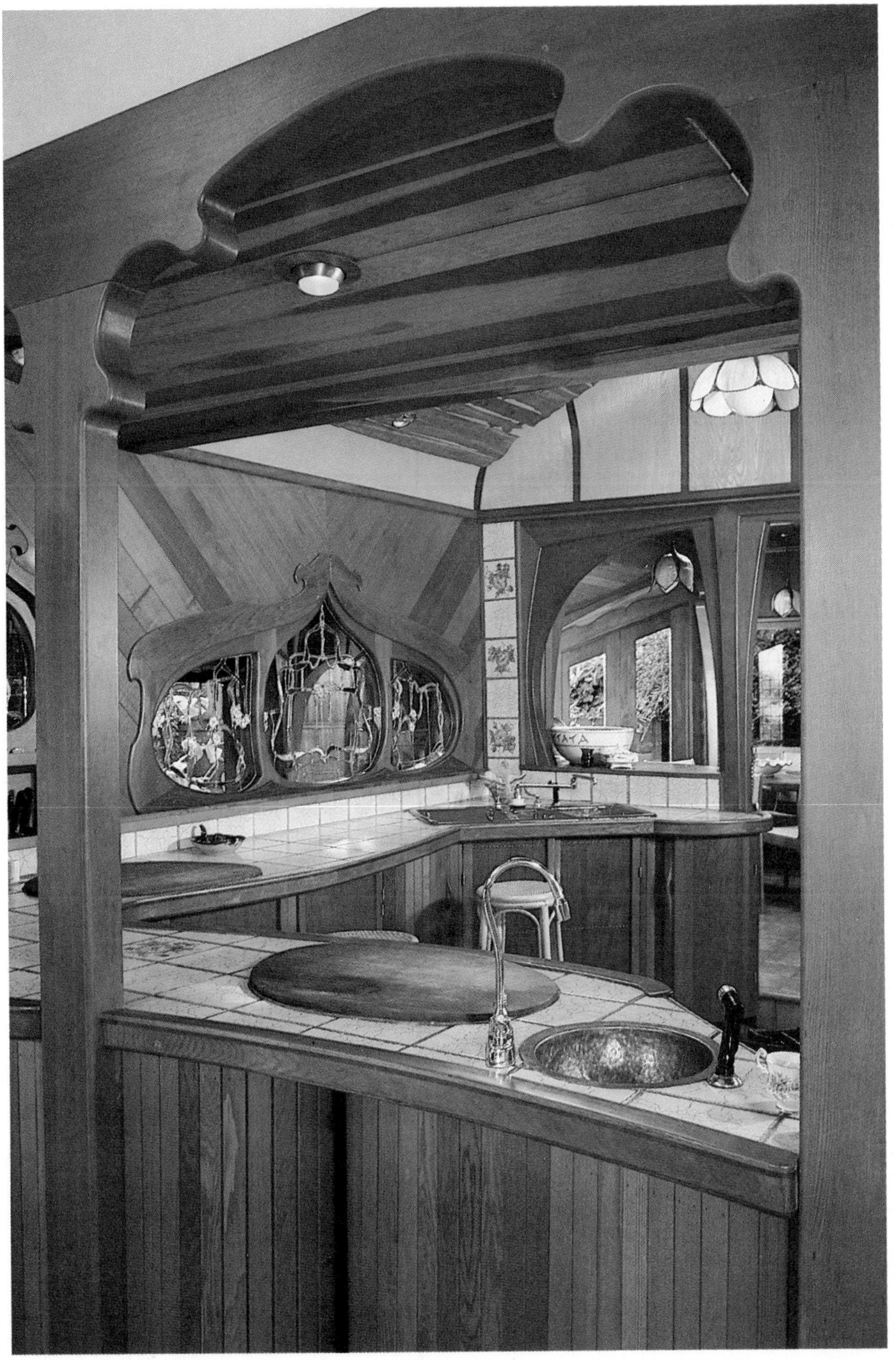

The color of wood can be important. In some instances, muted colors are desirable. But in a wonderfully uninhibited environment like this kitchen, something with pizzazz is in order. The redwood used here complements the dynamics of the curves—layer upon layer of them—and at the same time casts a warm glow over the entire kitchen.

meaning a good 40 years ago, and never got around to using.

But some of this old wood is in fact recycled wood. Ripper says there are still a few chestnut telephone poles in his area. One such pole was the source of the chestnut in his wall cabinet. I have a friend who (though he isn't a woodworker) relishes knowing—and not telling—where there's an old, old barn made almost entirely of walnut. There are real hazards—nails particularly—in preparing such materials for use, but it can be done.

Buying at the source requires a trip to a sawmill. And this is the real trip in woodworking. It puts the woodworker closer to the source, closer to the tree itself. At the sawmill is where the promise is unlocked.

As a tree, wood is pure promise. It can remain a tree and fulfill one promise. It can be cut down, sawed into boards, turned into utilitarian cabinets or shelves and fulfill another promise. It can be crafted into a custom-made dresser. It can be sculpted into a work of art. But it can also become firewood.

All these promises lie in the hands of a succession of workmen. First the logger, then the sawyer, then the woodworker. What each extracts from the wood depends upon his abilities, his frame of reference, his sensibilities, even his state of mind.

A logger with no thought in his mind but firewood may butcher a perfectly marvelous old walnut tree. One who is more thoughtful, more caring, will turn that tree to a higher use. The sawyer will process the butt log—the section of trunk between the stump and first branches—into boards. A shrewd sawyer *may* sell this log to a veneer mill; he'll get top dollar for the log, and the wood in it will be spread over far more cabinets than 5/4 boards sawn from it could make.

George Nakashima is horrified by this practice. He *abhors* veneer. In his book, *The Soul of a Tree,* he speaks of contemporary lumbering practices in splenetic tone. Slicing prime logs into veneer makes him particularly angry. He calls it "the psychology of match-stick manufacture," and rails against "the tragedy of once-in-a-lifetime timbers cut into veneers so thin the light can shine through."

Nakashima is best known for the table created from a single slab of wood, usually a wood that's both exotic and breathtakingly beautiful. Its shape—not square, rectangular or round—is dictated by the tree.

"Every tree, every part of a tree, has only one perfect use," he says, and he seeks to find that perfect use. Hence, the key part of his work is unlocking the promise each log contains. In his book he writes: "The sawing of logs is of prime importance. Each cut requires judgments and decisions on what the log should become. As in cutting a diamond, the judgments must be precise and exact concerning thickness and direction of cut, especially through 'figures,' the complicated designs resulting from the tree's grain. If a figure is cut properly, the beauty locked in the tree will gradually emerge. If cut improperly, most is lost."

The cutting of the log is so important that Nakashima, though he regards the sawyer as "one of the greatest craftsmen of our age," personally directs the operation. "Cutting logs is a great responsibility," he explains in his book, "for we are dealing with fallen majesty. There

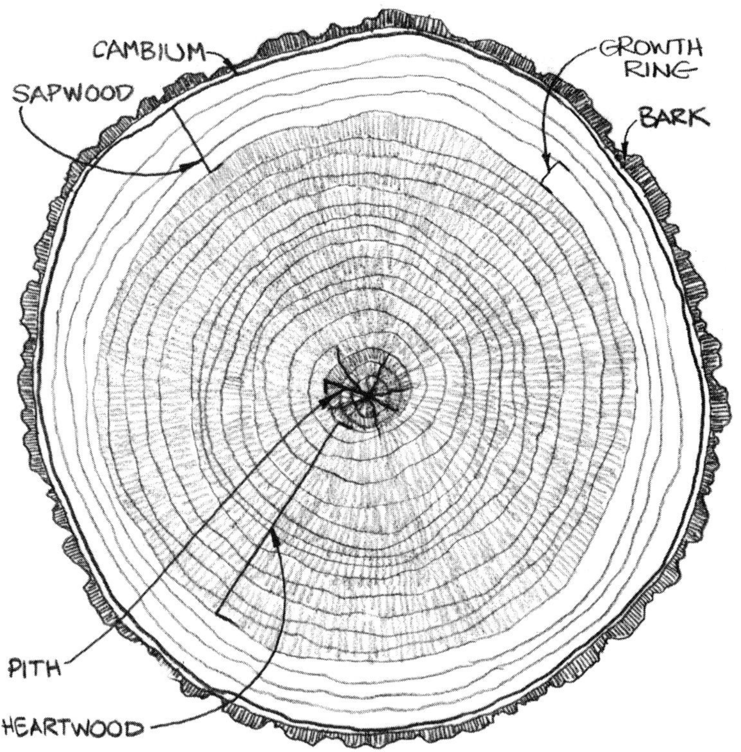

Bark *is a tree's outer covering.* Cambium *is the new growth; each year's growth is delinated by a* growth ring. Sapwood *is the conduit between roots and leaves; it is usually lighter colored than heartwood.* Heartwood *is composed of rigid, dead cells that support the tree and store food. In a softwood, the sapwood area is larger, while in a hardwood, the heartwood area is larger. The* pith *is the tree's core.*

are no formulas, no guidelines, but only experiences, instinct and a contact with the divine."

There can be no dispute that it is the wood itself—the spectacular figures and colors and shapes of the wood—that *make* Nakashima's furniture. And of course he is not alone in his unrelenting search for appropriate wood. Most woodworkers have at least one special nerve ending that's ever alert for material with special potential.

The travels to sawmills are just one part of their search. They, like Larimore, shop through the mail. They scan ads in woodworking magazines, in local newspapers and in shopper-swapper classified ad publications, looking for new places to try. They try to acquire promising logs, even if they must fell the tree personally. Some use chainsaw mills to turn logs into lumber, but usually people who get a sawable log or two have a local mill do the sawing for them.

I've done this. In return for helping fell a couple of big, old cherry trees, I got five logs. For a truly modest charge—less than ten dollars as I recall—a local sawmill flitch-cut them, just as I asked. It wasn't done while I waited; I didn't confer over the angle of each cut or anything. The mill operator insisted on waiting until his saw's blade, a frightening disk as big in diameter as each of my logs was in length with probably a hundred and a half bolted-in-place teeth, was ready for sharpening. My assurances that the logs weren't from line trees—those growing along tree or fence lines between farm fields—notwithstanding, the sawyer seemed to know he would run into nails or wire or staples imbedded in one or more of the logs. No sense imperiling the equipment.

And he was right. Just recently I extracted twisted strands of rusty fence wire from one of the six-year-old flitches, a good 2 inches into the wood from the bark edge. Decades old, it was. And representative of the perils of recycling old barn beams, telephone poles, line trees, even residential and roadside trees. A lot of mills

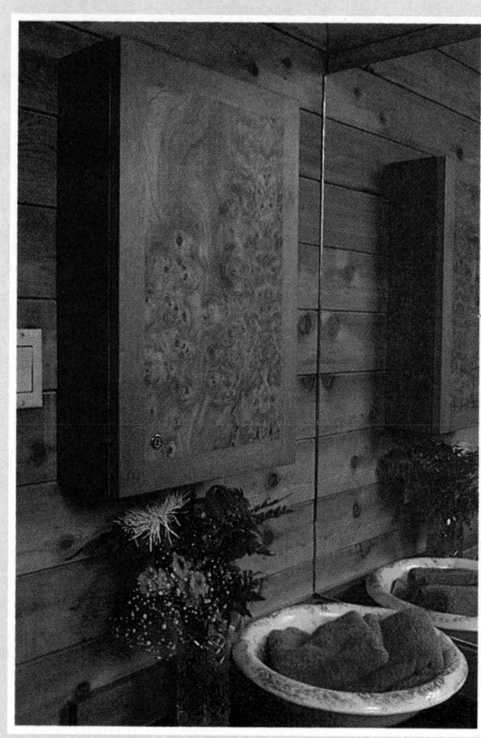

won't cut any of these under *any* circumstances.

This particular mill, Bailey's Lumber Company, is surely typical of those that will deal with individual woodworkers. They seem to exist wherever there are trees to be cut and sawed into boards.

Bailey's is set in a sawdust desert. A handful of employees process logs and sort lumber year round. Equipment for making pallets is on hand, though it's only used occasionally. The lumber is sold primarily to wholesale customers, but also to area farmers and woodworkers. I've purchased poplar, oak, cherry, walnut, some sassafras, and white pine there. That's what grows around here; that's what they saw.

Sawing logs can be done several different ways. The boards I've bought have been plainsawn. In this method, the sawyer slabs off a strip of bark, creating a flat face along the log, which will be the face of the first board. The sawyer saws off board after board until a defect—most likely a knot—is uncovered. Then the log is rolled 90 degrees and the process is repeated. The method is sometimes referred to as "rolling the log."

Ripper, for one, prefers this method for butt logs. "Butt logs," he says, "make the best lumber—the clearest and the oldest, so I usually have them plainsawn, depending upon the size of the log. The heart is usually more subject to checking and defects, so I discard a 3-inch by 3-inch heartwood core."

In *Understanding Wood,* R. Bruce Hoadley points out that the clear wood is generally right under the bark. Branches arise in the pith, and since the branches are the source of knots, the pith—the core of the log—is where the defects will be. Plainsawing gives the maximum yield of clear lumber. Clear lumber is what a cabinetmaker like Ripper wants, so that's the way Ripper has logs sawed.

Another approach is quartersawing. In this method, the log is halved, then quartered. Then each quarter is sawed into boards, so that the widest boards are perpendicular to the log's growth rings. This method yields boards that are largely edge-grained. Edge-grained boards finish and wear more uniformly than flat-grained boards, and they are more dimensionally stable across their width. The big disadvantage to this method is that it is slow (there's a lot of extra handling) and the yield of reasonably wide boards is limited.

How can a woodworker on a budget execute a cabinet in kevazingo blister? Only through the use of veneers, which are thin slices of wood that can be glued to a sound but otherwise undistinguished base wood.

James Connelly of Huntingdon Valley, Pennsylvania, made the smashing medicine cabinet, left—and several matching bathroom cabinets—using veneers. The cabinet and door frame are solid teak, but the door panel is a veneer of Carpathian elm burl applied to a basswood base.

Applying veneer is a simple though risky procedure. The woodworker prepares the base, applies glue evenly to it, lays the veneer in place, quickly aligns it, presses it firmly to the base using a roller or a veneer hammer, then clamps it in a veneer press. Problems can arise if the base is unstable or poorly prepared, if the glue spread is uneven or the veneer inadequately clamped, if individual pieces of veneer are not carefully matched or jointed.

Nevertheless, for a lot of woodworkers, veneering is a viable technique. Connelly offers a couple of suggestions.

He recommends that the woodworker go to the veneer mill to select pieces, because buying a veneer "skin" from a retailer can be risky. The log yielding the veneer may have been felled in one country, then shipped with little haste to a veneer mill in another. After slicing, the veneers may be air-dried and/or kiln-dried, stored for protracted periods in uncontrolled environments, then shipped to manufacturers or retailers. By traveling to the mill, the woodworker can eliminate some of these variables, and, in the bargain, select skins sliced from a single log, so a true match of color and figure is obtained.

Connelly also recommends that 2-ply veneers be used, because they are less frail and thus more easily worked than the traditional 1-ply skins. A 2-ply skin is created at the veneer mill by gluing a desirable veneer to a reinforcing veneer sliced from a compatible yet less treasured wood. These veneers are still only 1/16 inch thick.

Both of these methods are scorned by Nakashima. Rolling the log, he says, is "one of the most barbaric of practices." His technique of choice is known as "sawing through and through," or flitch-cutting. The log is not slabbed, it is not rolled, it is not quartered. It is simply cut into a series of slices, called flitches, which make full use of the log's width.

Curiously, Hoadley identifies "through and through" sawing as the type used on logs with numerous defects because "little may be gained by turning." The defects, of course, are the source of some of Nakashima's most favored displays. Clear lumber is seldom what he is looking for.

Traditionally, lumber is stacked with stickers just as it comes off the saw. "Depending

Particle board as a finish material is just the sort of selection one would expect of Larry Golden. And it works. Golden made these shelves using torsion box construction. He first built a gridwork frame of 2 × 2s for each shelf and fastened it to the walls. Then he glued and nailed high density particle board to both top and bottom of the frame, edging the shelf decoratively with redwood. The shelves are extremely strong and, says Golden, "They're real pretty."

upon the design of the project and what it will look like," Ripper says, "I try to use all wood cut from one log, for reasons of matching texture and color, and because it is likely to be more uniform when treated with stain or finish." Grouping the boards by the log from which they've come allows him to do this. Moreover, grouping the boards in sequence allows a cabinetmaker to bookmatch doors and drawer fronts.

Drying lumber is important because wood fresh from the saw is "wet." For rude sorts of constructions, it can be used that way. But for its cabinetmaking promise to be realized, it must be carefully dried, or seasoned. The cabinetmaker who buys from a sawmill must season his own wood. The one who buys at a lumberyard can and should insist that the material be kiln-dried.

When I say that wood coming off the saw is wet, I mean just that. With a good-sized machinist's vise you can literally squeeze water from a freshly sawn board. In drying a board, most of the water is removed, either through free or forced evaporation. Eventually, it will dry to a point called equilibrium moisture content (EMC). It is at this point that the board is ready to be worked.

EMC is not a static point. It changes from season to season, and even from week to week, as the atmospheric humidity and the temperature change. This is because the board can not only surrender its moisture, it can take on moisture.

Two important things happen to a board as the water leaves it. It loses weight and it shrinks. The weight loss provides a way for cabinetmakers to monitor the seasoning process.

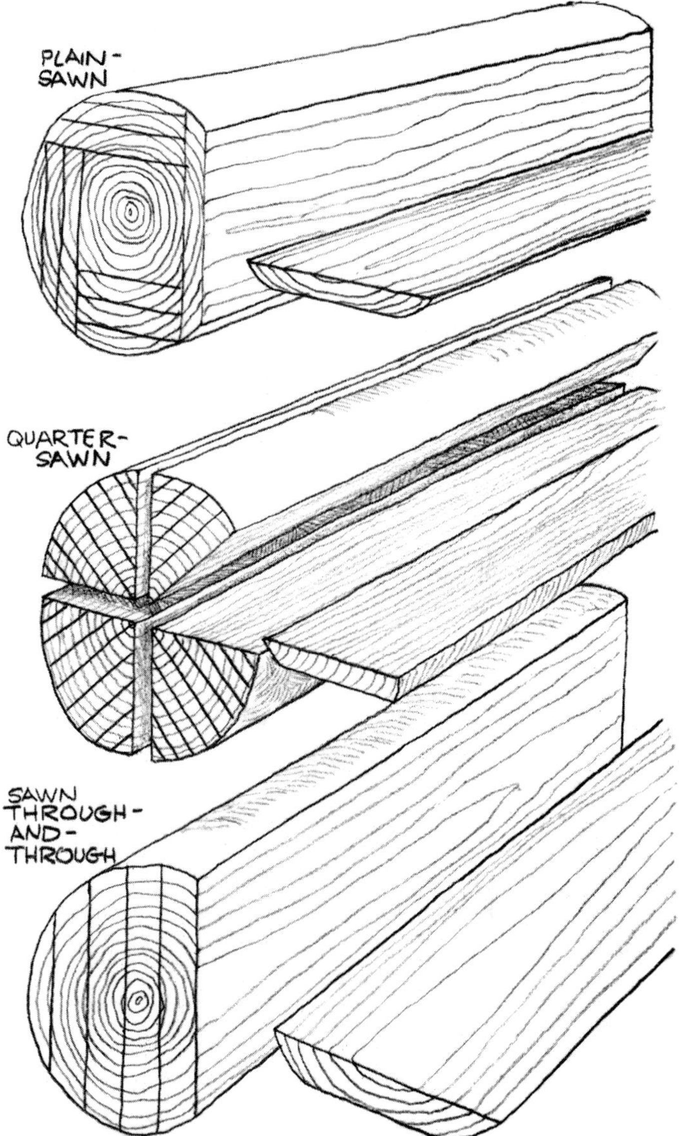

Plainsawing, also referred to as "rolling the log" or "sawing 'round the log," is the most common log-sawing technique, producing predominantly flat-grained boards and maximizing the yield of clear lumber. Quartersawing is the most laborious approach, producing a lot of waste and mostly narrow, albeit edge-grained, boards. Sawing through-and-through is usually "quick and dirty": the log is reduced to boards quickly, but the yield is of widely ranging quality with very few clear boards.

The shrinking is one part of the dimensional instability that the cabinetmaker worries about in designing and building cabinets.

The way the water leaves the board has a lot to do with the shape the board is in when the process is completed. If you were to drive the water out with a great deal of dry heat, you would get a very dry board, but you'd also get a warped, checked and probably case-hardened board.

In this situation, the outer layers of cells, forming what is called the shell, give off their water. They then find themselves under stress because the still-wet core won't allow them to shrink as much as they would like. But they place the core under stress, too. Eventually, as the shell stabilizes, the stress on the core changes. Now the core is drying and trying to shrink, but the shell is preventing it. Serious case-hardening can result in honeycombing, in which fissures open in the core.

Even if the case-hardening doesn't result in honeycombing, the wood is defective. The problem, though, is that the board doesn't appear to be defective. But when it is resawed, cut or machined, the board warps as the stresses relieve themselves.

Air-drying and kiln-drying are the two ways to season wood. Some cabinetmakers like to debate the virtues of one approach over the other in terms of the finished product. Some believe the heat and steam of the kiln deaden the color of wood. Others detect differences in the way the wood yields to tools.

"There's just something about it," Steve Ripper says of air-dried wood. "I don't know what it is. It's just a dream to work, especially with hand tools." And in fact, most if not all of Ripper's projects are made using air-dried wood.

Phil Gehret, though he believes air-dried wood is more resilient and thus makes better tool handles, doesn't see much practical difference. "The average person can't tell the difference between air-dried and kiln-dried wood in cabinetmaking," he says. The material he uses for his personal projects is air-dried. Were he to take on a cabinetry project for someone else, he'd go right out and buy kiln-dried wood at a lumberyard.

Drying wood in a kiln can take a month or more. The kiln is well-insulated building with equipment to control the temperature, humidity and air circulation. Green wood is stacked in the kiln with stickers between the layers so air can circulate fully around each board. Following a proven sequence of steps, in the aggregate called a kiln schedule, the operator slowly reduces the humidity and increases the temperature in the kiln. The goal is to accelerate the drying process to just shy of the point at which it would induce checking and case-hardening. The wood is actually taken below the desired moisture level. The last step in the schedule is to inject steam to reintroduce moisture to the surface layers of the wood, bringing the wood to the desired moisture level, and, at the same time, relieving internal stresses. This process yields "kiln-dried, stress-relieved wood."

Ripper admonishes all woodworkers who buy kiln-dried wood to ensure that it has been stress-relieved.

The approach the cabinetmaker is more likely to take to season green wood is to air-dry it. He will have everything ready for the wood when he brings it home. He will stack it carefully with stickers between each layer of boards, he'll shield the stack from the direct sun and rain, and slowly the wood will dry. In the end, if he isn't neglectful, and if he is modestly lucky, he will have a stack of relatively inexpensive material.

The cabinetmaker must monitor the seasoning process. If the wood dries too quickly, as evidenced by the development of surface checks, he must try somehow to retard the process. A plastic tarp covering the stack will hold in moisture. If fungi develop on the boards, air circulation must be improved. Perhaps the stack is in too dank a location and needs to be moved to a drier, more breezy spot.

Never does a good cabinetmaker rely on such rules of thumb for seasoning as: "Dry the wood a year for each inch of thickness." Doing that leads to neglect, which Hoadley identifies as a primary reason that material is ruined.

So the cabinetmaker must monitor the moisture level of the wood. There are several ways to do this, the easiest being to use a moisture meter. The meter shows the percentage of moisture in a piece of wood. Literature supplied with a moisture meter tells the user how to take readings and how to compensate for different species of wood.

A more laborious method for monitoring moisture levels is to periodically weigh a sample board and plot its weight on a graph. The board will lose weight rather precipitously at first, but eventually the weight will level off. When it does, the board can be assumed to have reached equilibrium moisture content.

Remember that EMC is the goal of the

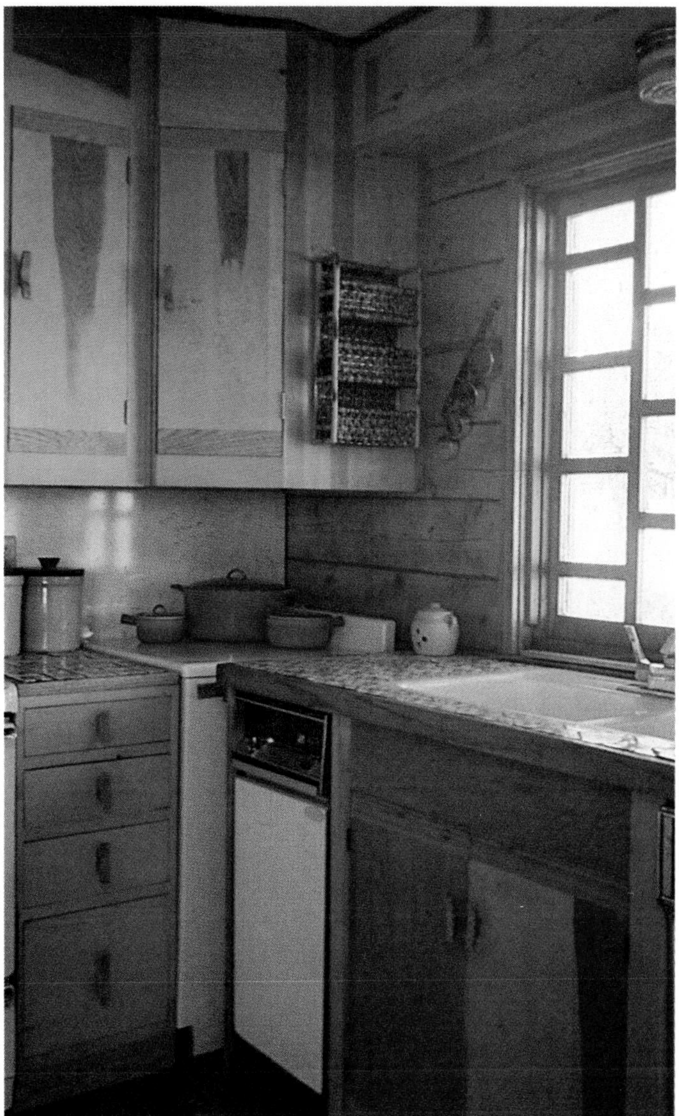

Both heartwood—the dark streaks—and sapwood were used by wood carver and cabinetmaker John Zoltai in making cabinets for his own kitchen. The contrast of colors is inherent and totally natural. Too, there's more interest than if only one or the other had been used.

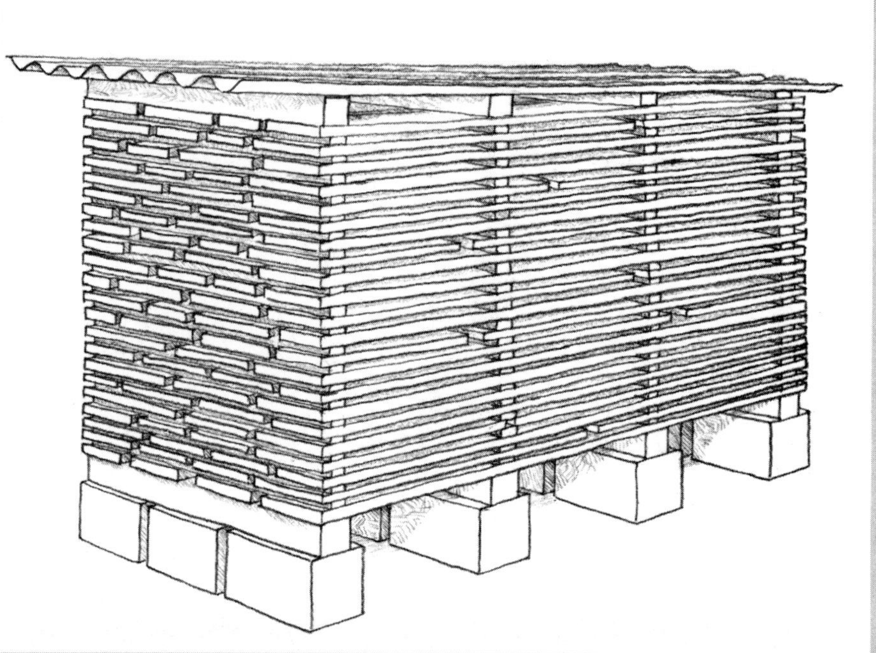

Stacking Wood

Wood begins drying as soon as the tree is felled. Sawing the log into boards exposes much more of the wood to the air, and the drying process accelerates. If the boards lie in a heap whilst the cabinetmaker scouts his yard or shop for a suitable spot for the stack, then collects the necessary foundation materials and stickers, it is likely he'll end up with lesser quality wood.

Having everything ready when the wood arrives is important.

Usually, the stack is built outdoors. Although the wood ordinarily is brought indoors for the final phase of seasoning, stacking green wood in a heated environment can prompt it to dry too quickly, leading to checking and case-hardening. The green wood can be stacked in an open shed, an unheated garage, or the like without problem. Wherever the stack is erected, it should have unrestricted air flow around and through it, but it should be protected from the sun, rain and snow.

Build the stack well off the ground. This is, again, to promote air circulation, but it is also to keep the wood away from the damp earth and the insects and fungi found there. Set cement blocks in rows the width of the stack and 16 inches apart. Lay dry timbers, say 4 × 4s along the block tops, then erect the stack atop them.

The individual boards should be laid in place with an inch or so of space between them. The ends should be supported so they don't bow or twist. As the first layer is filled out, position a sticker—thoroughly dry strips of 1 × 1 stock make good stickers—directly above a foundation timber. As subsequent layers are filled out, the stickers should be directly above other stickers. When all the wood is incorporated in the stack, cover it with a sheet of corrugated roofing or the like to protect it from the rain. Weights, like cement blocks, can be placed on top to help prevent warping of the boards in the top layer or two.

seasoning process. Remember too that the EMC varies from season to season and from the outdoors to a heated or air-conditioned house. Lumber must be allowed to acclimate to the conditions under which it will be used. Air-dried lumber should be stored in a stickered stack in a heated shop for several weeks (even months) before it is worked so it acclimates to the drier conditions. Kiln-dried lumber, on the other hand, may need to take on a bit of moisture to reach EMC. As Hoadley writes, " . . . [W]ood seeks to establish an equilibrium moisture content according to the relative humidity of the surrounding atmosphere. If this point is kept in mind, the rest will follow logically."

"The rest" includes the selection of joinery, for wood is *always* seeking an equilibrium moisture content, not simply during the seasoning process. Occasionally you read or hear of wood "breathing," which of course it never does. The person using the term is simply trying to convey the idea that as wood seeks EMC, it changes size, expanding as the moisture content rises, shrinking as the moisture content falls. One of Rodale's woodworkers, Fred Matlack, refers to this as "the come and go" of wood.

Matlack is inclined to view the come and go as more than a passing problem, especially for beginners or hobbyists. "I've seen people have a lot of trouble with that," he says. "Cut the pieces one weekend. Come back the next, and they're all different sizes." Obviously, assembly is a bit vexing in this situation.

But there's more to it than that. There's the matter of how to join materials that are

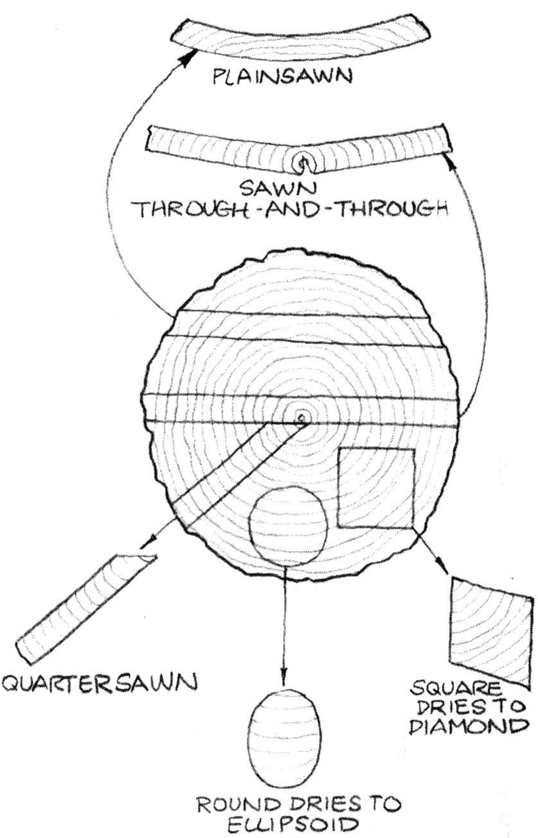

As wood dries, it shrinks and quite often changes shape. A flatsawn board will tend to cup, with the edges curling toward the "sapwood face." A quartersawn board will shrink relatively little and usually remain straight and true. One sawn through-and-through may be wide, but will crack and deform where it intersects the pith.

continually swelling and contracting. If the grain isn't oriented properly, if the wrong sort of joint is used, if allowances aren't made for movement, the wooden object can self-destruct.

It is to circumvent as much of this kind of trouble as possible that some woodworkers turn to plywood.

Plywood is woodworking's polyester. It has some very wonderful properties, but it is *déclassé,* proletarian, simply *beneath* cabinet-

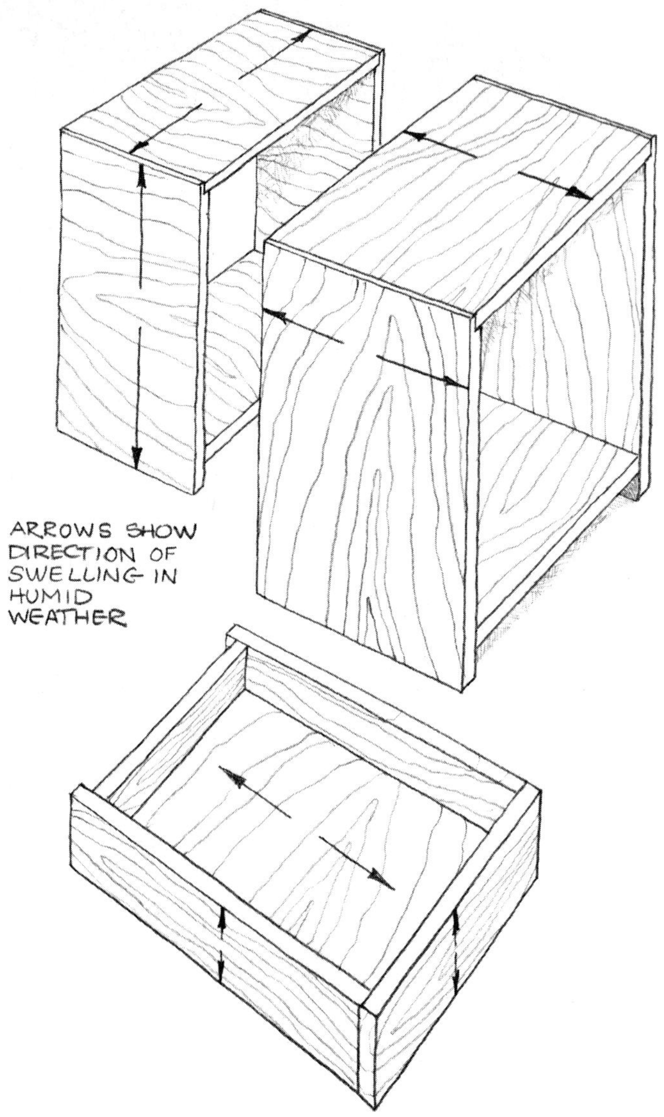

Orienting the grain properly in a solid wood carcass, top right, *makes the wood's seasonal dimension change, indicated by the arrows, manageable. If the grain is improperly oriented,* top left, *the change will be top to bottom and side to side, potentially pinching doors and drawers. In a drawer,* bottom, *the grain of a solid wood bottom must be oriented so the swelling is front to back, which is manageable, rather than side to side, which could knock the drawer apart.*

making's elite. Just as there are people who wouldn't be caught dead wearing a polyester shirt, there are woodworkers who would not be caught dead using plywood. For *anything.* Not for a concealed case, not for a drawer bottom, not for a hidden partition.

But other woodworkers have latched onto plywood as a marvelous material that takes a lot of the traditional worries out of their craft. They use it for everything: cases, drawers, doors.

Plywood has significant advantages over solid wood, all derived from its construction. It comes in huge sheets. It is strong. It is far more stable than solid wood.

As anyone who's read even a single book on woodworking knows, plywood is made up of very thin veneers of solid wood glued together in crisscrossing layers. Good plywood has an odd number of layers, with the greater number of layers having their grain oriented along the length of the sheet. While the prime strength of plywood lies in the direction of the face veneer's grain, it is strong in either direction.

There are two kinds of plywood, hardwood and softwood, and the cabinetmaker will use both.

Softwood plywood, made primarily for the construction industry, is assembled mostly from softwood veneers. The fact that the veneers are rotary-cut from logs gives softwood plywood that characteristic ugly figure. Waterproof glues are used almost exclusively these days, so "interior" plywood is virtually unobtainable: it's *all* exterior plywood.

Because of its crazy figure, plywood isn't a material you want to have exposed in a handcrafted cabinet. Oh, an artist may incorporate it to "make a statement" of some sort, but face it, softwood plywood is ugly.

Phil Gehret has used softwood plywood for kitchen and bathroom cabinetry where cost is a significant factor. The plywood is exposed on the insides of the cabinets, but hidden beneath a solid-wood face frame on the outside. "If the ends are going to be exposed," Gehret says, "then a ¼-inch panel [of hardwood plywood] can cover them."

A specialty plywood sometimes used for painted cabinets is called medium density overlay (MDO). MDO has a sheet of kraft paper sealed to each face, completely obscuring that plywood figure and giving the panel a wonderfully smooth surface. Many of those big green Interstate highway signs are made with MDO or its kin HDO (high density overlay).

The plywood most frequently used in cabinetmaking is hardwood plywood. It is made primarily for the furniture and architectural woodworking industries. The veneers in it are flitch cut; the face veneers are carefully matched in one of several ways to provide the optimum appearance. In addition to the all-veneer sandwich, hardwood plywood is made in lumber-core and particle board-core forms.

The usual problem with hardwood plywood is availability. Although it is made using a vast array of hardwoods—even exotic and uniquely figured woods—it is not easy for the individual craftsman to get. Lumberyards may stock birch plywood, but seldom any other hardwood plywood. For them it is a special-order item. There are dealers who specialize

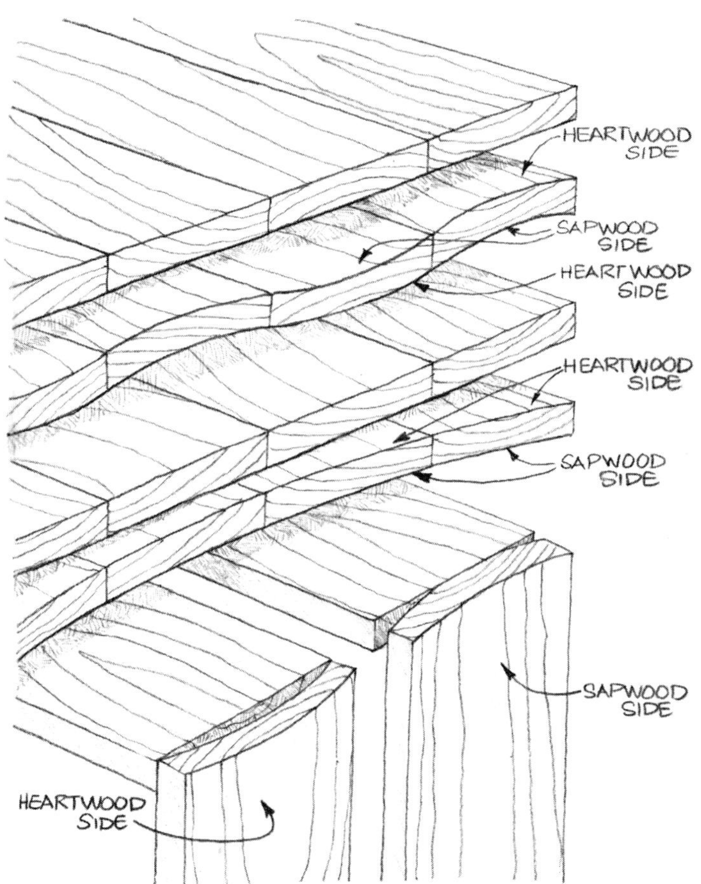

Properly orienting the sapwood/heartwood sides of boards (or, to put it another way, the growth rings) can play a significant role in the durability of a piece. Recall that wood is always swelling and shrinking in response to humidity and temperature changes. If the growth rings are alternated in a glued-up panel, the panel could get ripply (it's exaggerated here) as adjacent boards cup in opposite directions. If all boards are similarly oriented, the cupping of individual boards results in a more manageable deformation of the panel. Orientation in a case is important, too. If the sapwood side is out, the edges of a board can pull away from its mate, but if the heartwood side is out, the edges will push into the mate. The latter situation is usually regarded as the more manageable.

In some situations, the wood used for a piece is dictated by circumstance. The wall cabinet shown was part of the house's original cabinetry—it was built around the turn of the century. The current owner commissioned a cabinet to fit beneath the old sink. It had to match the old wall cabinet, of course, and that dictated the kind of wood to be used.

Plywood, below, *is a wood veneer and glue sandwich. Good plywood, whether hardwood or softwood, has an odd total number of veneers. Both have several quality levels, judged largely on the basis of the face veneer's defects or lack thereof. Only hardwood plywood is made up of flitch-cut veneers. These veneers may be matched on the face in several patterns,* right.

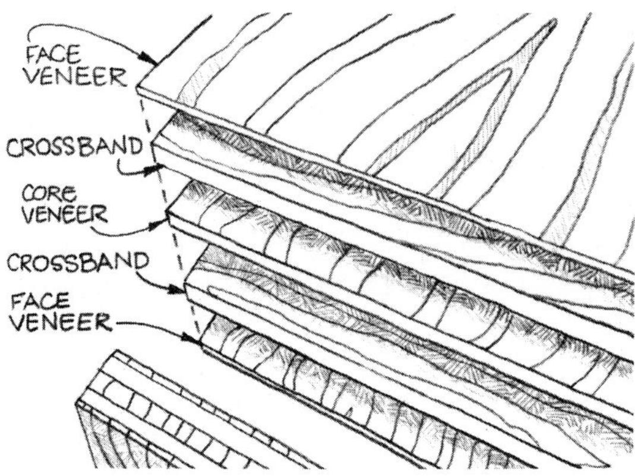

BOOKMATCH

RANDOM MATCH

SLIPMATCH

in hardwood plywoods and provide selection, but they aren't found in every town.

For cabinetmakers who don't feel constrained to use solid wood exclusively, plywood has a lot of appeal. "It's uniform," says Larry Golden. "It's strong. I like plywood as a material."

Gehret sees several other advantages to plywood. The stability and the cost are important to him.

Cost frequently enters into Gehret's woodworking equation. To him, plywood is a labor-saving material. Stan Griskivich, a woodworker featured in the Gallery (see page 144), has articulated the concept well. "You've got a big, wide case side that's 2 feet wide and over 7 feet high. To glue all that up from solid stock and sand it and square it up would take a lot of time, whereas you just cut the plywood out of 4 × 8 sheets and away you go."

This is a calculation that some would prefer to figure a different way. "The thing you find out is that a piece of walnut plywood costs as much as the walnut, so you might as well make it out of solid wood," Ellis Walentine told me. But in practice, it appears, he computes the equation just as Gehret and Griskivich do.

In describing a project he was designing for a pair of customers—"All they're concerned about is, when the neighbors see it, it rolls their socks down"—he admitted, "If I make it out of solid wood, it'll cost them $20,000, and they're not ready to spend that kind of money. So I'm making it of plywood." Walentine prefers to use solid wood, but he *does* use plywood, in some projects extensively.

The stability of plywood is the other key angle. "I can't see using—say in a wardrobe—solid boards where you know you're going to have trouble," Gehret says. "I would

Three woods—tan oak from California, paldau from New Guinea and ebony from Gaboon, Africa—were combined in these cabinets. The drawer handles and the accents along the countertop and around the door panels are ebony.

be inclined there to use plywood because of the stability." And he'd do it regardless of the cost. So would others.

Thus, a lot of casework is built using plywood. But plywood also turns up selectively in cabinets that are predominantly solid wood. The back of a bookcase or dresser may be plywood. So too may dust panels, drawer bottoms, panels in frame-and-panel doors be plywood. These are elements that present the biggest problem for the woodworker as he designs around solid wood's instability. These elements must be sized and installed to allow for movement, their own as well as that of the pieces around them. It is a tricky thing to do, and some woodworkers chose plywood for them so only the movement of the surrounding pieces has to be dealt with.

TOOLS

To put your knowledge of wood to use, you have to have some tools. But more than that, says Steve Ripper, "you have to have a knowledge of the tools themselves." You have to know how a tool works so, for example, you get one capable of doing what it is supposed to do. You must learn how to maintain the tool. You must learn how to use the tool efficiently and *safely.*

This is where the teaching of an experienced woodworker is valuable.

Having a grand array of tools at the outset isn't necessary, nor is having the very best tools. Jack Larimore has a practical attitude.

The work of cabinetmaker Gary Church exemplifies the point that design and joinery need not be unusual to yield a smashing appearance. Good materials choices can make the difference. For these bathroom cabinets. Church built birch plywood carcasses using very straightforward joinery. He then clothed them with face frames and drawer fronts of tan oak. The doors are also tan oak with paldau panels accented with ebony.

Glass Shelves

Most of the shelves seen in these pages are wood. Here and there are shelves that incorporate glass—in doors or as shelves in a wooden case. Stan Saran, however, has created a shelving unit that is entirely glass.

"These etched glass shelves," he says, "are very different and a relief from the usual wood shelves. Placed in a window, they catch the light and make everything on the shelves come alive."

The unit shown was made of sandblasted ⅜-inch glass, glued together with General Electric Clear Silicone Caulk.

To make such shelves, Saran recommends that you use ⅜-inch or thicker glass, since material less thick is too frail to support much of anything. Supports for each shelf should be no less than 24 inches apart. The glass can be purchased cut-to-size with its edges water-sanded (for safety and appearance) from a glass supplier.

Sandblasting the glass gives it a "frosty-like-ice" look and enhances the caulk's grip. The necessary equipment can usually be rented. Needed is an air compressor, a sandblasting gun, goggles and a good respirator mask. Ordinary builder's sand can be used, so long as you sift it through a kitchen strainer first. Use 35 pounds per square inch of air pressure. It is advisable to do the sandblasting outdoors unless you use a room or booth designed especially for the process. In any case, suit up carefully and be sure to use the respirator, because glass dust can cause irreparable lung damage.

Assembly is straightforward. Because the caulk "sticks like crazy" to the sandblasted glass, Saran recommends that you tape the glass adjacent to the joints to protect it. After taping, apply a bead of caulk to one of the mating surfaces, let it set for about 30 seconds, then squeeze together the pieces to be joined. The joint will air-cure within a half hour, after which the excess caulk can be cleaned away with a razor blade and the masking tape removed. The seal will completely cure in 24 hours.

"I'm not particularly romantic about tools," he says. "I talked to other people about tools and bought as good as I could afford. I don't lust after them the way some people do. I don't need to have the best."

Having the *right* tools for the jobs you want to do is essential. If your mode of research includes a course, you'll be able to use that experience to establish what you need to get started. At the least, do as Larimore did and talk to a cabinetmaker or two and get counsel before investing.

It is easy to deceive yourself. One cabinetmaker maintained that "the list of basic tools isn't long," until he counted the tools *he* considered basic. Depending upon what you want to do, the basic list can be very long, though it doesn't have to be.

So the first big question you have to ask yourself as you begin to tool up is: What am I going to be doing? And how?

Choosing a kind of tool—Should you eschew power tools in favor of hand tools?—need not be the either-or decision that novices sometimes make it. Sure, hand tools are romantic. Sawing off a board with a fine panel saw, hand planing it to a silky smoothness. Then using a rabbet plane to cut a rabbet. Or using a beautiful boxwood-handled chisel to rough out a dado and a router plane to finish it. Color the scene in rich, warm colors. Reds and browns and golden yellows. The colors of hand-scraped, hand-rubbed oiled woods.

It is a romantic vision, all right, almost insufferably so. Every cabinetmaker uses some hand tools in his work, but those who make their living at it do only a portion of the work by hand. Visit one. Watch him work.

Steve Ripper's shop is in an old one-room schoolhouse. Where once pupils' benches were aligned in rows, Ripper has a collection of massive woodworking machines. In the center, like a miniature Arc de Triomphe, sits a 24-inch thickness planer. Flanking it are a squat table saw, a long and bulky jointer, a shaper, a towering old band saw. A couple of drill presses are squeezed in, along with several other floor-mounted shop tools. Racks of hand tools line the walls. Even when idle the place seems congested.

Ripper uses power tools as much as any craftsman, but he is a strong advocate of hand tools. He argues that finely crafted pieces can be created only through their use. "The machine," he says, "only helps us do the initial steps. Then we begin the handwork. It's hand-planed; it's hand-scraped."

It is the initial steps that can be an incredible burden to do entirely by hand. Michael Gorchov, who crafted the sewing room cabinet on page 186, found that out. He dressed all the rough lumber that went into the cabinet by hand. Not only did the job take considerable dexterity, it took a lot of time and caused a lot of sweat. That's why Ellis Walentine, who designed the cabinet, has a big thickness planer in his shop.

Sawing all the pieces of a cabinet by hand may be romantic. It may also be very good exercise. But it doesn't necessarily make you productive. In the time you saw off a single piece, your counterpart with a radial arm saw can have a dozen pieces cut.

Larry Golden has in his vast tool collection an old Stanley #55 plane. The precursor of the router, this multiplane was sold with more than a hundred irons, each designed to cut a slightly different shape.

"You know what I do with that plane?" he asks. "I look at it. If people will pay me to use that multiplane, I'll use it. But I'd just as soon take a router and 'Rrrrrrr,' " he says, working an imaginary board with an imaginary router. "I use electricity as much as possible."

Golden, of course, is candid about being little interested in woodworking traditions. He is interested in making what he sees in his head as well but also as expeditiously as possible. "Technique in and of itself isn't the point," he explains. "I do precise work with hand tools when I think it is important to the piece." Otherwise, he'll work with power tools.

Phil Gehret is capable of doing precise work with hand tools. But even in making reproductions, he doesn't always use them. Instead of cutting moldings with molding planes, he'll use a machine. "You can run them through the shaper in one-twentieth the time."

Ripper and Walentine, who put a lot of stock in hand-tool craftsmanship, differentiate between the hobbyist and the professional, suggesting that the hobbyist doesn't have to economize on time to cut the ultimate cost of a piece. Too, he has less reason to invest in the kind of machinery a professional needs, since his bottom line is seldom a dollars and cents one. For the hobbyist, they believe, there is economy in using hand tools.

"A lot of real close tolerance work can be done by an individual without a lot of machinery," Ripper explains. "He can afford to take time. He can use hand tools more to get the final shape."

The problem is that machines are expensive. Yes, they do the work faster, and yes, they enable the less practiced person to do good work. But a plane costs forty bucks, a thickness planer fifty times that. A professional will have both, a hobbyist needs only the plane.

I see in this discussion an element of pecking away at the risk involved in cabinetmaking. It isn't a matter of making woodworking less hazardous. Rather, it is a matter of making the outcome more certain. Tools can be pivotal, though the professional may see this more clearly than a novice.

David Pye, writing in *The Nature and Art of Workmanship,* dwells on the certainties and risks of workmanship. He defines the "workmanship of certainty" as that in which the result of every operation is predetermined and outside the operator's control. It is assembly-line work.

The "workmanship of risk" is that in which "the result of every operation during production is determined by the workman as he works and its outcome depends wholly or largely on his care, judgement and dexterity." The extreme here is handwork, in which "a tool is held in the hand and no jig or any other determining system is there to guide it." He gives sewing and writing as examples. Wood carving would be another.

The choice of tools enters in, since certain tools reduce the element of risk. "All workmen using the workmanship of risk," Pye

Scrap-Glass Cabinet

Although the word cabinetry brings wood immediately to mind, wood is not the only material from which cabinets are made. Metal is an obvious alternative. But glass has been used, too.

Even if you accept glass as a cabinetmaking material, however, you are bound to find the medicine cabinet, right, most unusual. The case is made of glass set in a metal framework. The back is a sheet of copper. The door is the *pièce de résistance.* It is not simply glass, it is textured stained glass, scrap glass and, yes, glass bottles.

With 12 years of experience in stained glass work behind her, Rhonda Dixon doesn't find working with three-dimensional glass objects a problem. The cabinet isn't her first such assembly. She's made windows containing Depression glass plates, broken canning jars, crystal stemware, lots of bottle necks, and "cullet" —waste glass discarded by the glassblowers in Silver Dollar City, Arkansas, which is near her home.

In assembling works of this sort, Rhonda seals all of the small glass pieces together with copper foil work and the larger ones with standard H-channel lead came.

Using the copper foil technique, she wraps copper foil around the edges of each piece of glass, assembles all the pieces according to the pattern, and secures them in place on her work surface with molding strips and tacks. Then she brushes powdered flux all over the copper foil lines and solders them along the entire length (rather than just at the joints) to create a lead bead. When she is finished, she turns the panel over and repeats the fluxing and soldering process.

explains, "are constantly devising ways to limit the risk by using such things as jigs and templates. If you want to draw a straight line with your pen, you do not go at it freehand, but use a ruler, that is to say, a jig. There is still a risk of blots and kinks, but less risk."

Using a jointer, thickness planer and table saw to square up and dress a rough board for use in a cabinet is the workmanship of certainty. Using an assortment of hand planes to do the job is the workmanship of risk.

It is a totally unromantic view. Yet few cabinetmakers can afford to be romantic about their work. Wharton Esherick, a highly individual woodworker, now dead, produced cabinets and furniture and sculpture that is admired and studied by many contemporary woodworkers, Larry Golden among them. He wasn't romantic.

"I use any damn machine I can get hold of," he once said. "I'll use my teeth if I have to. There's a little of the hand, but the main thing is the heart and the head."

Basic tools are those you must have to work wood. It is unlikely that anyone stepping into cabinetmaking for the first time is doing it totally without tools. The home handyman has an assortment of tools, some of which lend themselves to woodworking: a hammer, some screwdrivers, a tape measure, maybe a saw.

If he has done any home improvement work, even more woodworking tools are sure to be in his kit. How about an electric drill or a portable circular saw? a framing square, try square or combination square? some clamps, a miter box, even a set of chisels?

All of these tools can be used in cabinetmaking. That cabinetmaker's first thought was right: The basic list to get started in a limited way is not long. And Jack Larimore is correct, too: The tools on it don't have to be expensive, individually or collectively.

It depends upon your desires, for there are a lot of paths you can follow. You can invest in:

- Hand tools only. These tools will demand a lot of practice, hold your productivity down since each project will take a lot of time to complete, and, though the goal is to economize, could still cost you a lot of money.
- Portable power tools along with some hand tools. This mix of tools will speed up your production without letting capital costs get out of hand. But you will still have to practice, and, to get accurate work, you will have to cobble up jigs and templates.
- Selected shop tools, again to supplement hand tools, and perhaps portable power tools. These machines will speed up your productivity another notch, remove more uncertainty from your workmanship, but will boost your capital outlay.
- Professional shop tools. Machines of this kind will cost you a bundle, require a lot of space, and boost your productivity, but they will not allow you to avoid hand tools, practice or the exercise of dexterity, judgment or care.

Regardless of the path you choose to follow, there are certain basics you need. The first is a shop. Mitch Mandel works in the basement of his rowhouse. It limits him. Like the proverbial boatbuilder, he has to be sure that what

Two different approaches to ornamentation are shown here. The door with the applied ornament, left, *was found in a barn. After it was cleaned and stripped, a cabinetmaker was commissioned to build a cabinet to go with it. Following a different line, John Zoltai built the cabinet,* below, *then carved the ornament.*

he makes can be carried out of the basement. Larry Golden works in a shop above his garage. Its size prevents him from having several shop tools—a planer and a big jointer, for example—that he'd like. Larimore *shares* his shop with another professional. It is big and well equipped, yet it costs him only half of what his very own shop would.

Basic hand tools you will need, too: layout tools like folding rules or tape measures, try squares, perhaps a marking gauge, a scratch awl or marking knife; sharpening tools like a grinder and bench stones; hammers and/or mallets; screwdrivers. And lots and lots of clamps: quick clamps, C-clamps, pipe or bar clamps, hand screws ("You can never have too many clamps," says Golden).

Even if you do buy power saws and drills and sanders, you surely will want a hand saw, an "eggbeater" drill, a set of chisels, a smoothing plane and some other basic hand tools.

Equipment for the shop will be needed. You can *buy* a workbench, say, a massive beech or maple bench with trestle legs, a couple of wooden vises, mortises for bench dogs, a recess for tools that are being used, even a drawer or two. But if you are serious about your woodworking, you will design and construct your own. The same is true for the tool chest or cabinet you will need, the sawhorses, the rack for wood, the bins for scrap.

If you choose to focus on hand tools, you must be dedicated. You are in for a lot of work. But mastering hand tools is evidence of a commitment. The woodworkers who take that extra step, who "put that care" into their

Sharpening

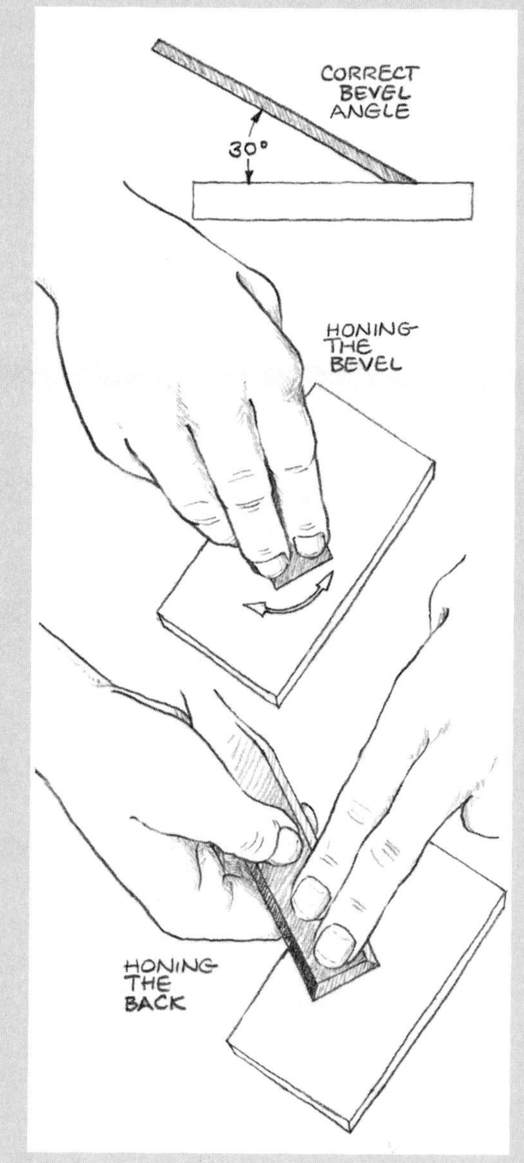

"Knowing how to sharpen tools is *so* important," says Ellis Walentine. "I think sharpening is the biggest problem any novice has to overcome."

Without a keen edge on that chisel or plane, he says, a dovetail is next to impossible to cut, a board can't be planed smooth and flat. "The *only* way you can do it is with a sharp tool."

How to sharpen tools is regularly explained in woodworking magazines, and every woodworking how-to book has a section on it. New—and often expensive—gizmos are advertised as miracle solutions to the sharpening problem. Yet sharpening remains one of woodworking's occult arts. Every craftsman has a slightly different idea about how it should be done.

Tage Frid, a longtime woodworking instructor and author of several highly respected woodworking books, recommends using a belt sander (stationary or a portable one secured in a vise) for sharpening, a buffing wheel loaded with polishing compound for honing. The specifics are explained in *Tage Frid Teaches Woodworking: Joinery.*

James Krenov advocates the use of a hand-cranked grinder for the initial sharpening and several grades of natural stones (with kerosene) for honing. To complement his hand-cranked grinder, Krenov uses a wooden toolrest he made so he can consistently grind a tool to the correct bevel angle. But this is only part of the job. *"Honing is just as important as grinding,"* he writes in *The Fine Art of Cabinetmaking.*

Walentine would agree. He favors the benchstone for sharpening. "People think hogging the metal away [with a grinder] is going to sharpen the tool," he says. "If they could learn to sharpen on a benchstone, they'd be better off."

To properly sharpen or hone a tool on a benchstone, most woodworkers demand you hold the tool, as shown, close to the cutting edge. "How you hold that iron (or chisel) is of great importance," writes Krenov. "One tendency is to hold it too high up, and not to support it properly. . . .Try holding the piece way down as low as possible, the fingertips of your fore- and index fingers nearly touching the stone."

Rock the tool forward and back on the stone until you "find" the bevel setting, then begin stroking. *"When you hone,"* says Krenov, *"long strokes are less easy to control than short ones.* To-and-fro is not as suitable as round and round or, even better, a short sidewise pivoting."

The bevel is honed until a burr develops. This is stropped off, either by honing the back of the tool with it flat on the stone, or on a leather strop dusted with polishing compound. When the job is done, both the bevel and the back of the tool should be polished clean of the most minute scratches.

Sharpening a new tool is laborious and time-consuming, for the back of the chisel or iron must be honed absolutely flat and all the tiny scratches on the bevel must be removed. Once the tool is sharp, the grinder or belt sander is resorted to only occasionally. You keep it sharp through routine honing. On a benchstone.

Plywood is often the material of choice for built-ins, such as this family room closet and shelf unit built by Alex MacLean. The parts are quickly cut from the plywood sheets, eliminating the need to glue up wood to the necessary widths. MacLean's practice is to band any exposed plywood edges with strips of the same wood as the face veneer, in this case, red birch.

This bathroom vanity has a lot in common with the unit on the facing page. It's made almost entirely of hardwood plywood. Exposed edges are banded with solid wood. By having the doors and drawer fronts overlay the carcass edges, the need for a face frame is eliminated.

work, to echo Jack Larimore, are the ones who do master hand tool use, regardless of how rigorous the apprenticeship.

Take planing, for example. Hand planing will give you a finished surface that is matchless in smoothness. Ellis Walentine asserts that if he were to compare a board he had run through his planer with one he had hand-planed, the hand-planed board would be smoother and flatter. Moreover, he says, the hand-planed board would be very nearly ready for its final finish. No laborious sanding through a range of grits from coarse to fine, only a bit of hand-scraping would be needed.

The plane is illustrative of the work that must go into mastering hand tool skills. You *may* be able to learn how to use a plane from a book, but the key ingredient is practice. "How do you learn to ride a bicycle?" Ripper shrugs. "You fall off and get back on."

I suspect it goes best if you get occasional advice and encouragement from a knowledgeable, experienced mentor. Such counsel will do more than break the tedium of making shavings. The goal is the unbroken 10-foot curl of wood. Walentine can produce such shavings routinely, but only, he says, because he uses a well-tuned, well-sharpened plane. Practicing alone, you may never happen on the well-tuned, well-sharpened combination, but working with guidance, you'll find it.

The next path to tooling up, which may well be simply a second step in a progression rather than a pure alternative to the first, is to blend in the use of portable power tools. It is using electric power to replace muscle power in crosscutting and ripping boards, cutting dadoes, grooves and rabbets, drilling holes, and so on.

But you can swing into this step without having grappled with the arcana of chisels and planes and such.

If you simply want to make functional pieces, don't want heavy investment, and are willing to design simply in terms of appearance and structure, you can do a lot with *basic* hand tools and portable power tools. Read in the Gallery about the bookcase Carl Wies built (see page 108). He did it using only portable power tools and simple hand tools.

Think about it. A portable circular saw with a good-quality carbide-tipped blade will make excellent cuts through plywood (or any other wood). Clamp a straight-edged board to the sheet as a fence and, so long as you measure with care, you'll get precisely sized pieces. Even though I have a table saw, I prefer to cut plywood this way, simply because full-size sheets of plywood are too unwieldy to maneuver on a table saw without help.

A router cuts grooves, dadoes and rabbets quickly and easily. If you are making a tall bookcase and are using dado construction, you will probably find it easier to cut the dadoes with a router than on a table saw. You have to move the workpiece over the table saw's blade, remember. That can be awkward if the piece is very long or very wide.

Of course, you can't cut fancy joints like lock miters with these tools, but you probably won't use such joints on early projects anyway.

If you want to use hardwoods, you can subcontract the basic preparation of the stock to a craftsman or a business set up for such work. (This is true for any woodworker who doesn't have a planer and a jointer.)

The move to stationary power tools, shop tools, floor tools, machinery—whatever you choose to call these devices—brings you to an important crossroad. Up to this point, you have been investing in tools you need, regardless of the level of your interest. Now the per-tool investment takes a quantum jump, and you have to be either rich or serious about woodworking.

There are lots of things you must consider. Many different machines are available. Certain machines are touted as multipurpose, while others clearly do but a single job. The range of cost for given tools is incredible: one model will cost $400, another five times that. How do you decide what to buy?

Start off with some expert advice. Look at the expert's tools, find out why he bought what he did, learn the order of his purchases, and ask him what he'd do if he were just starting out.

If you talk to a craftsman like Ripper, you'll learn that serious cabinetmakers get the right tool for each job, rather than a machine that does a dozen different jobs, but not one of them to perfection. The radial arm saw may be the prime example.

"The home handyman tries to do everything with a radial [arm] saw," explains Walentine. "It's all they have, and they come up with all these jigs. Well, more power to them. I view a radial saw as strictly a crosscutting saw. It's too dangerous or difficult to do anything else."

Shop visits reveal that most cabinetmakers are set up with immense machines, quite unlike the home shop tools hawked by Sears, Penney's and the like. "Weighs a ton" is no figure of speech when used to describe these babies. A 10-inch table saw, harboring the very same blade my saw uses, has a table as much as 4 feet square, a 2 to 4 horsepower motor, and underpinnings like an iron bridge. A jointer, though having the same 6-inch capacity as my Delta, dwarfs it, with tables extending 6 feet end-to-end.

"The bigger, heavier tools are more rigid," explains Walentine.

Contrasts abound in this kitchen. Chestnut boards, dark with age, were used to make the cabinets. Punctuating them are stark white porcelain knobs. The island is topped with a white marble countertop. The contrasts extend beyond the colors. The wood is old, the sink and other accoutrements are spanking new.

Wood doesn't have to be the only material used in cabinetmaking. This striking kitchen was created by combining wooden cabinetry with stained glass work for the door panels.

"The bearings are heavier," adds Ripper. "They are made for everyday, continuous use. They don't lose their setup or begin to wobble."

Don't feel *compelled* to follow the professional cabinetmaker's lead here. You may want to do that, but you don't have to.

Skimming through the book *Tage Frid Teaches Woodworking: Joinery* reveals that the key machine of this respected furnituremaker and teacher is not a woodworking behemoth. To me, it looks a lot like my Contractor's Saw. Frid says in his introduction that the equipment shown in the photographs is his equipment, which he uses regularly. That is encouraging. Gargantuan industrial machines aren't requisites for good work.

Cabinetmakers are unanimous about the first purchase: the table saw is the cabinetmaker's basic machine. "To me," says Gehret, "that's the first and most important tool for your workshop."

"You'll find the table saw the most used piece of equipment in your shop," Frid points out in his book, "so don't stint on quality." He advises getting a 10-inch or larger model with tilting arbor, no less than a one-horse motor, and big table and rail extensions.

Like Walentine, Frid doesn't view the radial arm saw as a substitute for a table saw. It is, he writes, "limited in function, much more difficult to use, less accurate for fine joinery or cutting." Those cabinetmakers who have radial arm saws use them for crosscutting.

After the table saw, there are a variety of tools that can be purchased: a band saw, drill press, sander. But if you take woodworking seriously, think about a jointer and a planer. If you expect to get into dressing rough stock yourself, you will need these machines.

Frid writes: "After the circular table saw, I feel that the jointer and the thickness planer are the most important big machines in a workshop, especially for the person who wants to make a living from woodworking. These two machines are a big investment, but will pay for themselves over the years." He recommends buying no smaller than a 6-inch jointer and no smaller than a 12-inch planer.

After setting yourself up with the three basic machines, let your interests dictate what you buy next, or even *if* you buy any other machines.

Buying used tools is an option every woodworker has to consider. Good floor tools cost in the four figures these days. Even a Contractor's Saw costs $800 new. Good hand tools cost a lot, too. Page through a catalog. A set of four chisels can cost $50 to $60, a smoothing plane $40.

In the face of such capital costs, used tools, old and rusty though they be, look pretty good. But many cabinetmakers buy used tools for a reason other than economy. They believe that old tools are better tools.

"There's nothing wrong with used equipment," opines Golden. "My feeling is the older tools are better." Golden, though he is enamored of the latest woodworking technology, does have a collection of old tools. Some of them, like the Stanley #55 multiplane, he "looks at," but others he uses regularly. His favorite handsaws are a trio of turn-of-the-century Disstons that were given to him by an old friend. They are of a quality that Disston itself doesn't match today, he says.

Ripper seconds the opinion. "A lot of the old tools were made with better steel. At one time," he points out, "Stanley made three or four hundred kinds of planes. The older Stanley tools are very good. The new tools are designed for the guy who needs to cut a 1 × 6 in his garage."

These opinions, of course, relate to hand tools. But these cabinetmakers clearly feel the same way about power tools. Ripper's 20-inch band saw is a relic he completely rebuilt. Walentine's pin router "goes back to the 1940s. They don't make them like that anymore," he says.

The places to look for such buys, they say, are auctions and used-tool dealers.

A problem that arises in buying used is the condition of the tool. This is where knowing tools is important. An old plane may be cheap, but it may be a poor buy at any price because it is warped—yes, even metal planes can be minutely twisted. The colossal cast-iron table saw being auctioned off at an old woodworking shop may seem to be inexpensive, but it may need a complete overhaul. If the brand or model is no longer being manufactured, replacement bearings and other parts may be impossible, or merely difficult and expensive, to get.

Carpenter's Machinery Company in Philadelphia specializes in used machinery. Much of the equipment sold there has been rebuilt, and comes with some backing in the way of service and replacement parts. It is one firm among many scattered around the country. Check newspaper ads, *Fine Woodworking* ads, the Yellow Pages.

When buying used tools, you may not get your tools in an orderly fashion, since you sometimes are prompted to buy something that's available at a good price, rather than buying what you really *need.* But you are saving money. And perhaps your illogical purchase is a tool you'd never get otherwise.

Shopping for new tools is no less perilous than shopping for used tools. You still have to be able to recognize good quality; you still have to shop around. The obvious sources—mail-order suppliers, the local hardware store, retail chains like Sears—are likely to be the best sources.

Larimore shops widely. "For a drill," he says, "you look first at Sears. For a router, you get industrial grade because you use it a lot." If he is seeking a particular brand such as Marples for chisels or Record for planes, he has no qualms about mail-order buying. For other tools and other brands, he may want to handpick the item so he gets a good tool.

Ripper is cautious. He's seen a lot of shoddy tools and doesn't want to get stuck with any. Try squares, for example, are often out of square, he says. You have to test each one by scribing a line along the tongue, then flipping the tool over and rescribing the line. If the tool is square, you'll have one line. If it isn't, you'll have two lines at slight angles to each other. Saws, for another example, frequently will have uneven teeth. "But that's the thing about tools," he says. "You have to have knowledge not only of the work to be done, but also of the tools."

Using tools safely, obviously, is important. Most cabinetmakers can tell some pretty grisly tales of fingers consumed by the tools of their trade. "Machinery is steel and metal, and the craftsman is flesh and blood. And the two do not mix," Steve Ripper says. As one who's missing a thumb, Ripper certainly is qualified to point out, "I'm not talking baloney here."

Larry Golden agrees. "You've got to respect those pieces of equipment. You can't take a tool that spins at 25,000 rpm for granted. They go too fast. So you can't be too cautious."

But a lot of folks who exercise all due caution around a table saw get blasé with a chisel and shed blood anyhow. "Any tool can bite you," says Larry Golden. "Even a pocket knife." Displaying a scarred palm, he adds, "Here's one. I had just gotten through sharpening a chisel."

The woodshop is a dangerous place, but the gory stories reflect only the obvious. The power saw that can zip off a finger also makes noise, dust, vibrations, all of which represent long-term hazards. The chemicals woodworkers use for finishing may be inflammable, caustic, poisonous and hazardous to the eyes, and their vapors may be toxic and explosively inflammable. So safety isn't simply a matter of using the blade guard and wearing goggles.

• Be ready mentally for work. Don't drag yourself out to the shop if you are tired, irritable, distracted or preoccupied. Steve Doriss lost a

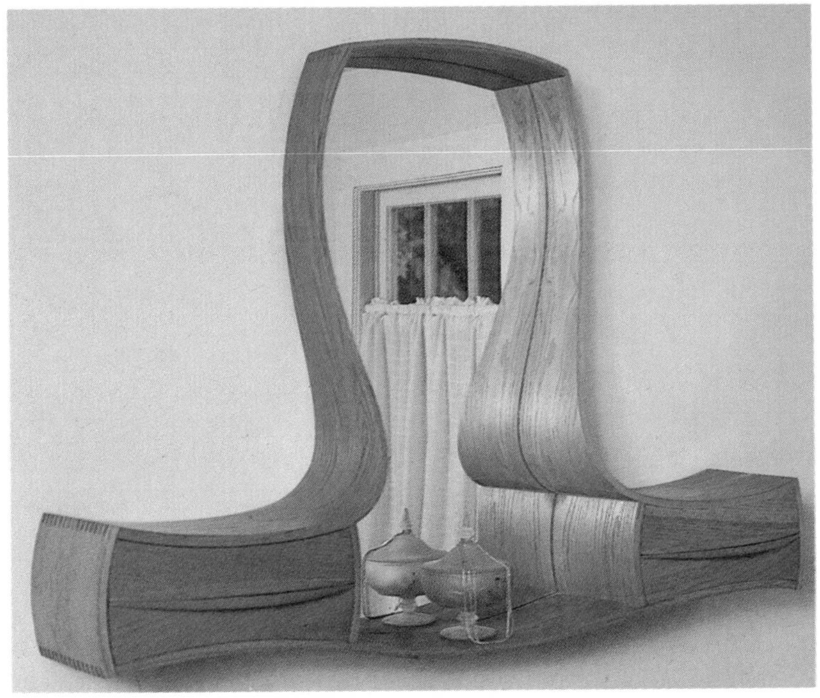

James Cottey wanted to try out lamination techniques, so he made this curvilinear jewelry cabinet for his home. The only square surfaces are inside the drawers. Cottey cut ⅛-inch veneers of white oak, then glued them up on special jigs to form the ½-inch-thick pieces for the carcass. These he joined using finger joints and stopped dadoes, cut with the aid of specially made jigs. Parts for the drawers were handformed, then joined with dovetails.

This huge room-divider cabinet, the work of Bruce McQuilkin, is actually three separate units: the base unit, the upper unit and the display case. Each is made entirely of California walnut, using dovetail joinery. The full depth of the base unit's center section is taken up by the drawers; on the living room side, false doors occupy the space. The same section of the upper unit is occupied by a television, hidden behind tambour doors on the living room side of the cabinet. The tambours shown are fixed and serve as the back of this section of the cabinet. Details of this cabinet are shown on pages 32, 76 and 106.

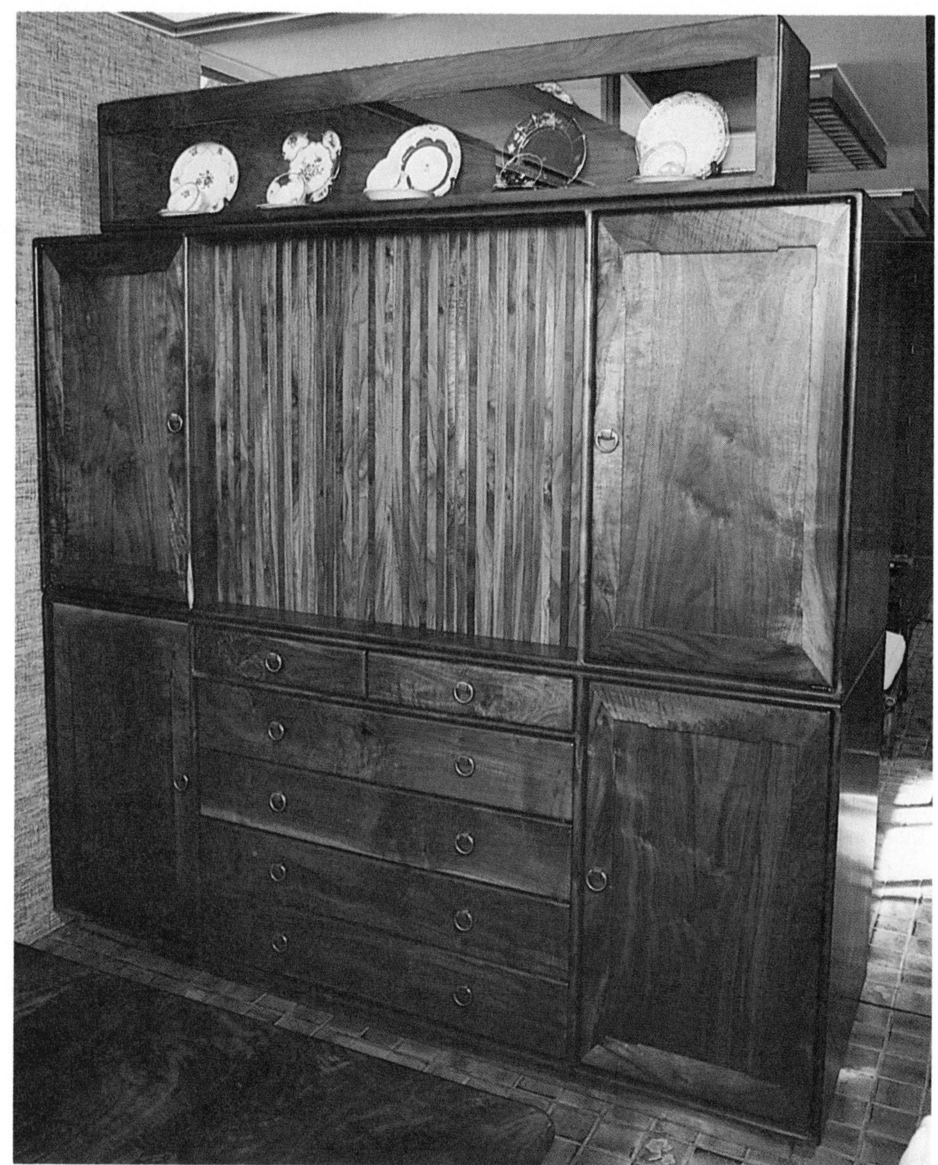

finger tip to a radial arm saw. "Like 99.99 percent of the injured woodworkers you talk to," he says, "I was tired, hassled and rushed. I now have very strict guidelines for myself. I don't use a tool if I'm in a bad frame of mind. If I'm too tired, it's just no good."

• Dress the part. Leave the jewelry, including your wedding ring and watch, on the dresser. Wear fairly close-fitting clothes and roll up your sleeves. If you are working with a power tool that generates a lot of sawdust, wear goggles and a respirator. If it is noisy, wear something to protect your hearing.

Because the sawdust of even some common woods like redwood is toxic, Ripper advocates wearing a respirator. "A paper dust mask is not enough when dealing with toxic dusts. You need a respirator with double filters to cover both nose and mouth."

As one who is experiencing hearing loss, Larry Golden is a strong advocate of hearing protection. "If I'm running my router, I put on my hearing protectors," he says. He does the same if he is using a table saw for more than a single cut.

• Maintain a well-ordered workplace. Sweep up when you finish work, picking up scraps of wood. Keep materials stored neatly, accessibly, *and* out of the way. Have a place for every tool, and keep it there when you aren't actively using it. Give yourself enough room to work around each shop tool you have, and don't use the tool's table as a workbench.

• Know your tools. Learn how to use each one properly. Read a book about it, or take a course, or at the least talk to an experienced cabinetmaker.

Commonplace materials can have some unusual uses. John Vugrin applied a blob of wood dough, ordinarily used to plug holes left when nails are countersunk, to a drawer bottom. Then he carved a leaf from the hardened material. To some, it is a decadent detail, to others, it is a legitimate surprise hidden by the craftsman.

Ripper is critical of tool manufacturers for their failure to explain the proper ways to use their products. "I don't think the industry that produces [the tools] makes it all that clear." He cites the danger of installing a molding cutter backwards in a radial arm saw as a hazard that's not made clear by manufacturers. Installed backwards, the cutter will *pull* the wood through, and likely the startled woodworker's hand with it.

But the onus of knowing what you are doing remains with the woodworker. "You *never* take a chance unless you are willing to accept the consequences," Ripper stresses. Take the time to set up for a task, using firm work supports and whatever clamps, jigs, guides or guards are necessary and appropriate. Every shortcut can endanger your well-being.

Finally, be prepared for accidents. Get a first-aid kit and keep it handy. Know how to use it. It is almost inevitable that you will get at least a splinter or two. Be prepared.

DESIGN AND CONSTRUCTION

If you ask a cabinetmaker how he'd make a bookcase, he'll turn on you with a buzz of questions.

"What do you want it to look like? That's the first question. Do you want it to be modern? Colonial?" Phil Gehret has asked these questions of dozens and dozens of customers over the years.

"What are you trying to accomplish? Is this going into an apartment, where you are going to move in six months? Or is this going into a home that is a hundred years old? Do you want to be able to move it from place to place? Is it going to be freestanding or attached to a wall? All these things enter into design. What's it being used for? Dishes in the kitchen? Towels in the bathroom? Or books in the living room? Is what it's going to be used for going to change? Are you going to want adjustable shelves?"

If you let the cabinetmaker know that you are seeking pointers

for a novice, new questions come up. "What sort of tools are at his disposal?" Larry Golden asks. "Does he have a shop? Is he familiar with the tools? What is his pocketbook like? Does he want it to be a one-day project? Does time matter?"

Ultimately, you'll get a brief recitation of how a bookcase could be built. If you ask several cabinetmakers—and I did—you probably will find that they all suggest essentially the same design with variations that reflect personal differences and preferences.

Jack Larimore, for example, usually combines traditional and modern approaches in his work. So he points out that "in a lot of instances, book*cases* aren't needed. What the client is actually looking for is nice shelving."

Given a choice, he says, "I would rather make standard shelves with interesting face treatment. The shelves themselves would rest on wall brackets. It's a lot less expensive for people that way." The face treatment can make the finished product look deceptively like a bookcase (see page 117).

But Larimore isn't inflexible about it. "If it's decided that it's to be a bookcase, a piece of furniture, is it to be made of solid wood or veneered plywood? There are a couple of issues here," he explains.

"There's a relative shortage of good hardwood. I usually opt for veneered shelves if the client is agreeable. You have to put edging on it. Quite often, the cost is not that much different, but the expenditure for quality hardwood is kept to a minimum."

The other issue is structural. "It is difficult to mix major elements of a bookcase, some being solid wood and some plywood. A plywood case and adjustable solid wood shelves is okay," he says. "Plywood is stabler than solid wood."

Larry Golden has a definite preference for plywood. He would almost always use a plywood, he says, a hardwood plywood for appearance, a softwood plywood for something that was to be painted.

"I think what would be nice," Golden says, "would be to get a piece of fir plywood. Rip it into 11⅞-inch widths." From the four 8-foot pieces, the woodworker could make an 8-foot-tall bookcase with four 4-foot shelves, or a 6-foot-high unit with the same four 4-foot shelves, or a 4-foot-high unit with three 6-foot shelves. "If they didn't want to put a back on it, they could just put some gussets in the corners."

He would construct the piece using dado or dado-and-rabbet joints secured with glue and nails. An alternative would be to join the plywood to strips ripped from 5/4 stock using tongue-and-groove joints; Golden used this technique in building the dresser shown in the Gallery (see page 134).

Strips of pine or a hardwood would be used to edge the plywood. He would make the shelves adjustable, using metal tracks and clips.

But Golden isn't dogmatic about any of these suggestions. "I'll give you different ways to skin the cat. If someone wanted to use pine boards, they could do pretty much the same thing. Buy some 1 × 12."

This approach is favored by Phil Gehret. "I'd use a stock-size lumber to begin with," he

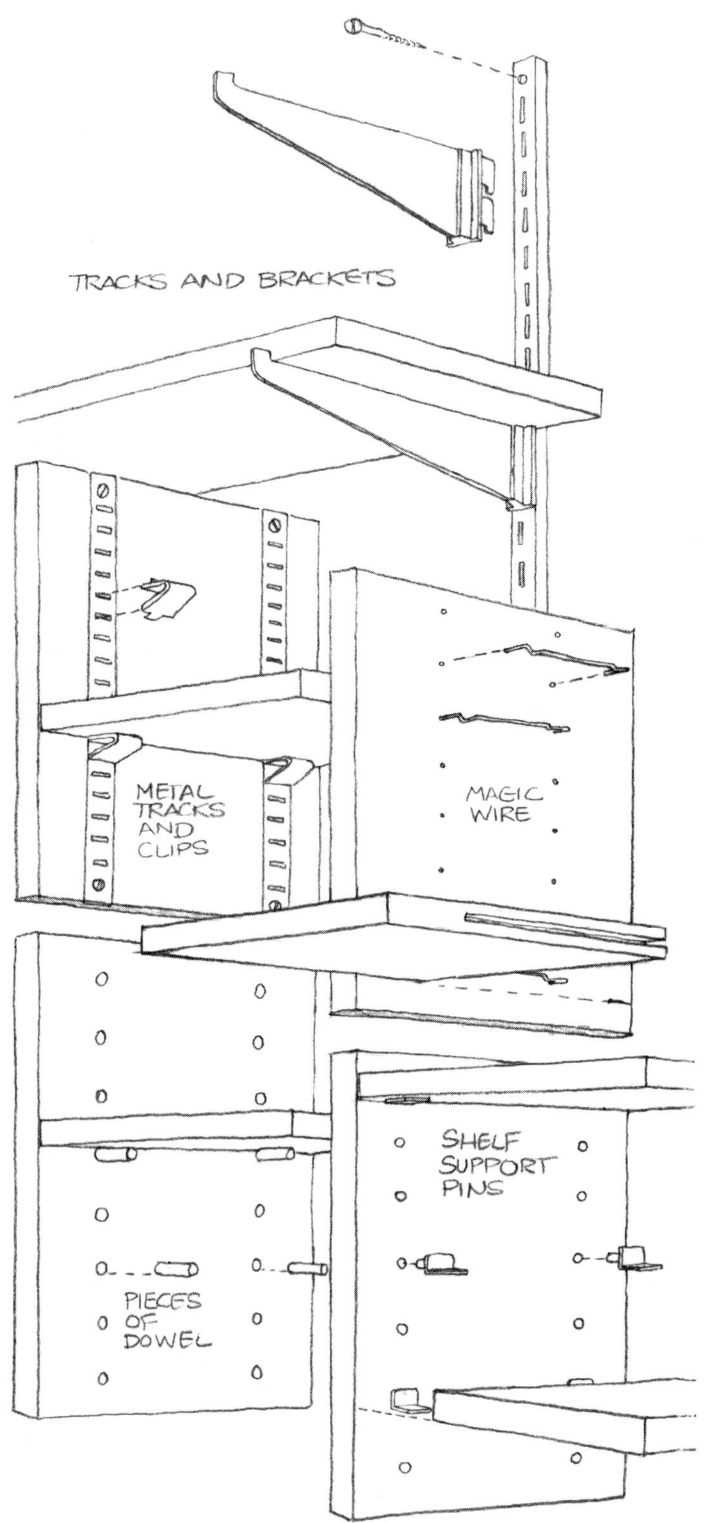

Shelves can be made adjustable in a variety of ways. Track and bracket hardware is common, quite inexpensive, and marvelously flexible. For cased-in applications, various kinds of hardware can be used, or pieces of dowel can serve as support pins.

says. "If you want it freestanding, you put a back on it. You use ¼-inch plywood for the back; I'd let it into a rabbet. I would prefer some sort of facing, which is only a decorative thing, really." This he would embellish with a simple bead.

"I'd probably make some of the shelves fixed and some adjustable," he continues. "The fixed shelves I'd let into the case sides. For the adjustable shelves, I'd use shelf pins. I'd keep the bottom shelf up, give it a toe space. Maybe only ¾ inch, but a toe space." The shelf would be elevated 3½ inches—the width of a 1 × 4—and a plinth beneath the shelf would be recessed that ¾ inch.

While butt joints would be simpler, Gehret would use dado or rabbet joints because "they help position" the pieces during assembly. Glue and nails would hold the pieces together.

The upshot is that the entire piece can be made using hand tools. "You can do it, but it's difficult," Gehret says. "Because you are going to set the back in a rabbet, you need to rip all the shelves ¼ inch. If you have a table saw, you can do it all easily." Failing that, Gehret figures the work could be done without too much difficulty using a router and a portable circular saw.

Ellis Walentine interrogates himself. "You ask yourself questions about design. You figure, if this is 6 feet high, I better tack it to the wall, because it might fall over." You ask yourself, he continues, "what are the odds that a 4-foot pine board is going to support 4 feet of books? And the odds aren't good." The solution here, he says, might be to add a ledger strip to the bottom of the shelf. Next, you have to consider torsional rigidity. "If it is freestanding," he says, "you have to have some kind of triangulation in it to prevent racking."

Walentine would prefer to use solid wood and would prefer that it be a hardwood. He speaks of walnut. He doesn't see problems in its use. "You don't have much expansion and contraction in a bookcase," he points out. "Drawers are where you *really* run into problems of expansion and contraction."

Joinery is another aspect to consider. "There are all sorts of ways you can do it," he says. Dadoes, blind dadoes, even sliding dovetails. With the latter, he explains, "the sides won't bow out and pull the shelf apart."

Through this process of mentally poking and prodding the possibilities, Walentine says, "you get your structural considerations taken care of." The visual possibilities he doesn't consider, because "the aesthetics question is specific to the situation."

Steve Ripper, in his turn, wends his way through "the levels of the job." One of his principal considerations in contriving a bookcase is the time frame within which the builder is working. "Does the guy want something he can get done in six hours? Is he open to the six-month job? It all depends upon one's facility and what he wants from the finished piece. You want to address the practicality and still have a sense of satisfaction."

In 6 hours, says Ripper, a reasonably practiced woodworker can do something with stopped dadoes and screws. In 20 hours, he can do a piece with through tenons and wedges. In six months, he can create a piece with tapering sliding dovetails, cut by hand.

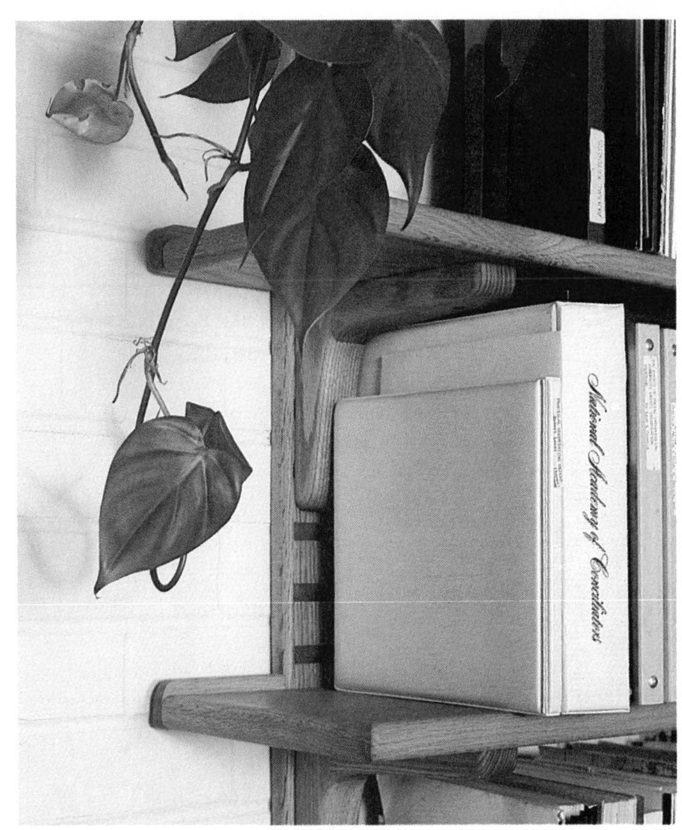

This all-wood adjustable shelving system is the work of Ted Scherrer. The standards are made by cutting angled slots in an oak strip, then enclosing them by gluing solid strips along each edge. The brackets have two extensions joined in a mortise-and-tenon joint; a tongue to engage the standard's slot is glued into the back.

Clearly, what Larry Golden has said is true: There is more than one way to skin a cat. Every woodworker has pet processes, materials, design touches. The process of converting a stack of wood into a battery of cabinets *is* frequently idiosyncratic. But for the beginner, it's best if the quirks can be eliminated from the process, for the more methodical you are, the less likely you are to make mistakes.

"There are certain basic mistakes that accrue to a lack of experience that you make and learn from," Larimore says. "Quite often they have to do with understanding the materials or with unforeseen relationships (things maybe not fitting, like a door), things that are hard to visualize. You have to limit the margin of error as much as you can."

One way to limit the margin of error is to start with a carefully thought out design.

DESIGN

Ellis Walentine has a design philosophy. For him, design is a problem-solving exercise, and the problem has five distinct aspects: function, aesthetics, engineering, materials and construction.

The functional problem is simply to define the purpose of the piece. Walentine couches it as a question: "What motivates the piece?" The aesthetic problem is that of making the piece attractive enough to satisfy both the customer and the designer. Hinging on the answers to these questions are the engineering and materials problems. The engineering problems are structural: what structure will serve the aesthetic without collapsing under the function? The materials problem is simply that of choosing which ones to use.

After all these are solved, still remaining are the problems of getting the piece built as designed: What procedures must be followed? What tools used? These are construction problems.

The solution process is not a linear progression. Each aspect of the overall problem impinges on every other, so you go through the sorts of interrogations that Phil Gehret and Ellis Walentine have demonstrated. You need to see *all* aspects of the "problems" you are trying to solve.

The information needed to come up with a reasonable bookcase design is actually quite simple. To design a dresser or a vanity or, worse, a battery of cabinets for a kitchen, much more must be known and considerably more variables must be dealt with.

"You always have to go through the same thought process to come up with a design," Gehret says. If the cabinetry is extensive, "the design process is basically the same, it's just more involved."

For instance, with a kitchen cabinet, you may have space restrictions. You may have to make the new piece blend with existing pieces. You may have to determine where to leave openings for plumbing.

Moreover, Gehret points out, "there is a standard that you *should* consider. It doesn't have to be gospel, but you *should* consider it. The standards have been developed for a specific reason." In the kitchen, for example, a dishwasher will fit under a 36-inch-high counter, but not a 33-inch-high one.

In addition, you have the practical questions to deal with. What materials will you use? What joints should be used? Can you make those joints?

"He [the beginner] has to keep his own abilities in mind," says Gehret. "I guess after 30 years of doing something, the ability becomes second nature. You *know* what you can do." An experienced cabinetmaker, then, doesn't articulate *every* question.

The design development path is not the same for every cabinetmaker. Nor is the starting point.

"Wood," Walentine says. "That's where it all begins. You have to start with the nature of wood."

And Steve Ripper adds, "You have to know some of the principles of putting wood together. The material itself does dictate a good deal as to what can be done."

"I go in looking at [wood with] a specific intention," Walentine says. "I come out with a specific design predicated on how I know wood works and how to make things. Sometimes it is awfully complicated to deal with anything but rectilinear things."

"The thing I try to do in my own work," Ripper says, "is create a balance between the design and the construction." He is not wedded to a single design routine.

On some projects, Ripper will spend hours at the drawing board sketching out the details of

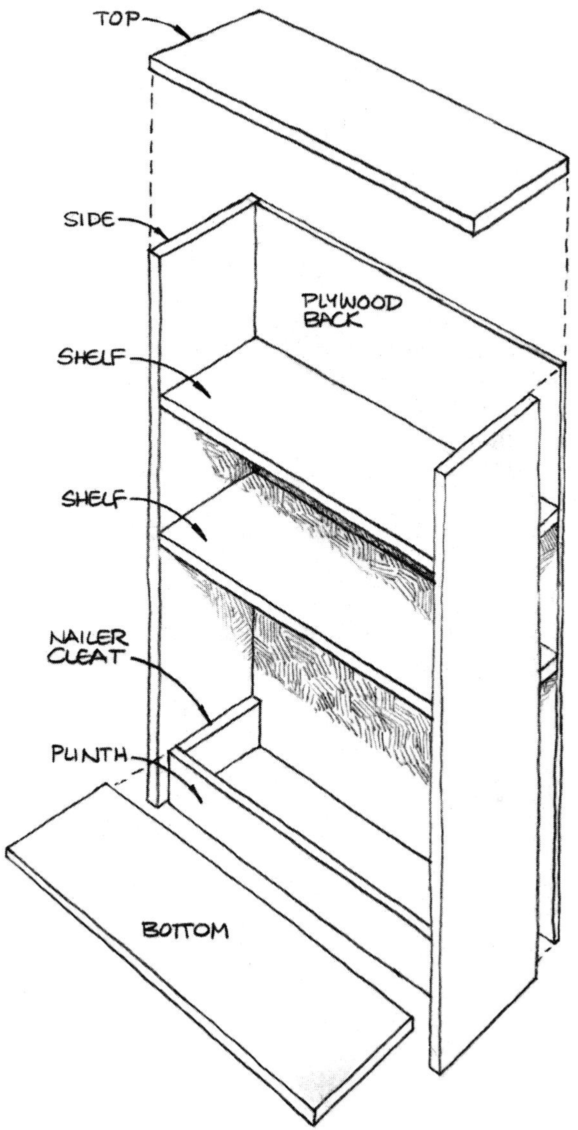

Bookcase assembly is here revealed. It is the quintessential carcass. Shown is a unit that could be made using pine board lumber or hardwood. It uses butt joints, though it could be enhanced structurally by selectively using rabbet joints, dado joints or sliding dovetails. The back prevents racking.

Tom Larsen, a cabinetmaker working in British Columbia, designed these kitchen cabinets without the kind of knobs that could catch the clothes of a busy cook. Rather, the doors and drawers have oval finger holes: slip a finger or two in and pull open the drawer or door.

what he proposes. He spends more hours sorting through his wood stacks, seeking just the right boards. It is a very time-consuming process, all done before a single cut is made. But the results—the dressing stand on page 10 is one—can be rewarding.

A different routine dispenses with the paperwork and the agonies of the woodpile. The walnut bookcase that graces his home (see page 8) was spawned through it. "It's like composing," he says. "You have a pile of boards, and you want to create a pleasing composition. For me, it is a spontaneous way of working. It's quick, it's fast. Unlike the dressing stand."

Larry Golden's routine has a lot in common with this latter approach. He doesn't labor at a drawing board. He doesn't sweat at the wood pile. "It's like the make-do school," Golden says. "If I don't have *one* thing, I can usually find something else that works. That's the chance part that I like."

Other aspects of the design problem lie beyond the interrogatories and the routines—aesthetics for one, the level of the job for another.

"Aesthetics" can encompass board-by-board selection of material, the piece's proportions, the degree and character of ornamentation, even the choice of joinery and whether it is exposed or concealed.

Taste is what aesthetics often get planed down to. Some cabinetmakers, like Ripper and Walentine, prefer serious, low-key, meticulously crafted cabinetry. Others — Larry Golden is one — like bold contrasts in color and form. Those like Jack Larimore design with a twinkle and a smile, working carefully but trying not to be too hidebound. Still others wonder what all the fuss is about.

Walentine, as you might expect, has definite ideas about aesthetics. "My personal inclination is to make the piece understated," he says. "Gratuitous ornamentation does not contribute to the function or the integrity of a piece. Surprises are fun — they add an element of discovery, another dimension. But they rarely make sense as design elements. A perfect, hand-cut dovetail or a hand-planed surface can be just as rewarding to discover yet much more elegant."

Designing for different level projects is less controversial a concept. Gehret draws distinctions among future family heirlooms, kitchen cabinets, and a cabinet or shelf for the shop or barn. He'll lavish money and effort on an heirloom, but not on a strictly utilitarian piece.

Walentine draws a distinction between freestanding cabinets and built-ins. To him, they usually are different levels of work.

"If a piece must stand alone, it should be approached with a different set of standards," he says, "because it becomes an objet d'art — movable, showable, collectible — as opposed to built-in work, which is designed with a whole new set of parameters."

Built-ins, on the other hand, "actually become part of the architecture. Since built-ins cannot be moved, shown in museums, passed on to new generations (except in their original place)," he explains, "they generally are not thought of by the customer as having the same investment value as a discrete piece of furniture, which in fact they don't. The value of houses as real estate is tied more closely to locality, number of rooms, than to how exquisitely they are detailed."

The upshot is that on built-ins, the customer tends to hold the craftsman back. There is the occasional exception. In creating the cabinetry shown on the cover and on pages 5-6 and 186-191 — all of it is in one house, all of it is built-in — Walentine had "the opportunity to define the spaces *and* set the style. This isn't always the case — in fact it's the exception. In addition, I was working with a customer whose ideals were as high as mine in many respects. He was willing to pay for solid wood throughout and for the attention to detail usually reserved for fine furniture," he says.

As the design nears completion, new problems can crop up. For a professional, they may be the taste and budget of the client. For the amateur, they may be his own budget, equipment limitations, even inexperience.

"I've developed a way of relating to a problem that involves trying to reach the ideal solution at the outset," Walentine says. "I feel that this is the only way to end up with the best possible compromise — to know what my bargaining position is. Then I can modify it to meet the other requirements."

To put it another way, he says, "I design to my ideal and then back up to his pocketbook."

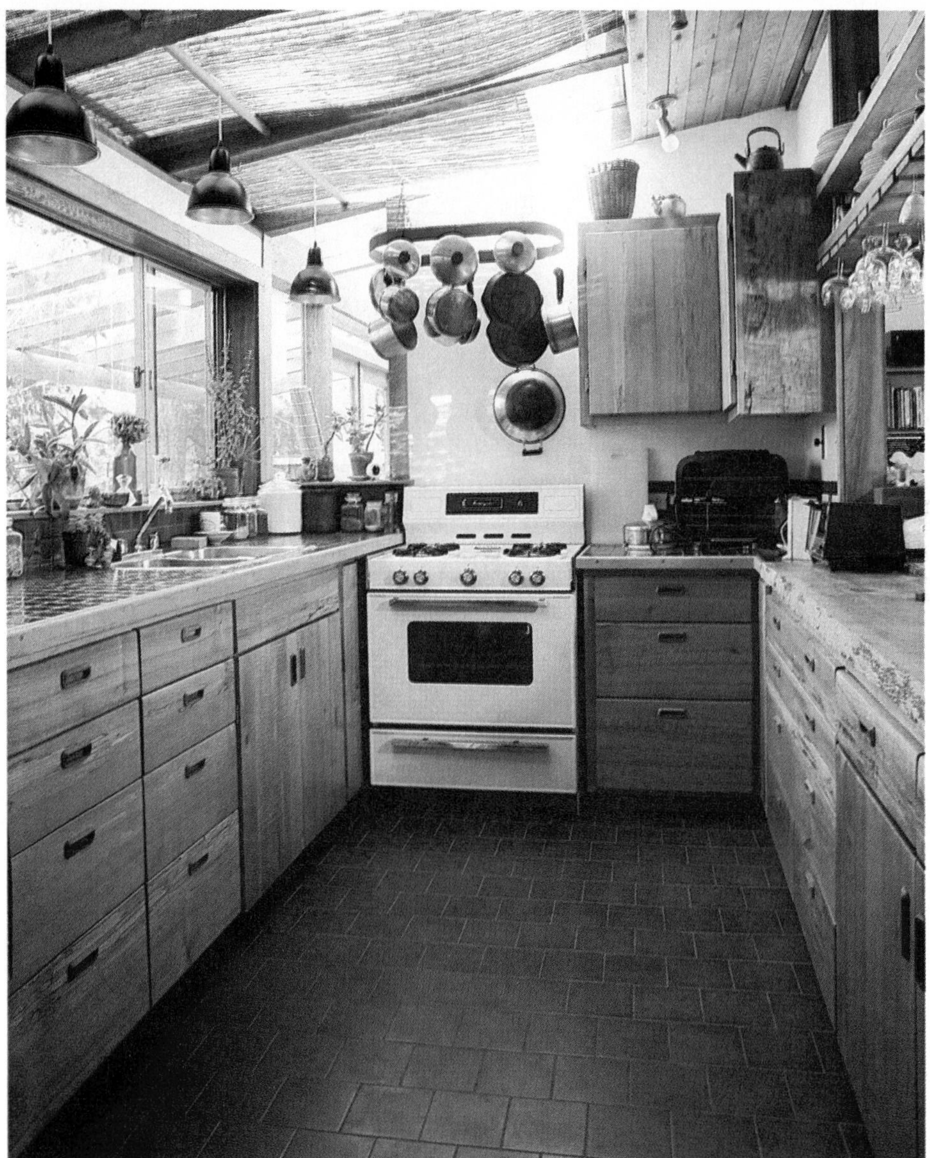

Some of the best-made cabinets are the most low-key in appearance. Paul Summerlin made these kitchen cabinets. His design allows the wood to do the talking, rather than fancy design touches or elaborate, exposed joinery. Doors and drawers fit flush, obviating the need for a face frame to hide the carcass construction.

The amateur in essentially the same position can do much the same thing. Design the ideal, then alter it to make it something he can both afford *and* build, given his tools and skills.

JOINERY

Joinery is no different than any other aspect of cabinetmaking. It is fraught with differing opinions and practices.

It encompasses, in my book, the selection of joints as well as the fabrication and assembly of them. Joint selection depends to one degree or another upon the structural application, the level of the job, the whims of the designer, the skills of the workman, the workman's equipment, the material, and surely a few other variables. Cabinetmakers themselves tend to focus on a single element in

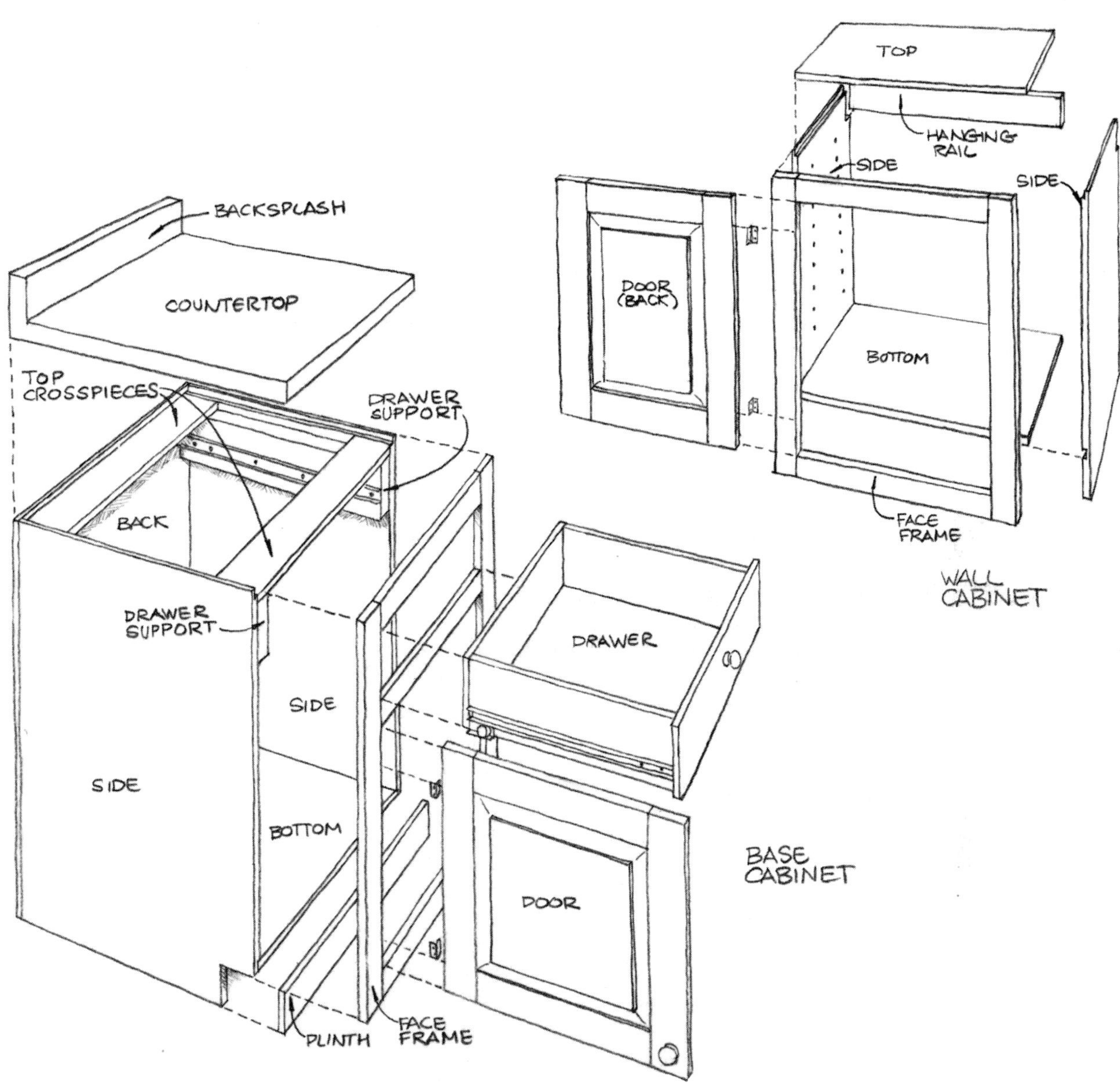

making a choice, though.

"You choose a joint because it's the one best joint for the job," Ellis Walentine says. It's the one that satisfies all the demands placed upon it, by the application, the aesthetics, the workman's limitations and so forth. There may be several that meet one or more of the criteria, but there's only one, Walentine judges, that will meet *all* of them.

And that's the one you use.

The basis for a built-in cabinet is the carcass or case, which, in its unembellished form, is almost exactly like the bookcase. The embellishments are the face frame, doors, drawers and, in the case of the base cabinet, a countertop. Usually, the carcass is constructed of plywood or particle board, and the appearance of the unit is established by the material and style of the embellishments. Here the cabinets have straightforward face frames, with flush-fitting drawers and doors, the latter being of the raised panel style.

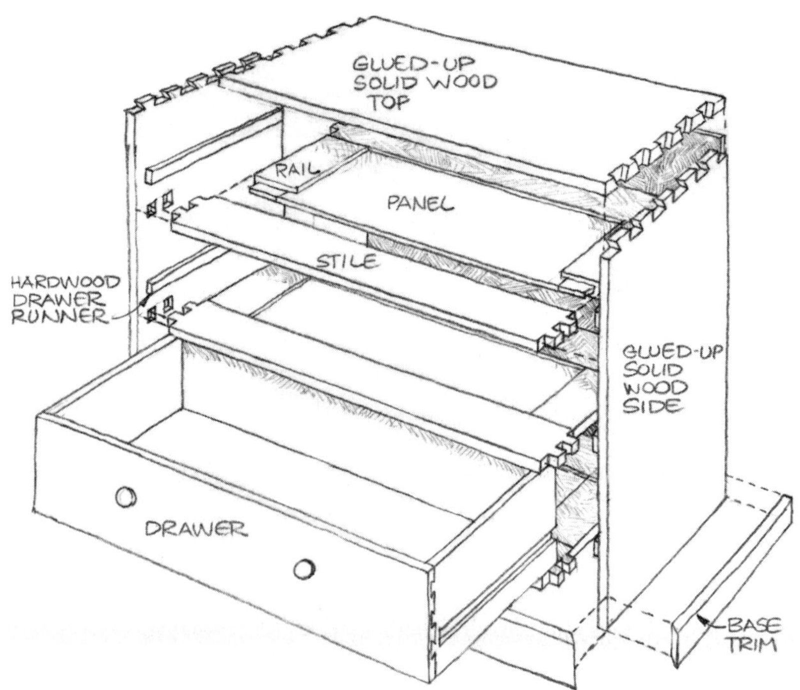

Traditional carcass construction uses glued-up panels of solid wood for sides and top and frame-and-panel elements for internal framing. Joints with the greatest mechanical strength are used: dovetails for the carcass, mortise-and-tenon for the frames. Since the entire carcass is solid wood, a face frame is unnecessary. Drawers are usually constructed in similar fashion and ride on hardwood runners.

"The choice of joinery depends on intention," Jack Larimore says in contrast. "There's nothing quite as satisfying as properly making a dovetailed carcass. There's nothing that so reflects one's abilities and caring. But given the glues we have today, it is not *necessary.* With the adhesives we have today, you can put two pieces of wood together any number of ways and they are going to stick."

Thus, in his view, the choice of joinery has less to do with engineering than with design and the nature of materials. "Do you want one board to be holding up the other, or do you want the eye to turn the corner smoothly," Larimore asks. "Or are you trying to imply evidence of handcrafting."

"It comes back to intentions," he insists. "The choice of joinery comes back to what you are trying to communicate."

The strength of a joint has to be a major consideration in the selection process.

According to R. Bruce Hoadley, there are "four critical considerations that determine the success of any given joint." These are "the stress system involved, the grain direction of the joined parts, wood movement in response to moisture, and the surface quality of the mating parts."

The stress system is what the joint must do mechanically in the structure. Joints can be in compression, tension, shear or racking (bending). Some joints withstand particular stresses better than others.

Compression stress occurs when one piece is pushed against a second. Tension stress occurs when one is pulled away from another. Shear stress occurs when one piece tries to move past another. And racking stress occurs when pieces are under both compression and tension stresses.

"Joints subject to tension and racking are usually most troublesome," Hoadley points out in *Understanding Wood.* "Although it is not usually necessary to figure the loads precisely, one must have a general grasp of the direction and relative magnitude of stress in order to design and construct good joints."

The grain direction possibilities are endgrain to endgrain, side-grain to side-grain, and side-grain to endgrain. Of these, side-to-side can be the strongest, end-to-end the weakest.

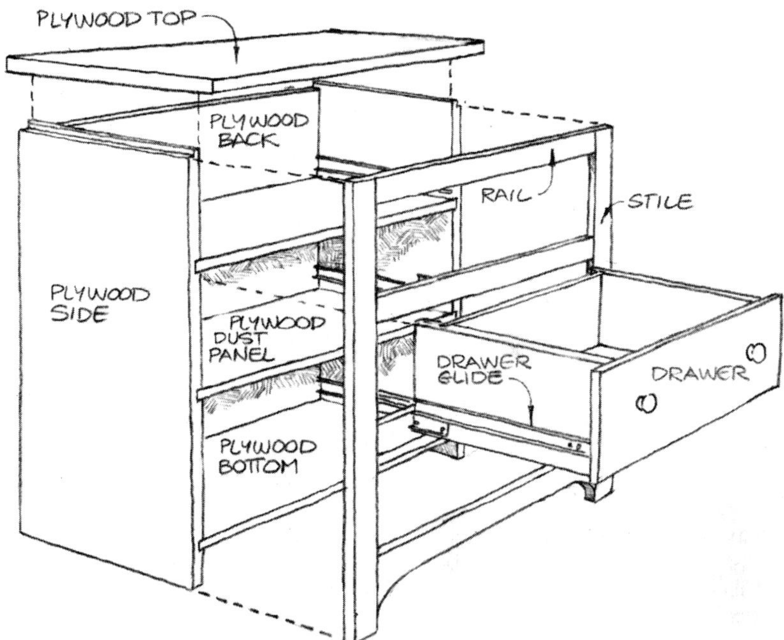

Case construction uses parts cut from plywood or particle board. Thus the back, top, sides and dust panels are single pieces rather than subassemblies. The case is joined using simple joints. The edges of the plywood must be concealed for appearance's sake, so a face frame is a necessity. In such constructions drawers are usually made of plywood and ride on commercial drawer glides.

Dimensional change, the third critical consideration, is probably the woodworker's biggest demon.

Dimensional change is seldom a problem in endgrain to endgrain or parallel side-grain to side-grain joints, because the growth rings of both pieces can be similarly oriented. But where the growth rings aren't oriented the same, the difference in the movements of mating parts can sometimes cause visual and structural problems. This is why many woodworkers are picky about how they orient the growth rings when gluing up a panel from narrow stock.

"In perpendicular side-grain to side-grain joints and in endgrain to side-grain joints," Hoadley writes, "the conflict between dimensional change along the grain and across the grain (especially where tangential direction opposes longitudinal direction) may become more important than the stress/strength of the original joint. *The potential self-destructiveness of such joints should always be anticipated.* A lap joint, for example, might be very strong when glued, but it could self-destruct as a result of dimensional change."

The condition of the mating surfaces is the last critical element. The joint can achieve maximum strength only if the fit is precise, with the mating surfaces being true and bearing evenly, and if the cells aren't too badly damaged by the surfacing process.

The use of the joint is another key item on the list of selection criteria. According to Tage Frid, there are two kinds of joints in cabinetmaking: those used to make frames and those used to make carcasses.

Among the former are lap joints and the many varieties of mortise-and-tenon joints. Among the latter are dado joints, rabbet joints, miter joints, dovetails and so forth.

A cabinet is usually made using joints from both of Frid's categories. The case and any drawers will be made using one or several of the carcass joints, while the face frame, doors and any frame-and-panel elements of the case will be built using frame joints. There *is* a certain amount of crossover, with some "frames" being assembled with carcass joinery. Exactly which joints are used where is deter-

(continued on page 90)

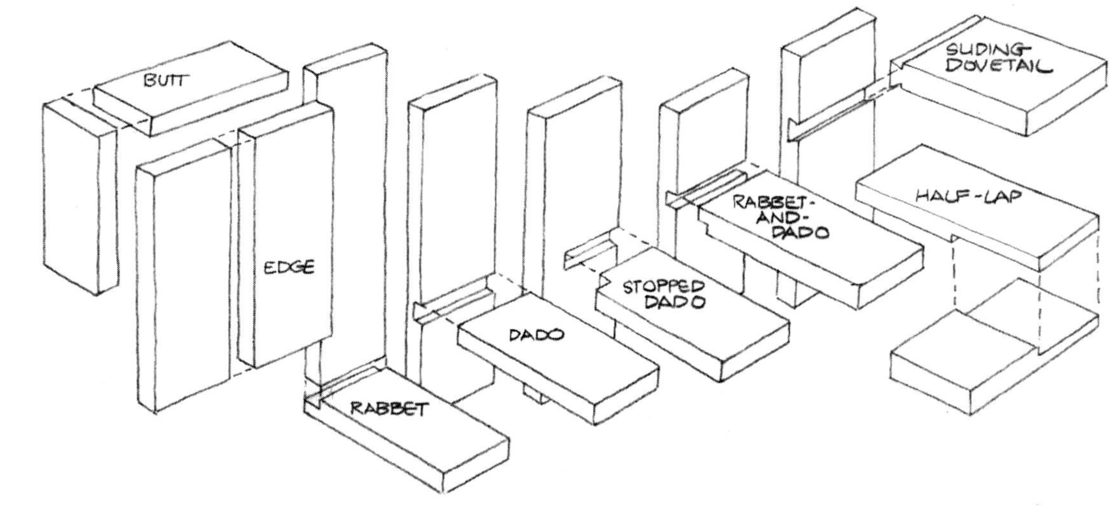

Joints

Joints are what joinery is all about. While a cabinetmaker is more than a joiner, he's got to have the joiner's skills mastered.

The joints you make in a cabinet will have a lot to do with its durability and its final appearance. There are more than a hundred kinds of joints that can be made, but they all fall into a few basic categories. While some cabinetmakers believe modern adhesives have reduced the need for some of the traditional joints—provided you make the simple joints accurately and carefully—others respect and use them.

Some basic principles still apply to all joinery. Use the simplest joint that will assure the strength needed in the construction. The joints you select must to some extent be determined by the tools and skills you have. If you have few tools but use them with care and skill, simple joints may be best.

Butt Joint This is the simplest joint, formed by butting two squared-off pieces of lumber together. Though it is inherently weak, it can be reinforced with dowels or a spline.

Edge Joint If you intend to glue up stock to make large flat panels, you will use some variation of the edge joint. Edge joints can be reinforced by several means, and the most common is with dowels. An alternative method is to use splines.

Rabbet Joint In its simplest applications, this is a slight elaboration of a butt joint. An L-shaped groove is cut into the end or edge of one of the pieces and the other fits into it. The width of the rabbet should match the thickness of the piece to fit into it, and the depth should be one-half to two-thirds the thickness of the board being rabbeted. A variation is to rabbet both pieces.

Dado Joint A dado is a groove cut across the grain. It is commonly used where the joint is to provide support for a horizontal member, as in a bookshelf or a cabinet bottom. You can make a blind or stopped dado by terminating the dado a short distance from the front edge of the supporting piece. The piece to be inserted will have to be notched accordingly, but the result will have the appearance of a butt joint and the strength of a dado joint.

For added strength and rigidity, a combination dado-and-rabbet joint has one member rabbeted and the supporting

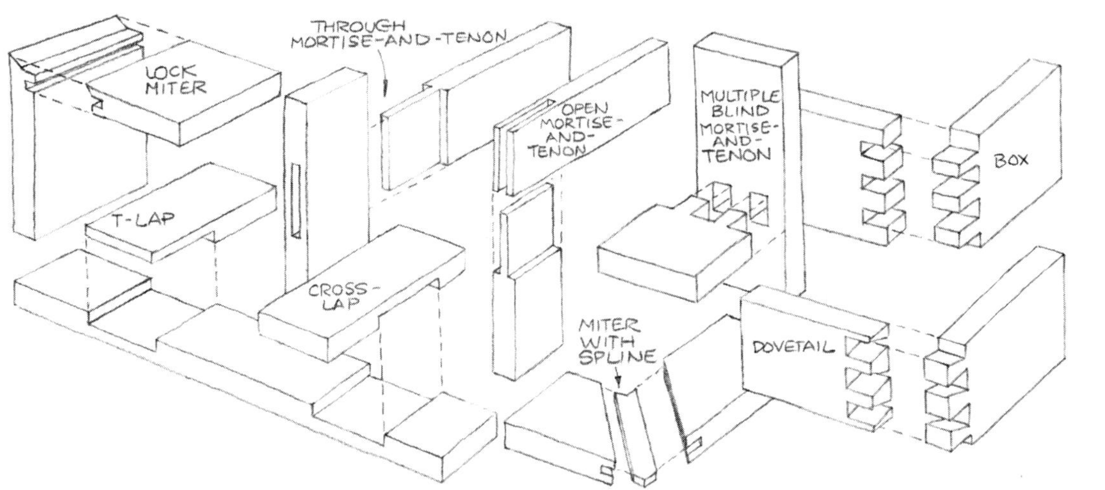

member dadoed.

A fancy, and strong, variation is the dovetail dado or sliding dovetail joint. The supporting member is dadoed with a dovetail slot, while the other member has a matching dovetail pin cut across its end.

Lap Joint A joint in which one member is notched to accept the other member is a lap joint. In a full-lap joint, only one piece is notched; the other's full dimension is set into the notch. In any of the half-lap joints, both members are notched, usually with half the total material to be removed coming from each piece.

Within these broad categories, there are many variations. In the end-lap joint, both members are lapped at their ends. In a cross-lap joint, the laps are somewhere other than the ends; the members can cross at any angle. In a T-lap joint, one member is lapped in the middle, the other at an end.

Miter Joint Pure miter joints are not particularly strong joints, and consequently must be reinforced with a spline, a key or dowels. There are a number of hybrid miter joints, such as the lock miter joint, used in casework. These combine miters with rabbets and dadoes and are stronger than simple miters.

Miter joints run in several main groups: the flat miters, in which the angled cuts run across the face of the pieces, the edge miters, in which the pieces to be joined are actually beveled rather than mitered, and the compound miters, in which the pieces are cut with combination miter and bevel cuts.

Mortise-and-Tenon Joint Mortise-and-tenon joints take many different forms. The basic elements are the mortise, which is a hole—round, square or rectangular—and the tenon, which is a tongue cut on the end of the joining member to fit into the mortise.

There are joints known as blind mortise-and-tenon, haunched mortise-and-tenon, open mortise-and-tenon. In constructing cases, a single joint may have several mortises and tenons.

Dovetail Joint This is the classic cabinetmaker's joint. When properly executed, the dovetail joint is extremely strong, and it is attractive to boot.

A simpler joint that resembles the dovetail is the finger or box joint. The interlocking pins, instead of being tapered, are parallel. They are therefore easily cut on a table saw.

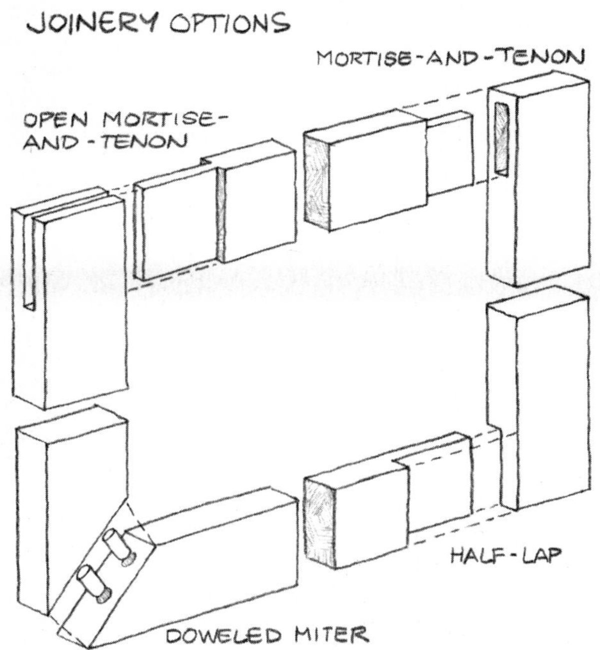

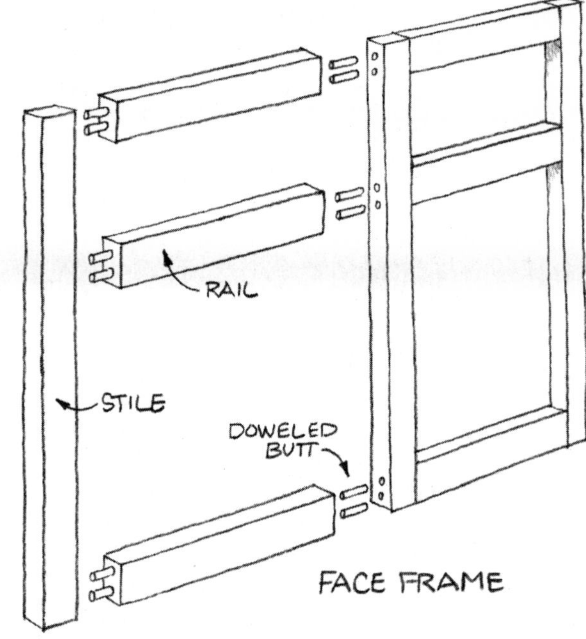

The face frame is an assembly of rails and stiles. Attached to the front of the carcass, it beautifies it and defines the spaces into which it is divided. Doweled butt joints are frequently used, since great joint strength is not necessary. Doweled miter joints lend a different appearance, while other joinery options offer greater strength without changing the appearance.

mined by balancing the strength the application demands against the many variables of particular joints (the joint's strength, its ease of fabrication, its appearance and the designer's intentions, and so on).

This is where Walentine's concept of the one best joint comes into play. But not all cabinetmakers are as dogmatic. "Unless I'm trying to do something decorative," Larry Golden says, "I'll choose the easiest solution to the problem."

The basic structural similarity between a face frame and a door offers some interesting points of joinery contrast. Both are frame constructions, built of vertical elements called stiles and horizontal elements called rails. But their uses are different.

"A face frame is going to be permanently in place," Gehret points out. "The door is not going to be held in a rigid position, and thus it must have a stronger joint."

For the face frame, Gehret suggests that "the easiest, depending upon your skill level, would be either a half-lap or a dowel joint. They're simple; they're the easiest. You can go with a butt joint, but there must be something under it to hold it in line."

Butt joints fastened with corrugated fasteners or staples are simply not strong enough, in Gehret's opinion, though they are widely used by cabinet manufacturers. The strongest joint would be a mortise-and-tenon joint, but it is more complicated to make and its strength isn't necessary in a face frame.

For a door, however, the mortise-and-tenon joint is much preferred. Gehret says that half-laps or doweled butt joints *can* be used, but he warns that they aren't really durable enough to withstand the racking stresses that a door sustains as it is yanked open and slammed closed.

Larimore is sensitive to the stresses of dimensional change that afflict the frame-and-panel door. If the door's panel were to be solid wood, which will add nothing to the overall strength of the door, Larimore says he'd use mortise-and-tenon joints for the frame. If the panel were to be plywood, which *will* add to the door's strength, he'd substitute an easier-to-make (but weaker) splined joint.

The case and the drawer have a lot in common, too. They are of vastly different sizes, but they use many of the same joints. Though the case is larger, the drawer is considered the acid test of the craftsman's skill. Because of all the pushing and pulling that a drawer is subjected to, it has to be well constructed to survive.

These shallow shelf units—they are mounted on drawer glides and slide into a wall cabinet—are a good example of solving a functional problem through design. Access to the area would have been difficult had it been handled in the usual manner—shelves behind a door. By installing these movable shelves in the space, cabinetmaker Alan Marks made it usable and *accessible.*

Cabinetmakers regularly come up with new solutions to the design problem presented by the drawer front. Stan Griskivich built drawers of plywood, above, *mounted them in a built-in using commercial drawer glides, then attached beveled-edge false fronts to overlay the face frame. Alan Marks made these drawer fronts,* above right, *in frame-and-panel fashion for a subtle contrast in figure. James Cottey used traditional dovetail joinery in these drawers,* right, *but plowed a groove in their bottom edges to be used instead of pulls.*

The dovetail has always been favored for both drawers and cases, in the old days because of its strength, but these days for what it says about the quality of the piece. Gehret uses dovetails in his reproductions, "one, because they are traditional and, two, because they are strong."

But not every drawer that's made these days, even by the most demanding of craftsmen, is dovetailed. "The only reason to use traditional dovetails in a drawer is to make that statement about craftsmanship," Larimore says. He generally uses through (not blind) sliding dovetails for the drawer body. The pin is cut on the ends of the sides, the slots are cut in the back and front. Gehret himself will make kitchen cabinet drawers using nothing more elaborate than rabbets and dadoes.

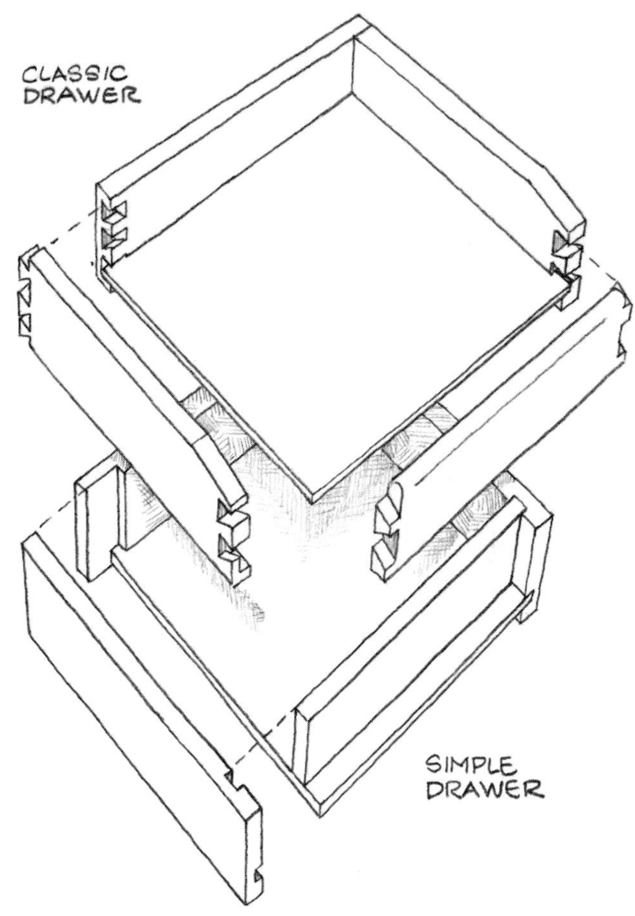

The drawer of classic construction uses solid wood throughout, even for the bottom, and hand-cut dovetail joinery. A more simple drawer may be constructed using plywood for the body and bottom and machine-cut dadoes and rabbets for the joinery.

The quintessential joint in cabinetmaking probably *is* the dovetail joint. What cabinetmakers say about crafting it can be applied to other, more mundane joints. The care applied to cutting pins and tails also goes into plowing grooves and paring tenons.

"People love and admire dovetail joints," Larimore says. "It is a connection between the craft and the consumer. The more subtle things sometimes go unnoticed." So these days, it is often used primarily for show. As Larimore has pointed out, the high-tech glues woodworkers use these days make the dovetail unnecessary.

Nevertheless, the dovetail *is* widely used in the best of cabinetry. Ripper and Walentine, who stress the traditional woodworking fundamentals in their work, use it, and not simply

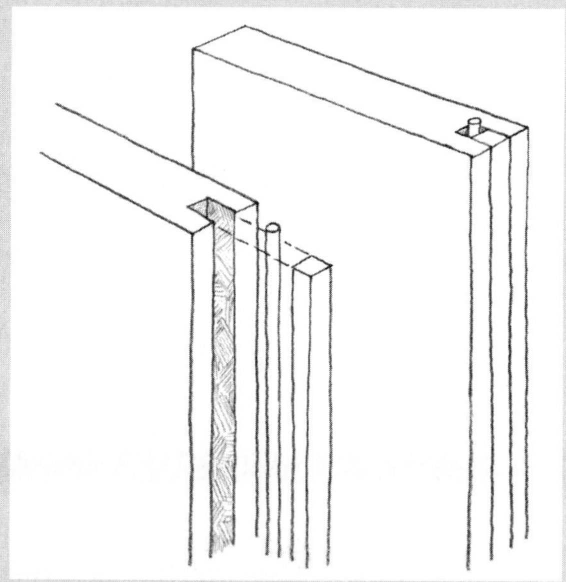

Handcrafted Pin Hinges

Dozens of different kinds of cabinet hinges are available, but there are cabinetmakers who simply don't want to use any of them. Steve Ripper is such a man.

In creating the design for the dressing table shown on page 10, one of Ripper's criteria was: "No exposed hardware." He was able to develop a way to mount the two doors so that "even when they are open, you can't see the hinges."

The secret is that the doors are mounted on brass rods that extend from top rail to bottom rail.

After completing the doors, Ripper plowed a groove in the edge of each outside stile, just wide enough for the rods. Then he crafted a strip of the walnut used to make the stand to fill each groove, leaving a hole the length of the stile for the rod. He glued a strip into each groove.

Holes for the rods were drilled completely through the bottom rail of the case and part way through the top rail. The gussets between the bottom rail and the legs hold the rods, and thus the doors, in place. By removing the gussets—they're secured with screws—Ripper can slide the rods out and remove the doors.

Ripper positioned the holes in the rails with extreme care since his design also called for the elimination of commercial catches for the doors. The doors are mounted so they have a minute sag when they are open. As they are closed, they ride up on a tiny wooden catch in the center of the rail.

The result? "You don't have a cheap metallic click," says Ripper.

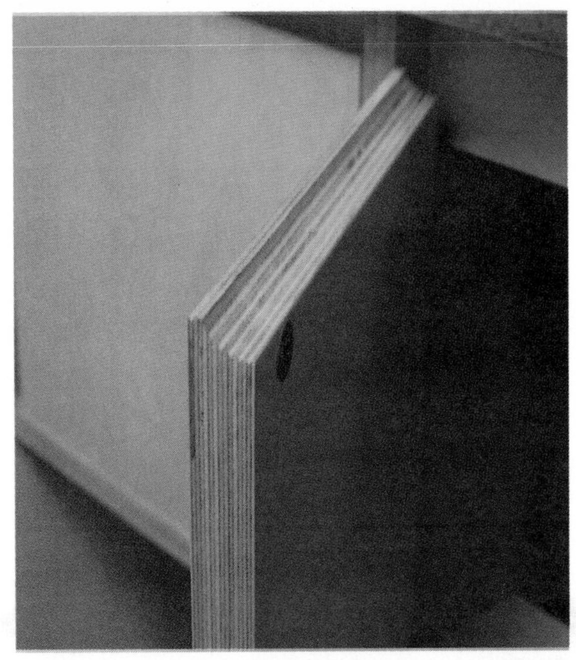

An unadorned plywood door can work aesthetically. Here, right, *the door is mounted flush, so three of the edges are hidden by the carcass. The fourth edge has a groove to be used instead of a pull. Glass doors,* below right, *provide visual access to the cabinet, while handcrafted pulls provide physical access.*

for its appearance. They use it for its mechanical strength. Its use does add to the cost of a piece, however.

Nowadays, a decent dovetail joint can be cut using a router and a special dovetail template. All the pins and tails will be of uniform size. The work goes quickly and the fit is the same every time. Cutting and fitting dovetails by hand is more demanding work. The joint must be precisely fitted or it will lack its valued mechanical strength.

In Gehret's opinion, the degree of precision necessary in the dovetail's final fit hinges on its location—"A drawer versus a case side to a top." Where looks are important, as in the exposed case, the fit must be very precise. In a drawer, Gehret *could* live with an easy dry fit. But, he says, in 90 percent of the situations, he'd want to have to assemble the joint "with a little persuasion." It is very rare, he says, that a cabinetmaker would want to achieve a one-time fit, meaning that the clearances are so exact that once the mating pieces are joined, they won't come apart again. He adds that "some finger joints are like dovetails in this regard."

"Wood is a pretty forgiving medium," Gehret explains. "You can do some things with it that you can't do with other materials. You *can* force it." In fitting dovetails, there is a margin of compression in the wood; forcing tightly fitted pieces together will work, but once the fit is forced, the wood is compressed. Repeated test-fittings, in other words, will alter the final fit.

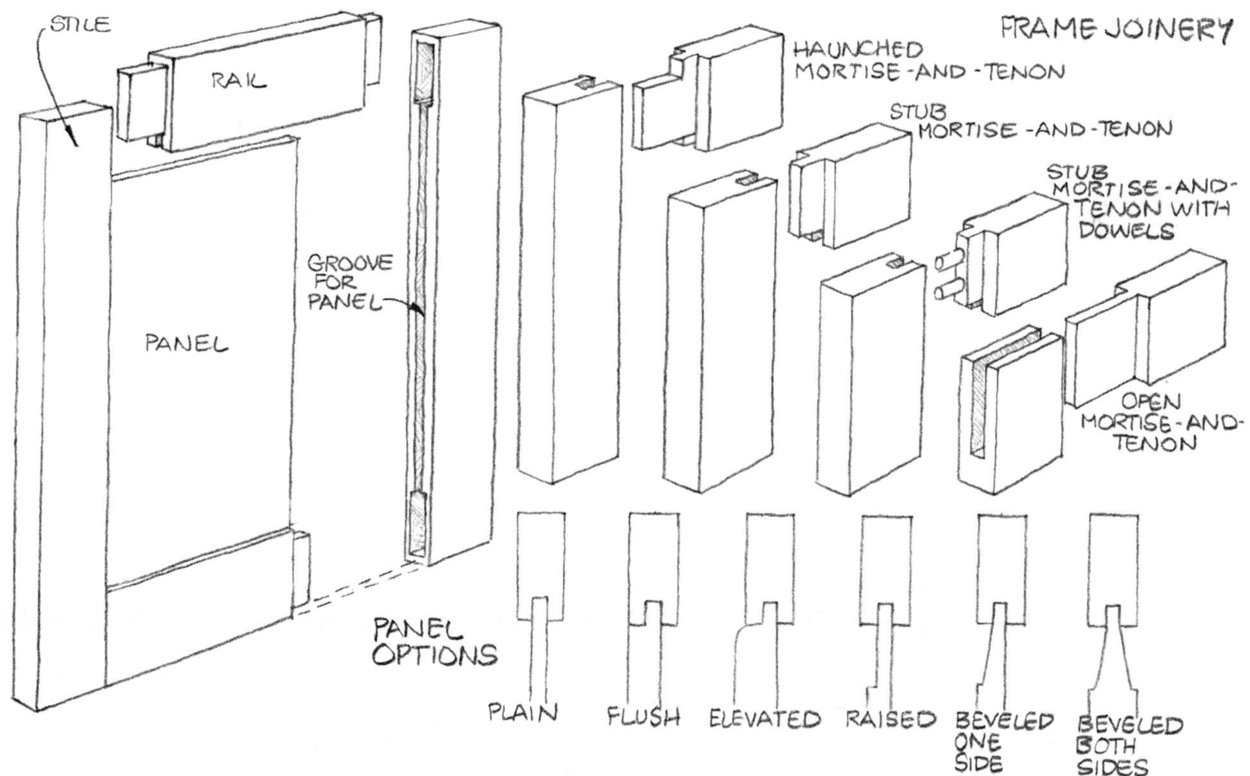

Options for the maker of frame-and-panel doors are many. For strength, the frames are invariably joined using one of the mortise-and-tenon joints; four of the many variations are shown. The panel can be plywood or solid wood. Using the latter makes possible the traditional treatments, such as elevating, raising or beveling the panel.

Gehret notes that the instability of solid wood can be vexing where dovetails are involved. It is wise to assemble the dovetails the same day they are cut. Otherwise, the fit may be off because the pieces change minutely in dimension. Dovetails are usually so precisely fitted that only a little extra humidity can thwart assembly. He says that dovetails are probably unique in this regard.

In any event, cutting dovetails may not be the best use of a novice's time. "I'm not saying you can't do a reasonable dovetail the first time off," says Ripper. "Most people's tools aren't sharp enough to do it."

Mitch Mandel tried dovetails fairly early in his woodworking experience. Laying out and cutting the first ones was "intimidating," and they didn't turn out all that well.

But Mandel has subsequently cut others and feels that he's improved. "For certain things they are appropriate," he says. "But if you're going to do them, I think you should do them by hand. Machine dovetails look like you made them with a machine." Besides, for Mandel, "part of the satisfaction of woodworking is doing it by hand and having it work."

Building the cabinet makes demands on the cabinetmaker beyond those of knowing how to create attractive and well-engineered designs and how to make tight, strong joints. You have to be able to work in the proper sequence.

"There's a certain religious attitude you

develop toward procedures, because procedures eliminate mistakes 99 percent of the time," Larimore says. "If you need to, you write them out. You think through it every way you possibly can."

The procedure that Larimore follows in making a case and bringing it up to a certain level of finishing illustrates the point.

"If there are details or cut-in joints, you have to do that before assembly," he explains. "You sand up to a certain point — 180 grit or medium grit — before assembly, too.

"The progression is," he continues, "that you dimension your stock, cut joints, sand the insides except where the joints are. Then clamp it up without glue if the joints are fairly complicated. Take off the clamps. (The dry fit prepares the clamps as well as allowing you to make adjustments.) Then there's the glue up. Immediately after the case is glued and clamped, check the case for square (the two corresponding diagonal measurements should equal themselves). Then try to remove the glue squeeze from inside. Depending upon the wood, you might wet-wipe or scrape.

"Then, in bookcases, add the face frame. You must wait until the case is glued up and square before attaching the face frame, but you should attach it before doing the final sanding," he says.

Many projects involve a certain amount of final fitting. "Usually the male element sits proud of the female element, so you can plane and sand those back," Larimore says. This is the case when using dovetails, box joints, rabbets, and through tenons.

The creative cabinetmaker is never limited by the knobs and pulls that are available at the hardware store. Alex MacLean handcrafted door pulls for a wall cabinet simply by cutting wedge-shaped slices off an oak burl, top. *He glued them to small blocks of wood, which were in turn glued to the doors. The obviously handmade pulls,* directly above, *suggest the sort of contribution a jewelry maker might make to a fellow craftsman's work.*

Finally, you sand the outside. Larimore says this is best left to sand all at one time, and he recommends that it be done last. "You take it up to a certain grit, depending upon the type of wood and the finish. It is hardly ever less than 200 or 220 grit," he says.

At this point, the cabinet is ready for its finish.

FINISHING

"Finishing is really important," Mitch Mandel points out. "I enjoy finishing, because that's when you see the thing really shine. That's when it finally looks good. You have to take your time in the finishing, or you *waste* all your previous time."

Finishing is often viewed as the application of a chemical coating to the wood: some sort of oil, paint, varnish, shellac or wax. But unless the surface is properly prepared for the coating, the piece won't look as good as it should.

The finish can be seen as a key measure of workmanship, for as Mandel says, "That's ultimately what people look at." When he's studying a piece he's going to photograph, he looks closely to see "if it's smooth and has no scratches and that everything fits. If it doesn't look good in the photograph, it doesn't look good."

The usual advice is to sand and sand and sand to establish that final surface. But Ripper and Walentine see that as fundamentally wrongheaded.

"The difference between a planed surface and an abraided surface is the difference between day and night," Walentine says. He explains that a plane makes a "crisply defined cut," while 600-grit sandpaper leaves "600 lines per inch." Most woodworkers never approach as fine a grit as 600; usually they quit at 220 or so. Not Walentine.

"I want to be able to *start* at 220 at the max. The last layer of cells that gets shown off is the bottom line. I sand only when it is necessary, only when the wood is so figured that I can't plane it smooth enough."

The approach Walentine and Ripper take in most of their work is to hand-plane every piece of a cabinet as it is fabricated. The final assembly is carefully scraped by hand, using a cabinet scraper. By doing this, the final surface is established through a cutting action rather than an abrasive action. The hand scraping is critical, in their minds, to establishing their work's custom character.

"The definition of custom is," Ripper explains, "that it has been made by me and a couple of other guys in my shop and the finish is hand-scraped and hand-sanded and there are no blatant machine impressions. What separates us from others is the knowledge, the understanding of how to use hand tools to achieve that finish." It is a theme both men return to again and again, with Ripper talking about "the nuances of hand scraping and hand finishing," and Walentine saying that "top work in this field is never cheap" because of the "extensive hand scraping and sanding."

Applying the finish can be quick and easy or slow and laborious. There are a welter

Wooden Hinges

There's something very special about wooden hinges, particularly in what they say about a cabinet and its maker.

Many very skillfully crafted cabinets have manufactured metal hinges on the doors. Usually, these hinges work flawlessly and either complement the overall design or are so unobtrusive as to have no effect on it. Yet open the door and there they are: harsh metal clashing with mellow hues and graceful figures.

A clever—and skilled—cabinetmaker may contrive a system of pins or rods that serves as a pivot around which a door swings.

Bruce McQuilkin, a San Rafael, California, woodworker, has gone one step further and made wooden hinges. Functionally, his hinges are kin to the concealed-pin approach, since the pivoting is done around a brass pin. But rather than mask the hinge, McQuilkin highlights it by crafting it of an exotic hardwood and recessing it into the edges of the door and case. In some cabinets, the hinge is flush with the door's face, in others it sits proud of the face.

McQuilkin makes the hinges by first preparing the cabinet. On a band saw, he cuts a notch in the door's edge and the case's edge with the sides of the notch converging toward its bottom. He machines a rabbet along the edge of the notch in both the face and back of the door, forming a tongue over which the hinge itself will fit. The pairs of hinge leaves are roughed out on a table saw, then carefully fitted so the female leaf fits over the tongue on the male leaf with but $\frac{1}{16}$-inch clearance. After drilling the leaves for the hinge pin, McQuilkin shapes them to match notches in the door and case, then cuts a groove around the mating edge of each leaf using a dado head in the table saw. Finally, the leaves are glued to the door and case.

The hinges look simple to make, but clearly it takes a particularly capable workman to pull it off.

In the 18th and 19th centuries, wood grain was painted on cabinets and walls. The kitchen of Nantucket's Maria Mitchell House is believed to be the work of itinerant workers.

of options here, and the substances and procedures that books talk of using can readily confuse an inexperienced woodworker. Whatever finish is chosen should enhance the appearance of the piece. And it doesn't *have* to be complicated.

"Finishes seem to be a real stumbling block for everybody," says Larimore. "It has to do with the fact that you are dealing with the chemistry of the finish, the wood, and your hands."

Larimore favors Minwax antique oil, which has a linseed oil base, for color. After that is applied, he sprays on clear lacquer very lightly. "It doesn't take much," he says.

"I like to keep finishes as close to an oil finish as I can," he says. "I think I'd oil most things if I thought people understood how to maintain an oil finish."

Ripper usually oils his pieces, applying as many as six to ten coats. On an open-pored wood like walnut, that many coats will fill the pores, obviating the need for a filler.

Filler is one of those substances that every book on wood finishing talks about. It is a pasty material you are supposed to apply to "open-grained" woods, like walnut, oak or mahogany, to clog up the pores and create a smooth impervious surface for varnish or shellac or lacquer. But not a single cabinetmaker I have talked to has mentioned using the stuff. And the finishes their pieces exhibit are flawless.

Those same wood finishing books list all sorts of elaborate finishing sequences: using stains and fillers and sealers and varnishes or lacquers. Few craftsmen, it seems, really use these finishes except on reproductions. Douglas Pinney uses the laborious French polishing method on some reproductions (see page 102). Steve Ripper experiments with different approaches.

In finishing the reproduction style wall cabinet shown on page 11, Ripper lavished time and energy on a multistep process.

"This walnut was stained and bleached out so the color of it is more like the old walnut," he explains. "It's very orange, a bright orangey color. It retains the yellows and the reds."

The idea was to have a finish that resembled that of the style of piece being mimicked. "A lot of old finishes have completely matted and crazed," Ripper points out, so to suggest that effect without actually reproducing it, he "built up alternating layers of oil and lacquer."

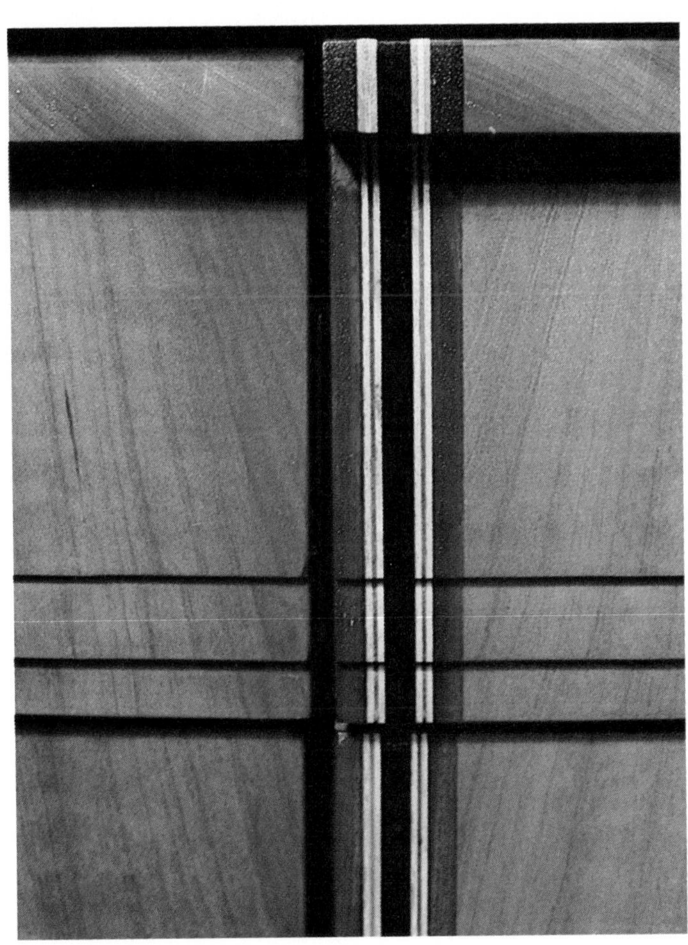

Gary Church wanted to create a lively motif for cabinets in a child's bathroom. He glued strips of reddish narrawood, light-colored baltic birch plywood and dark ebony to one edge of each drawer and door, creating a colorful stripe.

Phil Gehret has a fixed routine when it comes to finishing his reproductions. Because he has no separate finishing room, he gives his shop over to the process. This means, of course, that once he starts finishing a piece, he doesn't do *anything* else in the shop until the task is completed.

Part of the finishing—some of the sanding—is done during the fabrication and assembly of the piece. Individual pieces he'll plane, then sand with a fine belt on a hand belt sander.

After assembly is completed, Gehret will hand-scrape the piece with a cabinet scraper to ready it for its finish.

The finish consists of a lot of layers. The first is boiled linseed oil. Gehret applies it on a warm, sunny day. He brushes the oil on, waits 15 to 20 minutes, then wipes off the excess. The next layers are a wash coat of shellac (2 to 3 pound cut) followed by two coats of spar varnish. After shellacking the piece, which raises its grain, Gehret sands it with 220-grit sandpaper, wipes it down with a tack cloth, and brushes on a coat of spar varnish. He sands again, cleans up with the tack cloth, and applies a second coat of the varnish. When dry, this coat is hand-rubbed with a mixture of pumice and boiled linseed oil. When *that* is dry, Gehret carefully waxes the piece with paste wax.

This is the finish he applied to his walnut chest-on-chest (see pages 20 and 21). Gehret admits that the old finishes consisted of shellac alone, well protected by wax. But he thinks

French Polishing

A very beautiful technique for finishing fine furniture is called French polishing. It is a laborious technique, requiring a great deal of handwork. But because it is a traditional process, it is done frequently in finishing reproductions.

One cabinetmaker who does it is Douglas Pinney of Nantucket. "It's not a terribly durable finish," he says, "but it's so beautiful." The reproduction of a 1750 Queen Anne's lady's desk, shown right, establishes just how beautiful the finish is.

In brief, Pinney repeatedly applies alternating coats of linseed oil and shellac using a thumb-sized pad called a "wad." He points out that his is not the only approach that works, it is simply the one he uses.

Pinney prepares a piece, like the desk, in much the same way he'd prepare it for another finish, sanding and hand scraping it, then staining it.

Boiled linseed oil Pinney uses straight out of a can. He prepares his own shellac by mixing equal amounts of orange shellac flakes and alcohol and allowing the mixture to set for two or three days. It is strained through cheesecloth, cut with alcohol, and allowed to set several more days. Pinney cuts the shellac with alcohol as many as three times before using it.

The wad is a piece of cotton or linen cloth. Once it is charged with oil and shellac, it must not be allowed to dry. Any dried shellac can scratch the finish being applied. Between applications, therefore, the wad must be kept in an airtight jar.

Pinney applies a coat of linseed oil

first, covering but not saturating the wood. Then he applies a thin coat of shellac to the wood, working always with the grain. He is careful not to apply the shellac too thickly: It will take an excessively long time to dry—weeks, even—and it may very well crack after it *does* dry. After the first coat is dry, Pinney applies a second—linseed oil, then shellac—followed by a third and a fourth, maybe even a fifth. The first coat may dry in five minutes, but subsequent coats dry more slowly, with the last taking as long as six hours.

Each coat involves a lot of rubbing. The friction of the rubbing melts the shellac and forces it into the wood's grain. Pinney always works with the grain as he rubs. With the final coat, he mixes a bit of pumice or rottenstone with the linseed oil to help polish up the final luster.

The last step is to apply wax. Pinney uses either beeswax melted in turpentine or Johnson's Paste Wax.

In addition to being a lot of work, the finishing process is a sensitive one. The shellac is touchy. If it is too old, it won't dry. If conditions in the finishing room are not just right, it may cloud and spoil the finish. Pinney contends that even a slight draft across the workpiece can cause the shellac to cloud.

And even after the work is done, the finish is sensitive. The slightest bit of moisture or an excessive amount of heat can cause clouding of the shellac. It isn't durable. But as Pinney says, "It's so beautiful."

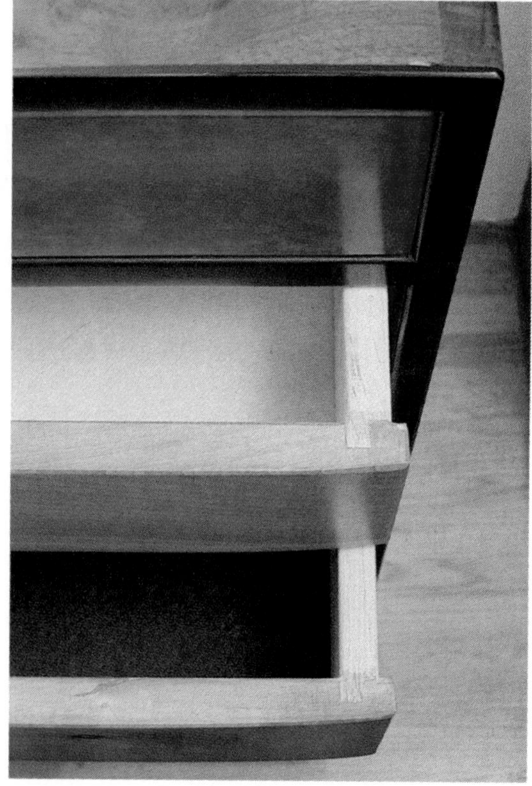

Old-world joinery and new-world finishing techniques come together in this dresser made by Arthur Espenet Carpenter. The carcass, made of California walnut, is joined with hand-cut dovetails. Madrone drawer fronts are joined to their bodies with rabbet-and-dado joints.

spar varnish has been available since the early 19th century.

Using paint, urethane varnish or lacquer finishes would save half the steps, Gehret says, so on a project of less personal significance, he'll be practical. A kitchen cabinet he will spray finish with paint, urethane (one thin coat, one normal coat) or lacquer (two normal coats on top of a sanding sealer). He points out that most spray finishing materials are available in a blend (retarding agents are added to slow the drying process) suited for brush-on application, too.

However the cabinetmaker chooses to finish a cabinet, he can't let up in preparing the surface or applying the finish. This is the difficult part. I always get antsy at this stage; I want the work to be done, so the piece can be brought into the house to be used and—I always hope—admired. But as Mandel says, the finish *is* critical to the success of the piece as an example of craftsmanship.

"The quality of the finished surface" is one of a few criteria Ripper and Walentine use to judge the quality of the workmanship of a piece. Among the others: "Tight glue lines," says Walentine. "Structural integrity," adds Ripper.

So the craftsman can't get antsy at the end of the job any more than he can at the beginning or in the middle. He has to maintain that intensity, that high level of care, in handling every little detail.

"Attention to detail," says Mitch Mandel. "That's the mark of the craftsman. Attention to detail."

Carpenter calls the dresser a Mondrian cabinet, since it honors the artwork of Piet Mondrian. The color is provided by blocks of felt glued to two drawer fronts, then sealed under clear casting resin. After gluing the felt in place, Carpenter applied masking tape around the edges, creating a dam for the resin. He poured a $^{3}/_{16}$-inch layer of the resin and, after it dried, buffed it to a high gloss. The black edging was created in similar fashion.

A GALLERY OF SHELVES AND CABINETS

Carl Wies

ARCHED FRAME SHELVES

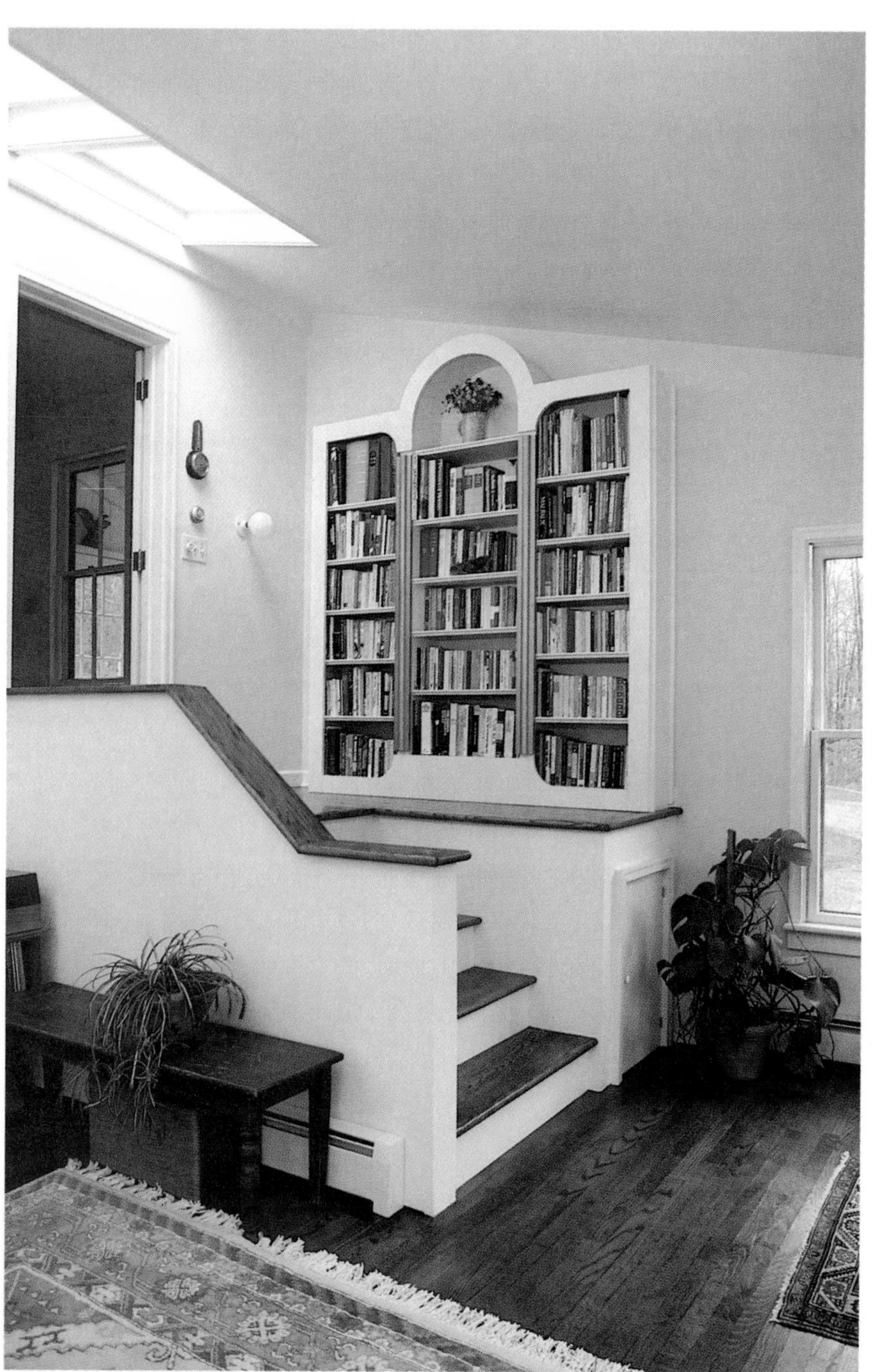

Before he designed and built this fanciful, free-standing bookcase, Carl Wies had only limited experience building furniture. He had few tools at hand, no shop, and not much interest in changing those situations. He just wanted a bookcase.

As an architect, Carl did have a ready vocabulary of architectural forms, and he had already made use of it to heighten the visual interest of his plain, turn-of-the-century house in Stony Creek, Connecticut. At the front, he added a quasi-Greek Revival entry porch, and at the back, a screened-in porch with a shed roof. On the sides of the house where the roof slopes down, he constructed three arches of descending heights. These alterations are discreet, and were deliberately chosen to appear as if they were part of the original house.

The arches on the outside of the house reappear in-

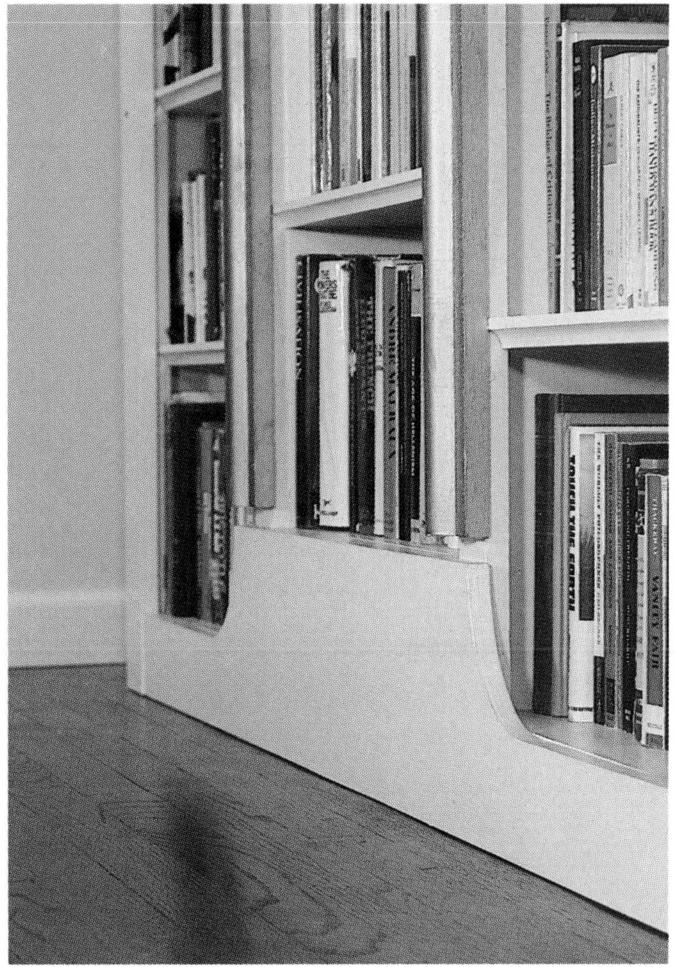

Clever design and very ordinary materials are the basis for Carl Wies's bookcase. An architect with no special affection for woodworking, Carl assembled the bookcase in a single weekend using common hand tools and portable power tools. The case is a straightforward plywood box. The face frame, from which the style of the unit emanates, is an assembly of plywood and pine, cove and half-round moldings.

doors in the bookcase. But to make it clear that in this case the columns have no structural function at all, he left a gap above and below them. And to avoid any suggestion of academic ponderousness, he painted them bright gold. They are really purely decorative molding.

Carl's design confidence made it easy to produce a plan in one quick doodle and proceed from there. He used the nineteenth century furniture in the adjacent living room as a starting point for a design that alludes to historical styles but is more modest in detail and technique. His site, a stair landing, dictated the 7-foot-square dimensions of the unit. The sloping ceiling suggested the use of some decorative device at the top.

Because of his limited supply of tools and time, Carl decided to build simply. He allotted himself one weekend for the task, bought plywood and pine moldings, then glued and nailed the unit together. He used his porch as a shop.

He cut all the plywood case members with a Skilsaw, then used a roller and quick-drying primer to paint them. The sides, top, bottom, shelves and two vertical dividers are ¾-inch birch plywood. The back and arched top are ¼-inch birch plywood. The face pieces are ¾-inch clear pine boards.

Carl began assembling the case by attaching the two sides and the two vertical dividers to the lower half of the back using temporary bracing to provide rigidity until the shelves were in place. He then nailed the upper half of the back to the sides and dividers. The two pieces of plywood, one above the other,

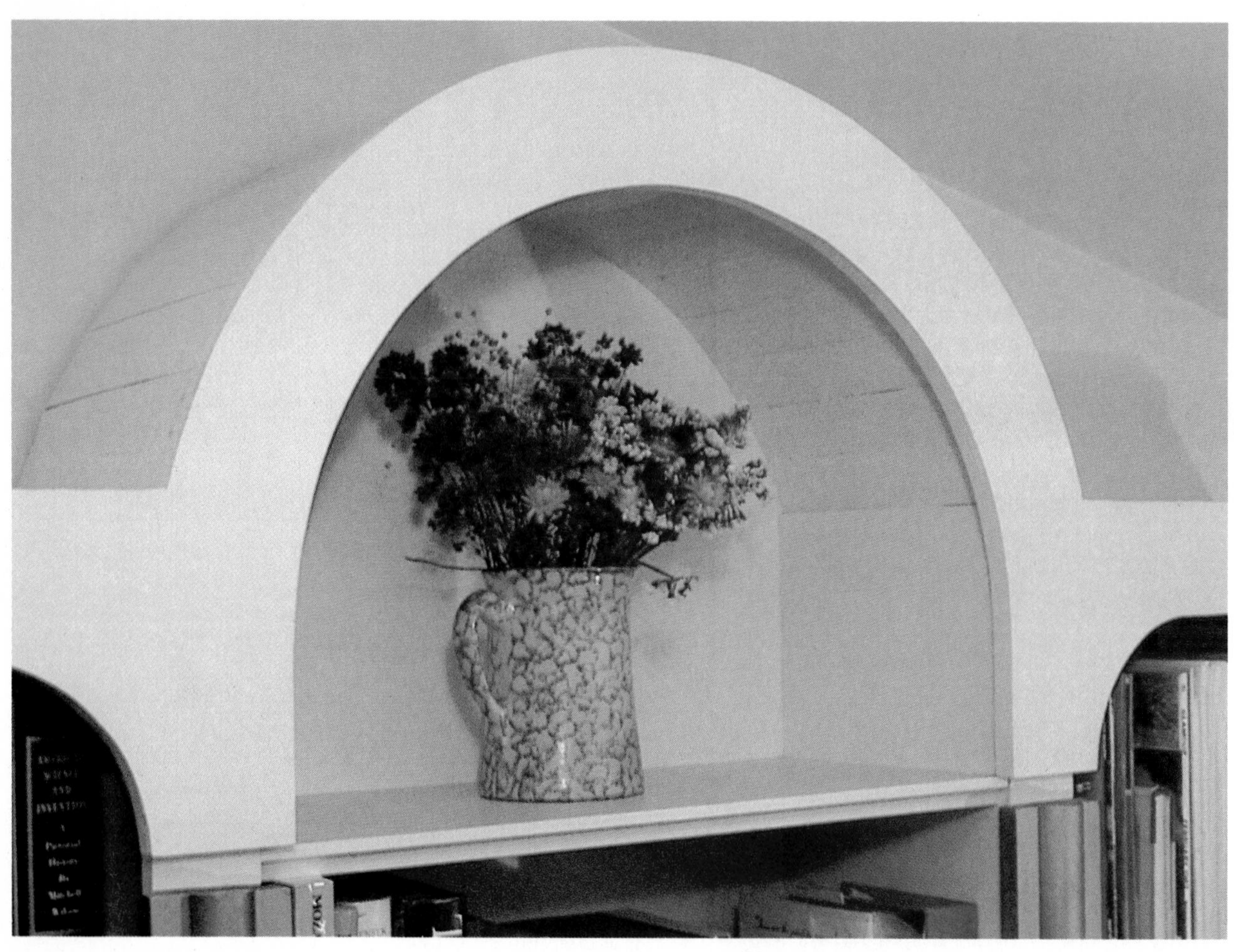

Carl elected to simplify construction wherever possible. Therefore, he formed the inner surface of the arch using narrow strips of ¼" plywood. While the result isn't as seamless as he would have liked, the effect is completely acceptable.

that compose the back, meet in a butt joint. That seam is covered on the left and right tiers of shelves by a shelf, and in the middle tier by books.

He marked the placement of the shelves along the sides and vertical dividers, then secured them in place with yellow glue and 6d finishing nails. In the middle tier, he placed the bottom shelf 5 inches higher than either of the side tiers to accommodate the design of the bottom molding he would later add.

To make the cabinet face frame, he cut and attached the vertical face pieces, which consist of 1 × 4 pine strips overlaid with 1 × 3 pine strips. He then added the bottom face, consisting of a layer of 1 × 4 pine covered with the scalloped plywood face piece. He used ¾-inch plywood for the bottom face piece because it had to be 8 inches high, and he thought pine might tend to cup. The top face piece, a ¾-inch plywood arch that spans the entire front, is also reinforced with 1 × 4s.

Carl built the arch separately. He cut the arch for the face from ¾-inch plywood using a saber saw for curves and a Skilsaw for the straight parts on the left and right. The ¼-inch plywood back he cut to the same radius in much the same manner. Running front to back between the face molding and the plywood back is a series of 2-inch-wide strips of ¼-inch plywood, one beside the next, that serves as the roof of the arch. He nailed each strip to arch-shaped pine blocking that is behind the arch molding and on the plywood back. There are two layers of these strips. The strips do not bend as readily as he had hoped and there are tiny visible joints between them. He may yet replace the strips with Formica, which he thinks will bend more efficiently to the radius of the arch.

Finally, he added the cove moldings along the shelf edges and the joints where the back and face pieces join the sides, and the half-round molding that covers the edges of the vertical dividers.

After countersinking all the nails, he puttied the holes, reprimed where necessary, and sanded lightly. He then painted the shelves ivory with oil-based, alkyd semigloss enamel. He masked the area around the columns and then spray-painted them a shiny gold. Though the gold paint on the pillars has faded a bit, it still serves to emphasize their wryly symbolic function as "pillars of knowledge."

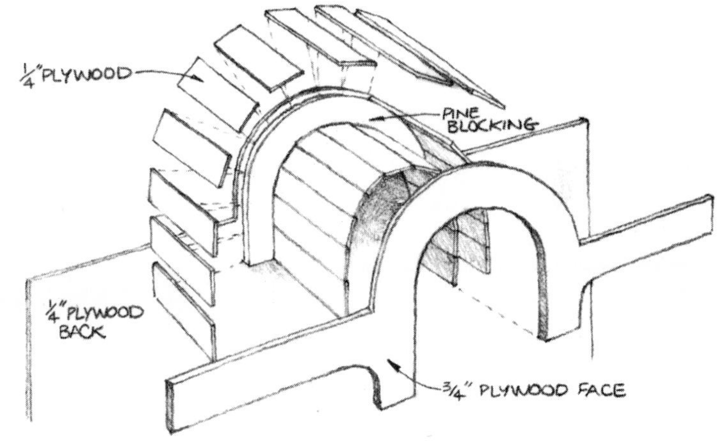

Exploded drawing of the arch section of Carl Wies's bookcase.

Carl Wies set out to make shelves that reinterpreted historical decorative motifs. But functional considerations were as important to him as aesthetic ones. With confidence in his own freewheeling design sense and in his skills, he got the results he wanted.

Marilyn Hodges

Jack Larimore

LIGHT SHELVES, PLAYFUL INTENTIONS

"If you're doing commissioned work," Jack Larimore says, "you have to be very connected to people." Jack has been doing commissioned work for a number of years, and since he has been doing it so well, he has more commissions than he genuinely *wants* to do right now. He must be connected to people.

Jack is a designer and builder of fine furniture and cabinets. Although he does occasional built-ins, and then only when he can control the design of the entire room housing the built-in, he prefers the discrete piece. And despite a backlog of commissions, he has of late been focusing his efforts on speculative pieces. He works out of a shop that he shares with another woodworker in the Fishtown section of Philadelphia.

His connectedness with people is manifested in a variety of ways.

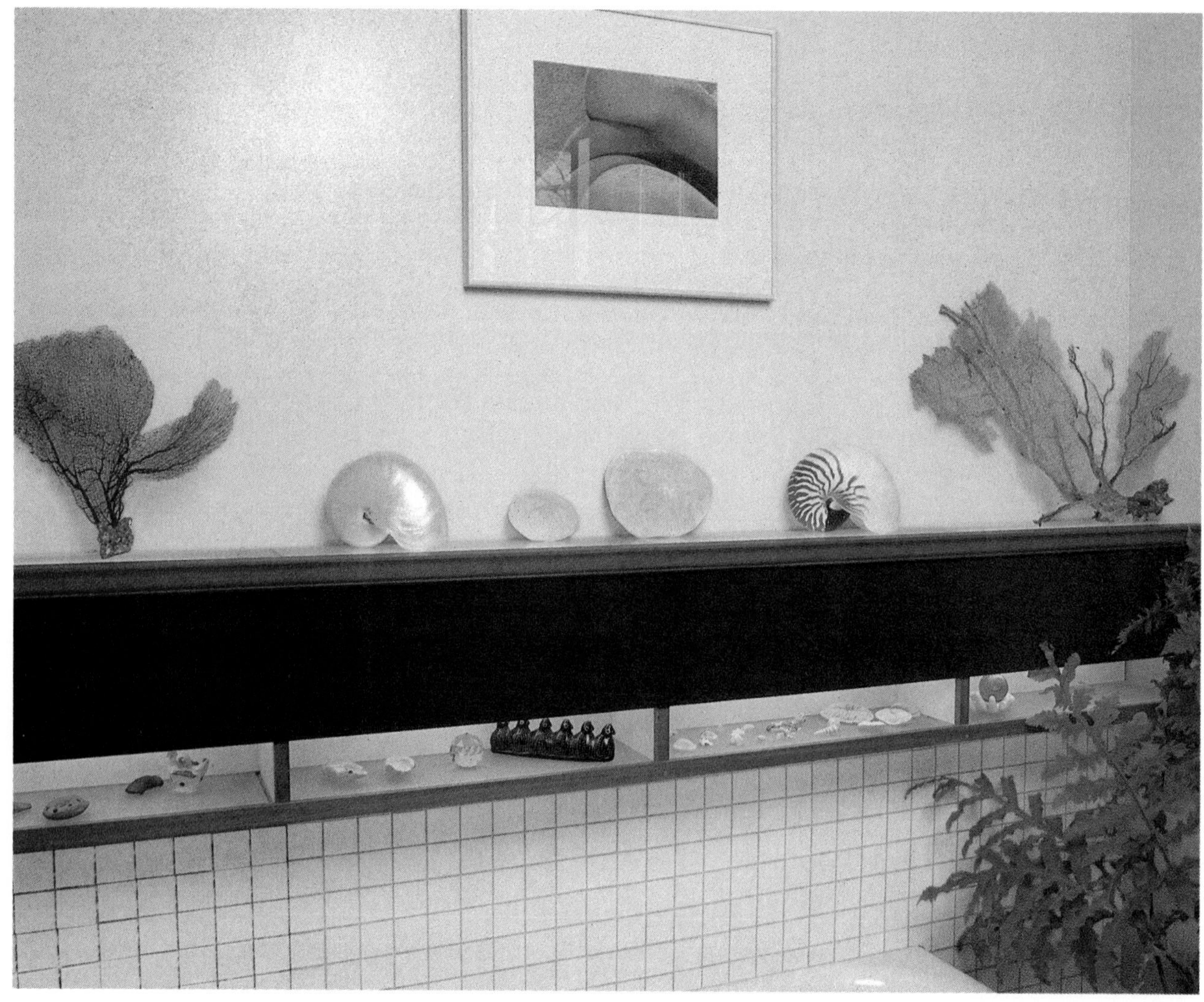

First, he's articulate and voluble, talking easily about art, craft, design, workmanship, woodworking, business and himself. Seldom are his thoughts couched in other than humanistic terms. When he talks shop, it is seldom talk of boards and tools and joints. "The fellow I share the shop with, Bob Ingram, we spend a lot of time talking about why we're doing what we're doing," he explains. "There's an architect I work with frequently, Cecil Baker. With him, it's the same thing. It has mostly to do with people."

When Jack is working on a commission, the people that he is working for become central to his efforts. As the creation of the two built-ins shown here demonstrate, it is not simply a design or a construction technique or a room that shapes a cabinet or shelf, it's the people who will own and use that piece that shape it.

He likes to pry as many design requirements as possible out of his clients right at the start. He acts as a catalyst to stimulate them to focus on what they want. "Once it's done, it's theirs, and they should have a feeling that they are a part of it," he explains. Once a basic rapport is established, he feels free to make suggestions and give advice.

Generally, Jack's designs are what is called post-Modern by people who concern themselves with labeling such things. Jack describes his work as being "clean and neat with a touch of antique." It is a blend, often playful, of the starkness of modernism with the grace and ornamentation of older forms. His intention is to create "an approachable aesthetic," and he is happy if his work evokes memory or mood, but lightly and in a playful way. His designs usually draw clients, like the Ostermans (for whom he created the light shelf), whose taste he describes as eclectic. And his designs are appreciated most when they evolve from a good connection between designer and client.

The Ostermans, Jack's former neighbors, asked him to design the master bathroom in their big old stone house in Villanova. The house began its life in the 1700s as the Green Tree Inn. For the last hundred years it has been a private residence subjected to frequent design shifts. Even its location has been changed to move it farther back from the road.

The Ostermans wanted a bathroom that would be exciting, uncluttered, and at the same time make reference to the rest of the house with its fine moldings, fireplaces, and elegant stairs. This apparently uncongenial combination of needs sat quite well with Jack. It's the kind of mix he likes: "Clean and neat with a touch of antique."

He and the Ostermans decided that the bathroom should be created from a small existing bathroom and a hall closet. The two spaces together would create a room about 12 feet square, give or take a few ins and outs.

Jack then designed the bathroom and built the vanity, medicine cabinet, and the light shelf. Because he believes a bathroom should fulfill needs beyond its obvious functions, he included the light shelf as an area for decorative display.

The fluorescent tubes mounted inside the case illuminate two frosted glass shelves and cast a soft light on the surrounding walls. The

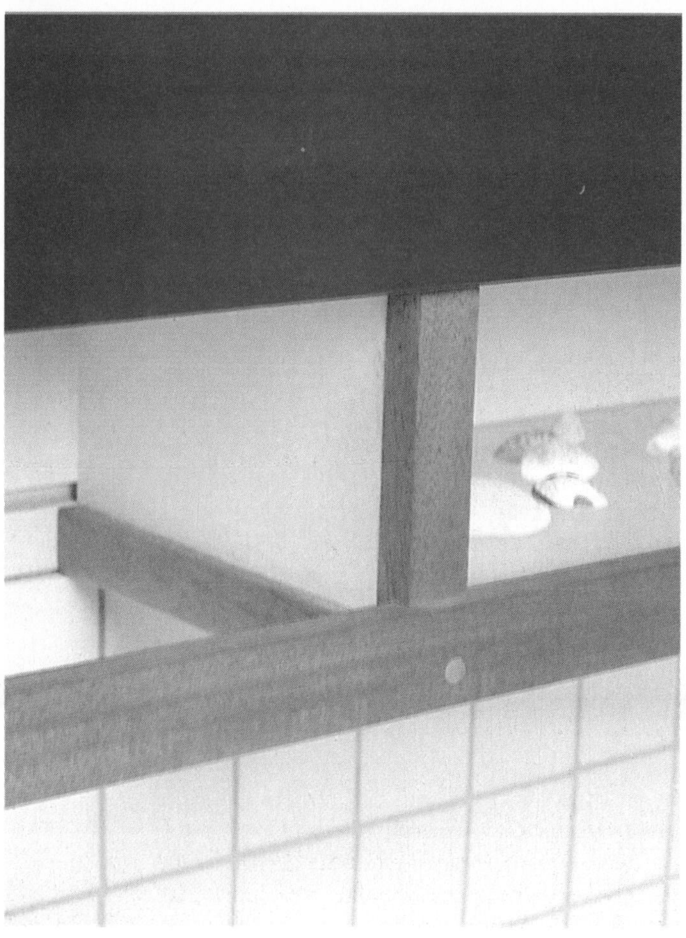

More than simply a shelf unit, Jack Larimore's bathroom display case is an orchestration of light, color and form—a harmonizing of the modern and the traditional. It brings together, for example, a stark, modern, electric blue panel with a time-honored ogee molding of mahogany. And the combination works.

effect, when the shelf unit is the bathroom's only light source, is warm and cozy, producing a feeling almost like that of natural daylight.

The shelf makes its allusions to the rest of the house, most obviously in its long expanse of ogee molding. Mounted at wainscoting height, the molding continues around the room, above the sink and vanity areas. Not only does it recall the moldings of an earlier time, but it is a nice chair rail conceit in a modern bathroom. Below it is tile, and above it are painted walls.

Jack built the whole unit in his shop, starting with a shop drawing and lists of the members he would need to cut, with their dimensions. The cutting list suggested the list of materials he would need to buy as well.

The case is birch veneer-core plywood, 7 feet long, 13 inches high, and 7 inches deep. All the trim is Honduran mahogany, in keeping with the handrail on the stairs, and the generally elegant feeling of the house. Cherry molding, he decided, would have been a bit too "country."

He prepared the mahogany by rough cutting it with a radial arm saw and a band saw. He used a jointer and thickness planer to dress it to finish size. The plywood he cut on a table saw.

He assembled the plywood members first, beginning with the ½-inch birch veneer-core back. He ran a groove all along the bottom of the back (to hold the frosted glass panels that would be installed just before the shelf unit was mounted). He then cut three vertical dadoes to receive the ¾-inch plywood divider panels.

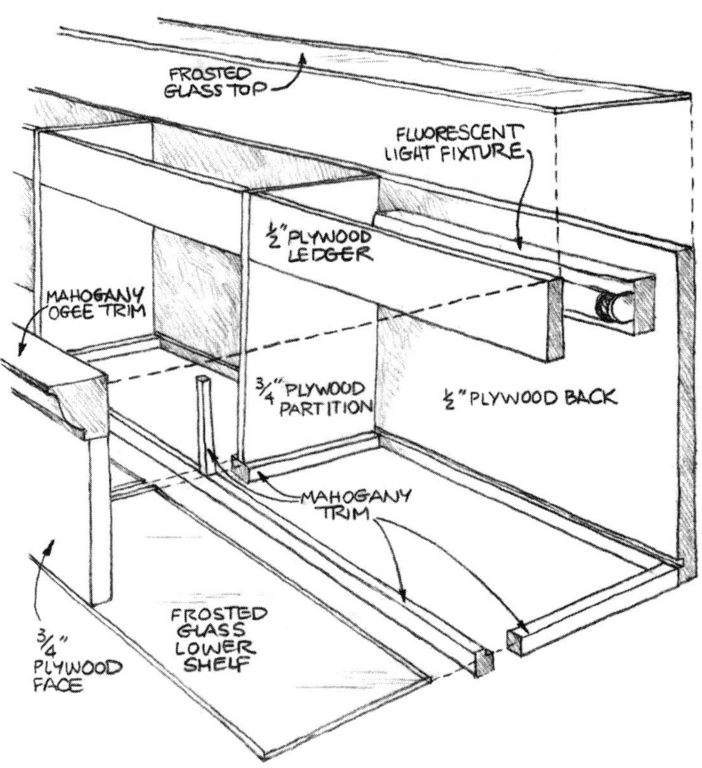

Exploded drawing of the Jack Larimore-built light shelf.

He also rabbeted the ends of the back to receive the sides.

In the ¾-inch plywood face panel, he cut dadoes that would be opposite those on the back panel when the shelf was assembled so the vertical dividers would connect the two together. He also rabbeted the face panel to receive the sides.

To assemble the case, he laid the back down, set the vertical dividers and sides in place, then put the face on top. He joined the parts together with an aliphatic resin glue, then clamped them. He glued ½-inch plywood ledger strips on the back of the face panel, fitting them horizontally between the vertical dividers, flush with their tops. They help support the top frosted glass panels.

Next, Jack molded his Honduran mahogany for the trim using an ogee bit in his shaper. He glued it to the top of the face panel, using the top edge of the face panel and the fronts of the ledger strips as his gluing surfaces. He cut a ¾- by 1-inch strip of solid mahogany to fit along the bottom of the shelf unit, then rabbeted it to receive the frosted glass panels. He screwed it into the bottom of each vertical divider with a brass screw, then plugged the screw holes with ¼-inch dowel. He also used solid mahogany strips to connect the front to the back, under the two case sides.

Finishing the unit required Jack to mask and remask it, since three different finishes were used. The front panel of the shelf unit has an ultrasmooth automobile finish. Jack sanded it as smooth as possible, then filled it with Nitro-Stan, a filler used on cars. He primed it, then sprayed on six thin coats of blue automotive lacquer, hand rubbing the finish between coats. He painted the inside of the shelf unit white. To bring out the color of the mahogany, he rubbed the strips with Minwax Antique Oil, then sprayed them with a clear acrylic lacquer for durability.

To mount the light shelf, he screwed it into the wall studs at eight places. Once it was in place, he mounted the four light fixtures and connected them to the wiring. Then he installed warm pink fluorescent tubes, each 30 watts.

Finally, he put the frosted glass shelves in place. The bottom shelf fits into the groove along the bottom of the back and the rabbet in the mahogany strip in front. The top glass shelf rests on the top edge of the back panel, the tops of the vertical partitions, and the ledger strips glued behind the face panel.

Jack and his clients never settled on what the shelves would display. He assumed they would set out glassware or pottery or their collection of brushes and combs. To his delight, the Ostermans arranged a collection of shells to perfect advantage on the bottom shelf. The connection was complete.

The light touch and the flowing lines that characterize the bathroom shelf unit are also part of the built-in shelves Jack made for the Starks, old friends of his who live near Trenton, New Jersey. They wanted a lounging corner in their bedroom, and they asked that it have a cozy, sensuous atmosphere. Jack responded with a design for a couch with a slanting, upholstered plywood base, and shelves above with a rounded center ornament that is frankly erotic. It isn't necessarily a design with universal appeal, but the Starks love it. The designer, again, had made the connection with the client.

The shelves are lumber-core plywood with a cherry veneer. The arched decorative molding on each shelf is solid cherry, and the balls are purple heart, a South American hardwood. Shelf supports are Rakks brushed aluminum standards and brackets.

Jack made the cherry molding in two pieces that appear to hold the ball in place where they meet at the middle of the shelf front. He cut the cherry strips for the molding with a band saw, then used a spokeshave to smooth off the edges.

To make the purple ball look so nicely tucked in at the front, he rabbeted the back of the cherry molding strips where they meet in the middle. Into this groove, he glued a ¾- by 1½-inch strip of purple heart, aligning it flush with the back of the molding and extending a little below it. To make the rounded ball that shows at the front of the molding, he glued a ½-inch strip to the face of the first piece of purple heart. This second piece protrudes between the cherry rounds at the front, and fits snugly, thanks to a little judicious hand carving. To make balls at the ends of each shelf, and on the ceiling, he followed a similar procedure.

Finally, he oiled the shelves with Minwax Antique Oil, and then added two thin coats of clear spray lacquer. The shelves have the look of a hand-rubbed oil finish. The low, flat arch of the shelf molding is vaguely classical, but it is the ornament that playfully suggests the room's mood.

This happy style of working wood does not in the least reflect Jack's training. His degree is in landscape architecture, but that's a career he jettisoned early on. When he renovated his own home, he discovered "that part of me that likes to design and *build*, to realize the design right away." With that revelation, it was good-bye to the world of growing things for Jack Larimore.

Several small contracting jobs followed, and then cabinetmaking opportunities. "Because I like more refined work," he remembers, "I was steered in that direction by friends and clients, so I got into cabinetry, then furniture." Now his connections are less with nature, more with people, and the medium is wood.

MARILYN HODGES

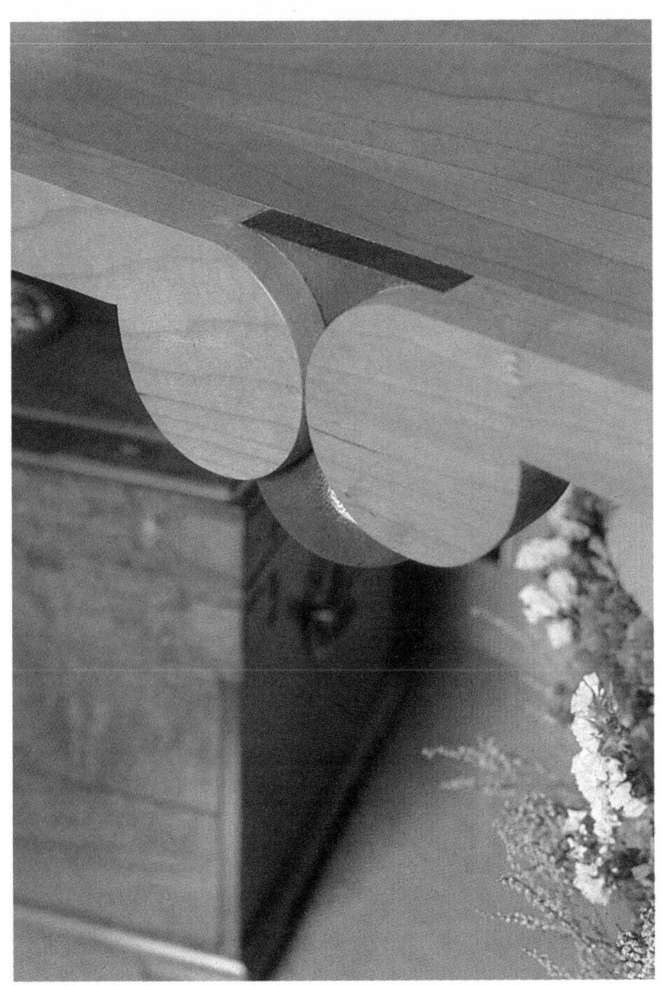

Jack Larimore acknowledged the playful and erotic purpose of this cozy corner of the bedroom in the ornamentation that embellishes not only the shelves but the ceiling and the headboard of the bed as well. The cleverness of the ornamentation, however, shouldn't overshadow the cleverness of the shelving design. Larimore used commonplace standards and brackets. But by breaking the pattern of association—plain boards are always used with standards and brackets—he made the construction seem to be more than it is. He broke the pattern by gluing decorative facing, incorporating the hand-sculpted purple balls, to the shelf-board edges.

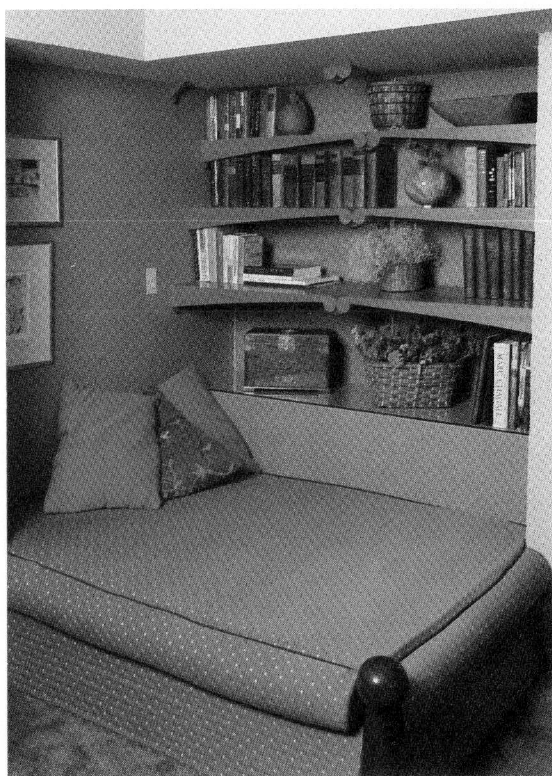

Rick Redden

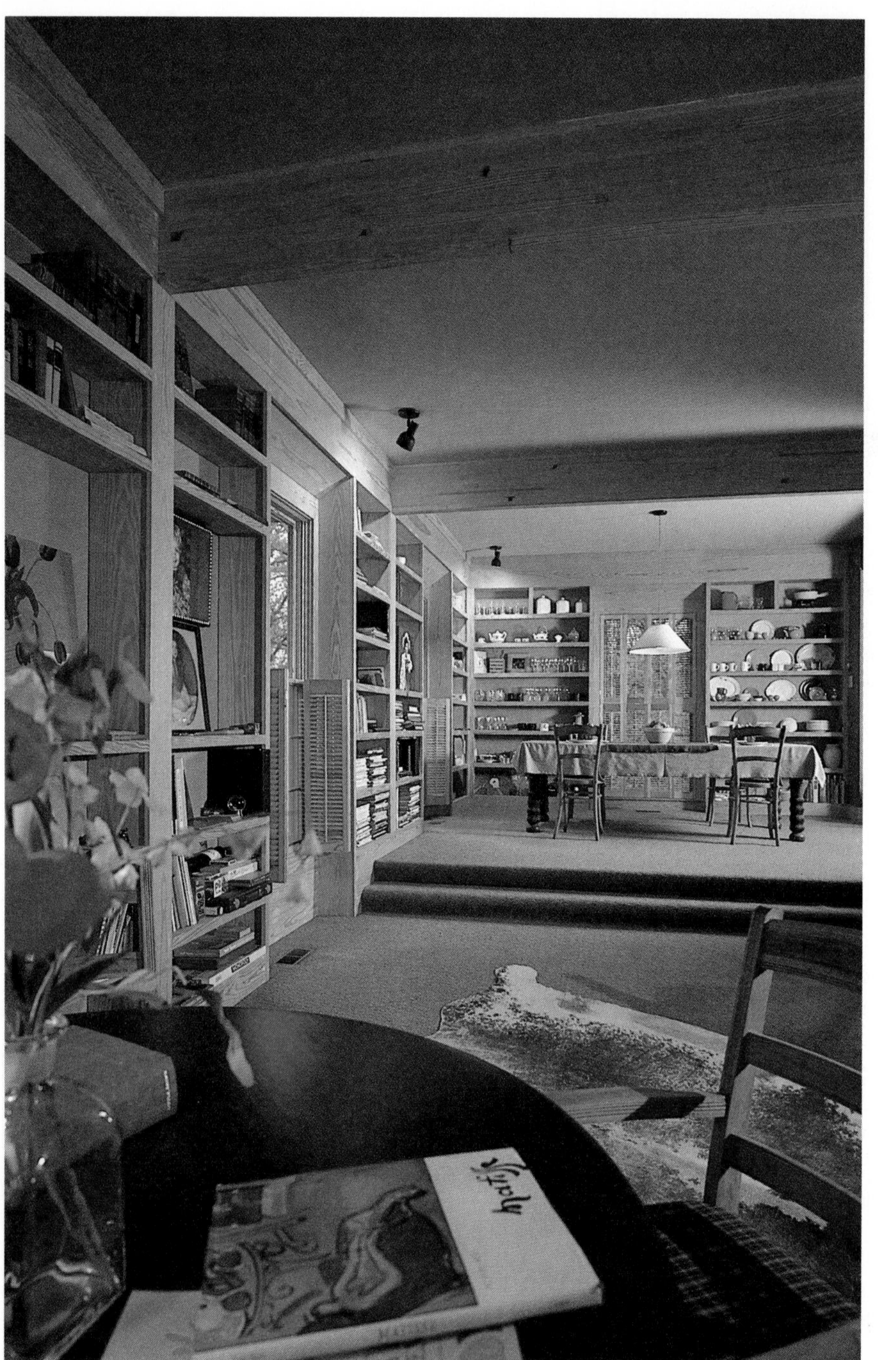

ROUND THE ROOM SHELVES

Architect Rick Redden and his wife Laura like the look of natural wood. They built themselves a redwood house in Little Rock, Arkansas, then made lavish use of local yellow pine to create a shelving system that dominates the first floor. Friends who came to admire their work looked at the humble pine and asked the Reddens when they were going to get out the paint cans and brushes.

But paint was never part of the plan. The golden expanses of shelves help to control light in the living and dining rooms, serving as a buffer between the bright light that pours in from all sides and the darker, light-absorbing walls. The window soffits, set at a 45-degree angle, offer an echo of splayed castle apertures that diffuse and soften incoming light. The pine shutters make infinite variations in intensity possible. The effect is just what the Reddens wanted—light enters the rooms gently, without glare.

In designing the shelf units, Rick was concerned that shelves and shutters work well together. He incorporated enough space on the sides of the shelves for the shutters to be neatly folded away. In addition, the shelves make the walls of this new house seem more massive, like the old, thick, European masonry walls that Rick admires.

Of course, the shelves provide useful storage. Like most people, Rick and Laura used to feel that they never had enough storage. Once the shelves were built, however, they were afraid they had created more empty spaces than they could ever fill. In time, though, their possessions expanded to nicely fill the shelves.

Rick and Laura simplified their building task by using all standard-size lumber, building the shelves in separate units, and nailing them together without any fancy joinery. All the shelves are nailed in place and require no additional supports. Where units meet, the seams are simply covered with trim.

The Reddens shopped for wood at a local lumberyard, and bought only boards that were clear, smooth and free of knots. Not only was the yellow pine they bought inexpensive, it was also fairly strong (more so than white pine), reasonably easy to work with, and sure to yellow as it ages.

They bought 1 × 10s for the shelves and the sides, and 1 × 12s for the valances at the top. To stiffen the shelves and make them look thicker, they bought 1 × 2s to trim the edges. They also bought 1 × 2s to trim the uprights, and 1 × 4s to trim the valances and cover the seam wherever the sides of the two units meet.

Rick sawed all the boards on a table saw and a radial arm saw. Starting with the units for the dining room, he built two units at a time, cutting the uprights first. He made the uprights 3 inches short of the ceiling so he would have sufficient room to tilt them up against the wall. He assembled each shelving unit on the floor.

First, he created an assembly jig by nailing two 2 × 4s to the floor. With uprights flat against the 2 × 4s, he fitted the shelves between them. He nailed through the uprights straight into the endgrain of each shelf using three 8d finishing nails in each side. The 2 × 4s provided a surface Rick could brace the unit against while driving the nails. Because he was not making the shelves adjustable, he varied their heights to anticipate different uses. The bottom shelves are all 14 inches high to accommodate art books. Most of the other shelves are 12 inches high, but in some spots he skipped a shelf altogether to make room for artwork.

To anchor each unit to the wall, he nailed a 1 × 4 nailer under the back of the top shelf and a 1 × 3 nailer under the back of the bottom shelf. He made the baseboard for each unit from a 1 × 6 the same length as the shelves above it and nailed it in from the sides. Each unit's base fits flush with the shelf surface, and between the vertical molding strips at the sides.

Once Rick had built all the shelving units, Mike Meyers, a finish carpenter, beveled the molding strips and nailed them on with a power hammer and 8d finishing nails.

Rather than have the shelves reach right up to the ceiling where they would be all but inaccessible, Rick topped off the units with a

In a single setting, you see a whole range of possible uses for shelves. Books, periodicals, art works, dishes, glasses and cookware are set on display and handy for ready use. Though the rooms are walled-in with shelves, there's no claustrophobia here. And the whole complex was simply though skillfully constructed of common board lumber using hand tools and hand-held power tools.

wide valance. Its substantial proportions also create a harmony with the laminated pine structural beams that crisscross the ceiling. He nailed the 1 × 12 valance around the top of the shelves, making it flush with the bottom of the 13¼-inch-wide structural beams. He then overlapped it with 1 × 4s to cover the gap between the top of the 1 × 12s and the ceiling.

The angled window soffits close the gap between the pine trim at the top of each Pella window and the 1 × 12 valance. To make each, he beveled the top and bottom edges of a pine board, tacked on a temporary wooden handle, and used it to maneuver the wood into place.

When all the shelves and molding were in place, he countersunk the nails and covered them and the nail holes left by the handle with filler in a matching shade. He then applied

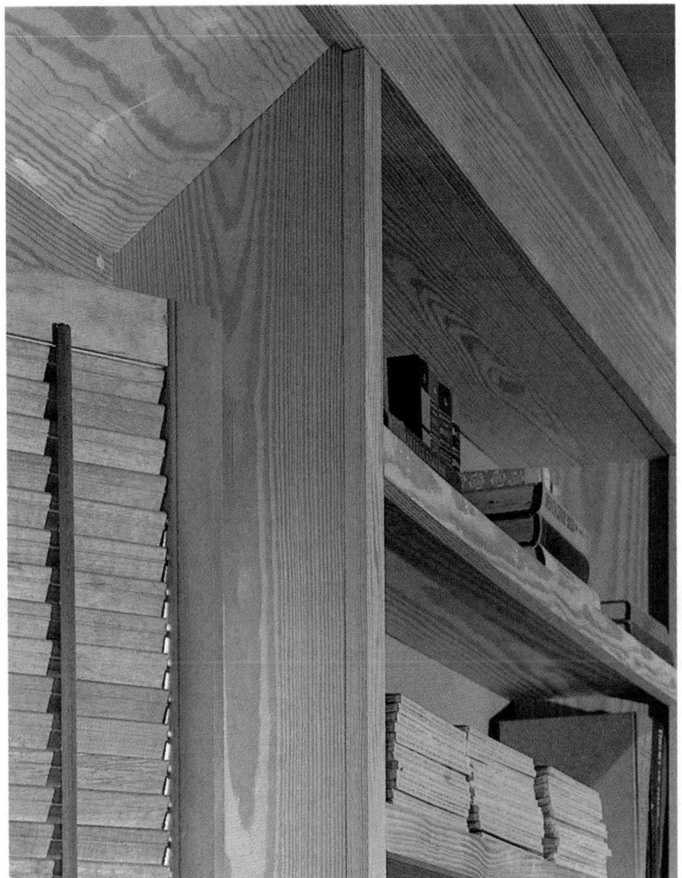

The basics of the Redden shelving units are evident. The shelves are simple boxes built of 1 × 10s. Though unembellished, the units gain a sense of substance from 1 × 2 strips added to shelf and upright edges as a face frame. The valance and 1 × 4 acting as a cornice molding visually tie the units together and to the ceiling, while sloped soffits tie them to the windows.

two coats of Watco Danish Oil, sanding between coats.

With the shelves in place against the soft gray green walls of the downstairs, Rick and Laura went on to create paintings that blend similarly well with their surroundings. Rugs and objects in the house show up in these paintings, creating amusing echoes of life in art. For a simple house, there is rich texture here.

The exterior of the house was sufficiently innovative to win an American Institute of Architects design award in Arkansas. Like the other houses in their old city neighborhood, it has a sloping roof and horizontal lap siding. But their house is redwood, and it has no entrance from the street. The entrance is at the rear of the sloping site and is accessible only through a separate gatehouse, which is capped with its own pitched roof. This rustic entrance separates the parking area from the house.

The years Rick Redden worked in Switzerland and England are reflected in the design of the exterior, in the open-plan rooms, and the careful planning of every inch of space to take best advantage of small quarters. Where wood is more scarce and more highly prized as a design element, Rick learned to make the most of the abundance he and Laura found at home in Arkansas.

Marilyn Hodges

Larry Williams

SHELVES FOR A VICTORIAN HOUSE

In Eureka Springs, Arkansas, the livin' is easy. The town's assets are its pleasant Ozark climate, 65 bubbling springs, and some of the best-looking Victorian houses in America. Two thousand people live here, many of them craftsmen, but even more of them busily restoring their own houses to their original summer resort elegance.

Larry Williams makes his living doing custom work in the old houses around him. He repairs exterior architectural details, fixes balustrades, makes doors and sashes, and (with the greatest enthusiasm) makes furniture.

In this town of Victorian gems, he thinks that Gloria and Jack Muzio have one of the best-proportioned houses of all. Their house was originally the summer home of a St. Louis industrialist. The Muzios themselves migrated east from northern California

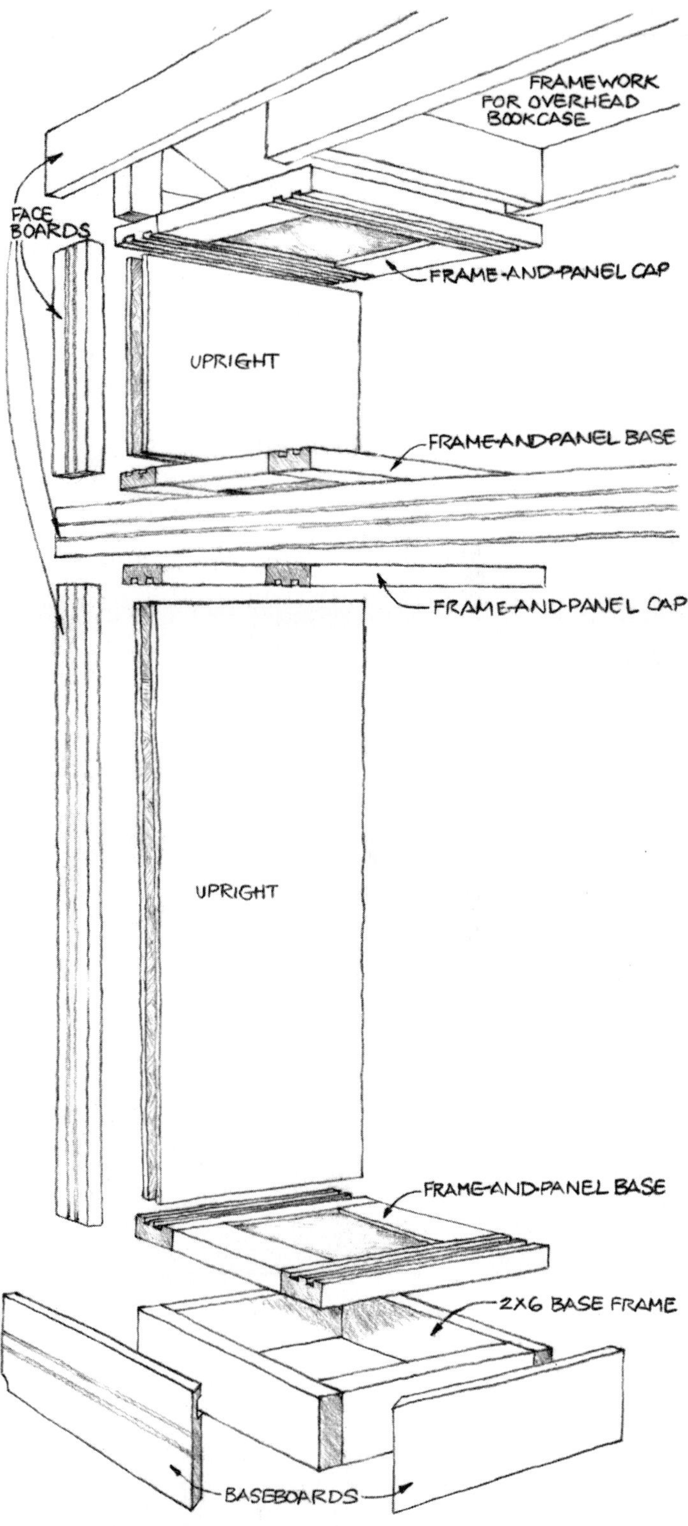

Exploded drawing of the major elements making up a single vertical bookcase unit. Clearly, there is more to it than meets the eye.

in search of the kind of unspoiled Victoriana they had both grown up with.

They asked Larry Williams to build them some bookshelves that would enhance the 10- by 15-foot wall behind the couch in their den but leave room for the Victorian advertisement for Lion Beer that hangs above the couch.

Larry took his lead from the Italianate molding on the outside of the house and used it to adorn the top of the shelves. He also let himself be influenced by the many choice pieces the Muzios already owned.

The design, worked out with the Muzios' interior decorator, Shirley Cantrell, fell into place easily. Working out the construction details was more difficult. Larry recalls that he stayed awake nights trying to solve the problem of creating shelves that would be strong enough to hold heavy books and resist crashing onto the heads of those sitting on the couch below. And rather than mar the original Victorian plaster and trim, Larry had to make the entire unit freestanding.

He finally settled on a very elaborate construction. Reduced to simpler terms, the unit was created by constructing two vertical bookcases, one for either side of the couch. A long frame is set atop these bookcases, spanning the space between them. The long overhead bookcase is suspended from this frame. Complicating this relatively simple design solution were Larry's decisions to assemble each major structural component from several pieces of wood and, for reasons of economy, to use two kinds of wood: oak and pine. The plan was to make and finish the components of the bookshelf unit in the shop, then truck them to

The bookcase is not as simple as it looks. Two different woods were combined in an elaborate construction. The upright element that appears to be a single board, for example, is actually four separate boards: two broad uprights and narrow front and back pieces. Other elements of the unit are similarly complicated. Much of the unit is pine, while all the beaded facing pieces and the scroll-cut corner braces are oak. It is Victoriana in more ways than one.

Exploded drawing of the center upright in the overhead bookcase unit. The shelves are actually suspended from the overhead framework by the threaded rods.

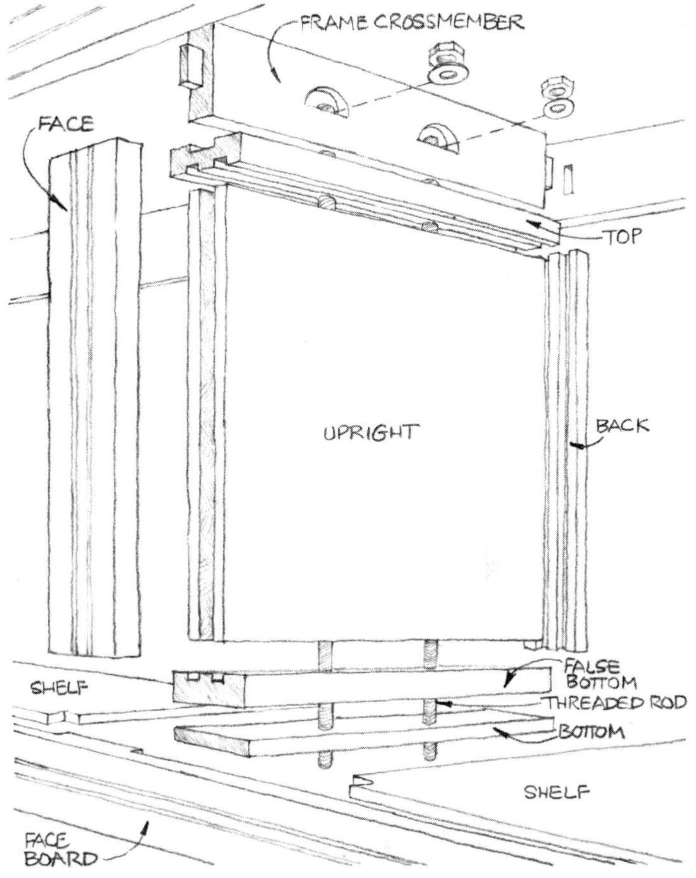

the Muzios' house, assemble them and complete the extensive trimwork.

Larry prepared detailed construction drawings, then went off in search of wood. He used oak for the visible parts of the bookcase, and pine for the parts that do not show.

He counts himself lucky to have bought usable old pine that had been stored in a barn for many years. He prefers air-dried pine to kiln-dried pine, because he inevitably finds the latter too damp, gummy to work with, full of pitch, and hard on his tools.

He was not as lucky with the white oak he bought. The boards turned out to be what Larry calls "case hardened"; that is, the exterior surface was relatively dry, but the core was still damp. As he resawed the white oak boards to make the molding, they cupped and twisted.

His solution, which delayed the project a month, was to cut the oak to rough dimensions, then stack it with thin strips of wood between the boards (called stickers) for additional seasoning. After a month, the boards had stabilized enough to remain warp-free after he cut them on his planer.

Following his construction drawings, Larry continued his work. His design for each upright consists of four boards: an oak face and a pine back, each 2½ inches wide, and two 12-inch-wide sides, either oak or pine depending on whether or not the wood shows. The sides are glued into grooves which extend the length of each front and back piece.

Larry decided to use frame-and-panel units both to form the bases that the uprights stand on and to rest on top of the uprights like a cap, tying them together.

Each frame-and-panel unit he designed has pine rails and stiles and a plywood panel. Each stile has double grooves cut in it to accommodate an upright.

Each vertical bookcase consists of a short case composed of a top, bottom and two uprights resting atop a tall case also composed of a top, bottom and two uprights. The overhead unit consists of a single central upright and two single-board bottom shelves.

In Larry's design, there are two critical elements to the overhead bookcase: the framework from which the unit is suspended and the central upright. The central upright is made just like all the other uprights, except that it has a top and bottom in addition to the front and back. The overhead frame Larry made from pine 2 × 6s, nailing them together in a straightforward boxlike assembly of rails and

Ornamentation relates the assembly to the rest of the house. The vertical bead cut into the upright fronts, is a detail found elsewhere in the house.

crossmembers. A key central crossmember is installed with mortise-and-tenon joints.

The top of the upright is butted against the bottom of the central crossmember. Tying them together are two ⅜-inch threaded rods, which extend from the crossmember though the hollow core of the upright and out its bottom.

Because Larry intended to bring the shelving system to the site all ready to install, he stained and finished the parts in his shop. His finishing procedures were complicated because the oak and the pine are different in porosity, grain and figure. The trick was to make the pine look like oak.

First, he scraped the pine with a cabinet scraper, then sealed it. Then he prepared the oak, using the cabinet scraper on the flat surfaces and sandpaper on the detail work.

He applied the stain to the pine and oak with a cloth, wiping it off before it got tacky. When staining the oak, he added a couple of tablespoons of paste filler to his stain mixture in order to fill the pores of the oak and accentuate its grain. When staining the pine, he mixed the stain with varnish to create a surface finish, since the sealer prevented the stain from coloring the wood.

Larry usually mixes his own stains, preferring to do so right in the room where the furniture will be, in order to see the effect of the room's natural lighting on the color. He uses universal tinting colors in a solution of 2 parts turpentine to 1 part linseed oil. The resulting stain has a thin, varnishlike consistency.

To obtain the color he wanted for the Muzios' bookshelves, Larry experimented with raw umber and burnt sienna, applying various mixtures to the oak and pine scraps.

After applying the stain, Larry applied a flat, clear varnish to both oak and pine, rubbing with steel wool after each of the two coats. He thinks varnish is best for dealing with daily wear and tear. Fuller-O'Brien is the brand he prefers because it contains turpentine rather than mineral spirits.

When Larry arrived at the Muzios' den, he had all the parts of the shelving system finished and ready to lock into place.

First, he set a 2 × 6 pine frame in each corner. Then he placed one of his frame-and-

The cornice, made of three separate moldings, integrates the bookshelves with the entire room.

panel units horizontally across the top of each frame to provide a base to stand the uprights on. He set up two double-wall uprights. On the top of these, he added another frame-and-panel unit to act as a cap.

On top of that frame-and-panel unit, he added another, this one with its grooves facing up to receive the two short uprights he then put in place above it. Another frame-and-panel unit caps these two uprights.

With the tall left and right cases built up almost to ceiling height, Larry was able to fit the overhead case. He installed the frame, then bolted the center upright in place. Oak shelves fit into rabbets in the bottom frames.

Larry assembled the bookshelves about 4 inches out from the wall, then maneuvered them into place. He added an oak facing and baseboards. The tops of the baseboards are flush with the tops of the bottom oak shelves. A ¼-inch bead runs down the face of the uprights and along the shelves and baseboard. It matches the ceiling and baseboard molding in the room, whose decoration is also cut into the wood. Larry cut all the beads using a molding head on his table saw.

Larry then added the adjustable pine shelves with oak facing. The shelves are supported by ½-inch birch dowels that fit into holes in the sides of the uprights.

Ornamental corner brackets came next. Each consists of two pieces of 1-inch oak that Larry face-glued together, then routed with a ⅜-inch double-fluted straight bit. He screwed the brackets in from the sides, drilling pilot holes first.

He made the ceiling molding, his next task, in three parts. The first strip of ceiling molding is ¾- by 1½-inch oak board with a 45-degree bevel along one edge. It is nailed to the 1 × 6 inch oak soffit. Butted against its underside is the second part of the molding, a ⅜- by 4½-inch oak strip. Overlapping this and also butted up under the ceiling molding is a ¾- by 3½-inch oak board into which is cut a decorative motif of arrows and broken circles.

Larry's wife Glenna took on the task of applying carnauba wax, which involved a lot of vigorous rubbing. The job of periodic waxing fell to the Muzios.

Larry is a self-taught craftsman, who first discovered the pleasures of working with wood when he restored an 1890s house in Denver a few years back. He and his wife run an art gallery in Eureka Springs, and he juggles that pursuit with his custom work. Immersed in Victoriana as he is, he hasn't had time to get around to another project he has a strong interest in—restoring his own Eureka house.

MARILYN HODGES

Paul Pugliese

HIGH-DESIGN STORAGE

Paul Pugliese is an architect for a firm in Stamford, Connecticut. On the side, he takes on challenging commissions as partner of Design Directions—unusual projects that demand both a high order of design and an innovative use of materials.

In designing a living room addition for a house in Greenwich, Connecticut, Paul gave particular attention to the built-in wall unit shown here. "Because the shelves covered a large area and had to incorporate so many different storage requirements," he says, "they had to be composed." In other words, his challenge was to reconcile the three-dimensional problem of storage (for such specific items as records, stereo equipment, books, display items, and even a dictionary on its own Selby roll-out TV extension shelf) with the two-dimensional problem of having the wall look pleasing. Paul took inspiration from the satisfying intervals

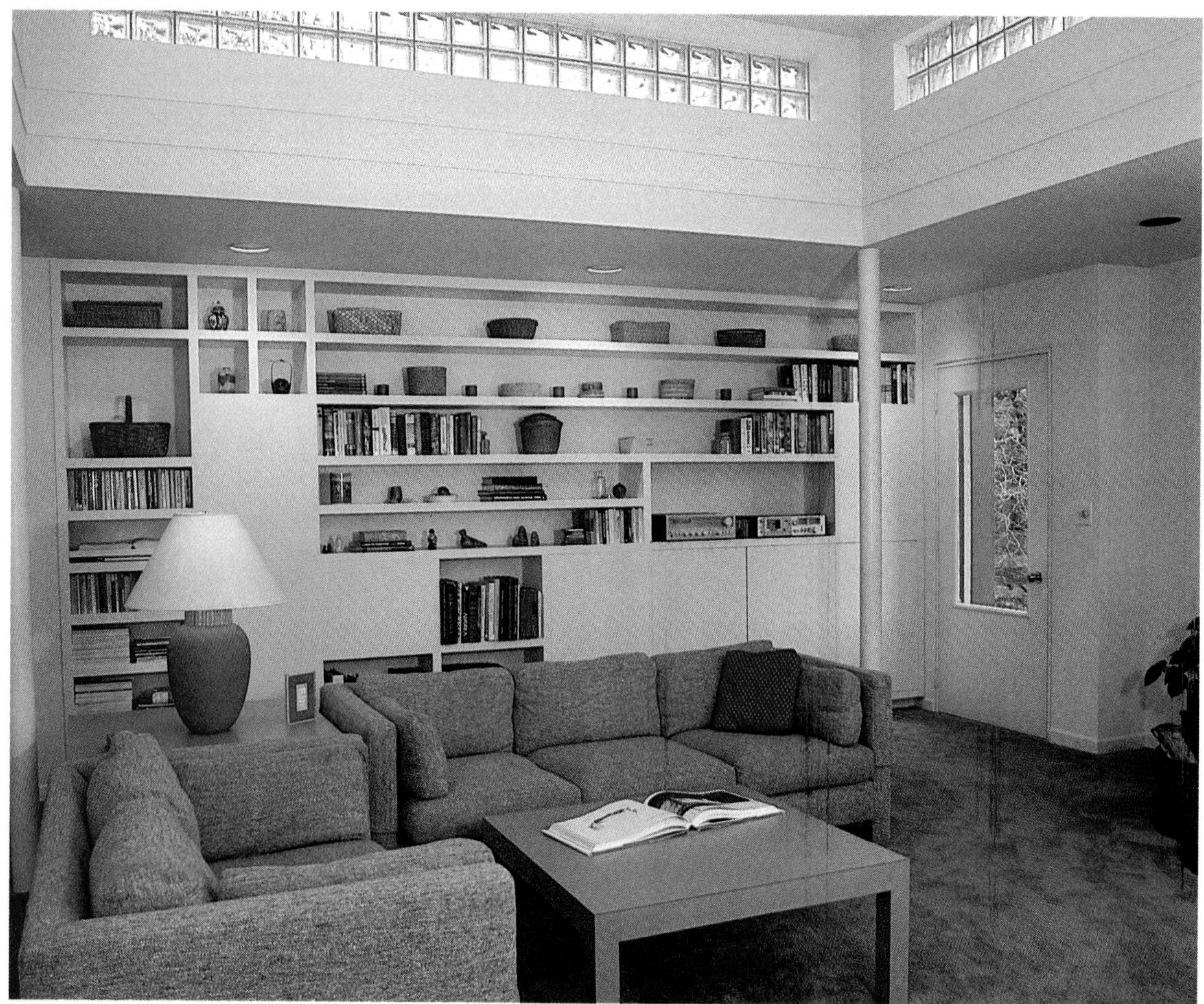

of bars and spaces in Piet Mondrian's paintings. He modified those intervals to accommodate his client's collections.

The resulting wall unit is a carefully thought-out composition of strong lines and rectangular shapes. Each of the lines is boldly stated with 1¾-inch-thick sandwiches of plywood. The flush-fitting cabinet doors and the solid face panels used to enclose dead spaces (on the far right side of the unit and below the grid of four display boxes on the left) contribute to the sense of mass.

Paul had the 16-foot-long, 8-foot-high unit built at the Westchester County, New York, mill owned by East Coast Wholesalers. The company, owned by his grandfather, had done work for him in the past. He was confident that the woodworkers there could handle this unwieldy piece of furniture.

They built the unit in two halves and then trucked them to the site. The halves weighed close to 700 pounds each, and yet when they were fitted against the clients' living room wall, the cut line was invisible. "Building this particular unit to this level of quality required a fairly good craftsman and definitely a good shop," Paul says. "This isn't the sort of project somebody's going to put together on a Saturday with a Skilsaw."

In spite of the scale of the wall unit, it was " . . . pretty much like building a standard bookcase. But instead of using ¾-inch-thick material, which is kind of flimsy, you're building a bigger piece of wood. If 1¾-inch-thick wood were available, and if it were dimensionally stable and free of checking and not extravagantly priced, then you wouldn't have to go through the trouble of making the sandwiches."

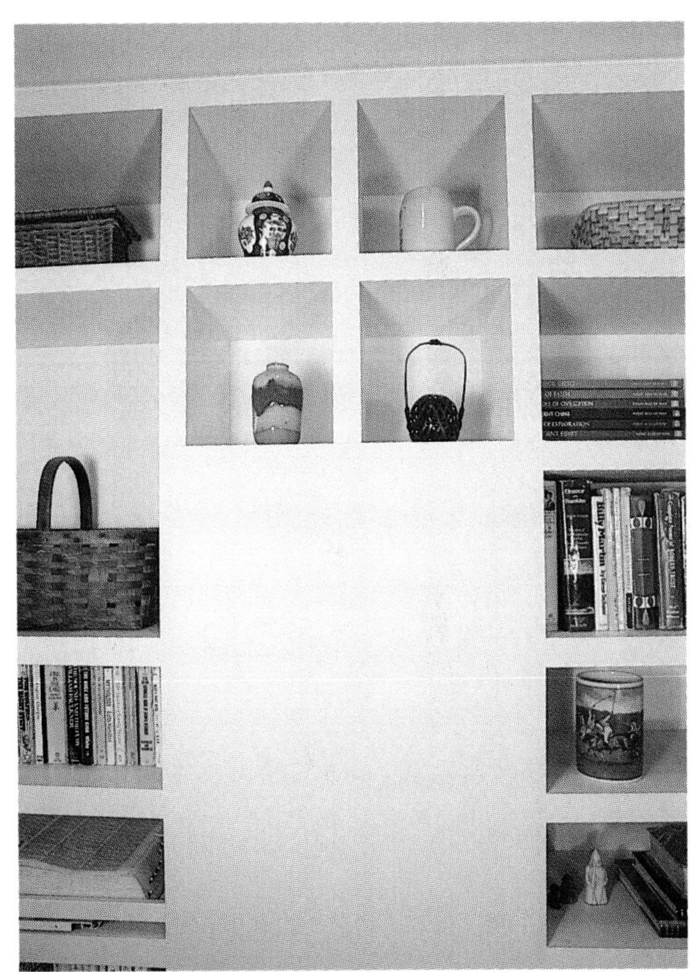

Inspired by the art of Piet Mondrian, architect Paul Pugliese "composed" this massive shelf and cabinet unit for a living room wall. The arrangement of boxes and negative spaces was designed to simultaneously accommodate a divergent collection of commonplace items and artifacts and to be interesting in and of itself.

Some of the negative areas in the unit are nothing more than blank white spaces. But behind other sections is concealed storage for records, games and other items that wouldn't display well. The plywood slab doors have no pulls to disrupt their surfaces, but they spring open at a touch. Because the doors are so well fitted, the distinction between dead areas and storage areas is evident only to the most discerning eye.

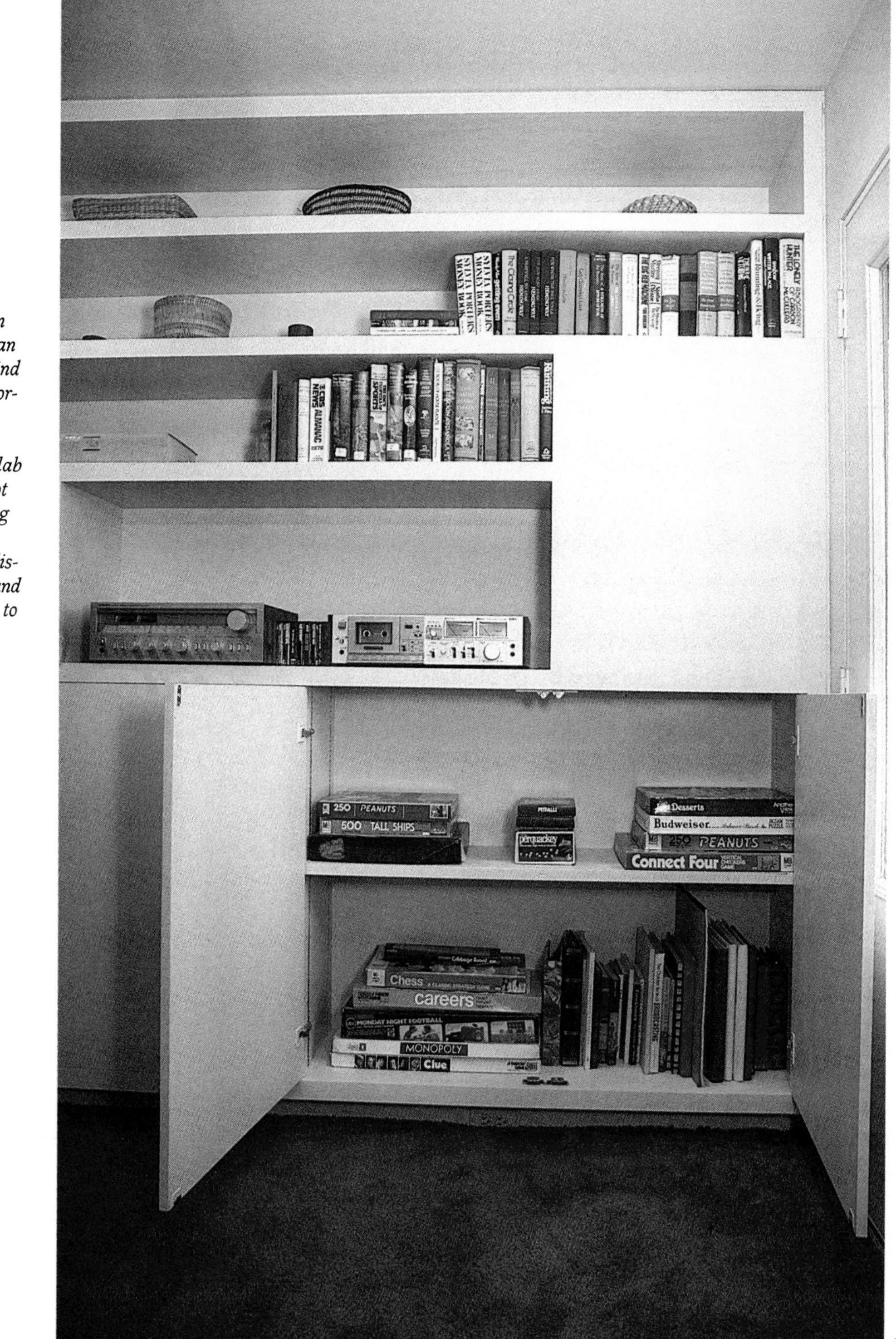

Much of the unit was formed of these 1¾-inch-thick plywood sandwiches—sides and bottom and top, shelves and vertical partitions—all dadoed into each other and into the ¾-inch plywood back. The sandwiches were made by cutting two sheets of ½-inch birch plywood to the size of the shelf and mitering the front edges 45 degrees to receive a mitered facing strip.

If you would like to make a scaled down version of the Mondrian-inspired shelves, incorporating the plywood sandwiches, use a very sharp blade to cut a clean miter. Lay down the first piece of plywood, beveled edge facing up, and arrange on it the battens that constitute the sandwich's filling: Paul suggests 1½-inch-wide strips of ¾-inch plywood, pine, or any dry and dimensionally stable scrap you have on hand. Run them front to back, spaced every 2 feet or so, with the end pieces flush with the left and right ends of the plywood. Glue the battens to the plywood and hold them in place with finishing nails. Next, spread glue on the top of the battens and lay down the upper piece of plywood, its beveled edge down. From ½-inch plywood, cut a 1¾-inch-wide facing strip with mitered edges. Glue and nail it in place to join the two layers of the sandwich. Use wood putty to fill in any gaps in the work.

The woodworkers at the East Coast Wholesalers mill shop assembled both halves of the wall unit of these sandwiches. They routed out the outer sandwiches (equivalent to case top, bottom and sides) to take the shelves and vertical partitions. Because the plywood used to make the sandwiches and back is only ½ inch thick, they cut dadoes just ¼ inch deep. Where shelves and vertical partitions appear to pass through each other, they hid the joinery by using stopped dadoes. To add stability to the structure, the woodworkers glued and toenailed together all the sandwiches and then attached the plywood back.

To further reinforce the longest shelves, Paul specified the use of concealed, inch-wide metal angles of 3/16-inch-gauge steel, spaced every 3 feet. The 8-inch vertical arm runs down a dado in the rear surface of the back; the horizontal arm goes 8 inches into the core of the shelf sandwich. The angles are screwed in place through holes predrilled in the arms.

The flush-fitting cabinet doors are featureless and therefore contribute to the sense of mass. They are cut from ¾-inch plywood, hung on Selby Sof-Snap concealed hinges mounted on vertical sandwiches. No visible hardware is necessary because the doors employ touch-latch catches.

After trucking the two halves of the unit to the site, the woodworkers prepared to assemble them. They laid down a base of two 2 × 4s, running parallel to the wall. They set the outer one in 3 inches from what would be the front of the wall unit. They nailed a ½-inch plywood kickplate to it. Then they lifted the two halves of the unit onto this base, and pushed them snugly against the wall. They installed the unit with a reveal along the top and sides. This gap, cut ⅜ inch wide and ½ inch deep, was then filled by a recessed strip of wood that plays up the transition from shelves to the surrounding walls. "You never can put a built-in unit right up against the wall without having at least a hairline crack," Paul explains, "so you make this joint into a feature."

A high degree of fit and finish was vital to making the shelves come off as sculpture. Paul points out: "Everything had to be very tight and filled. I didn't want to have cracks, or little lines where the doors fit in." The woodworkers filled the seams with wood putty, let it dry, and sanded the entire unit with very fine sandpaper. Then a painter applied two primer coats and a coat of off-white enamel. Paul believes that a superior paint job was important in making the design a success, and he is pleased with the job done by the painter—an enamel finish all but free of brush strokes.

Paul likes to consider light sources in working out a design. This wall unit is illuminated by Lightolier wall washer spots recessed in the ceiling. Rather than simply projecting a cone of light, these spots use a parabolic reflector that spreads the light across the wall.

On another job, Paul used a novel means of backlighting shelves that were to display pre-Columbian artifacts. The 8-inch-deep oak shelves have softly glowing backs of ⅛-inch Plexiglas, illuminated by a General Electric Bright Stick fluorescent light inside a soffit at the top of the unit. The Plexiglas goes up through a slot at the rear of the soffit, so that the light source is not evident.

Since Plexiglas will pick up light wherever it is scratched, Paul scribed the surface with a precise 1-inch grid, using a plastic cutter. This high-tech pattern contrasts nicely with the ancient artifacts.

Another of Paul's freelance projects was unusual enough to be featured in two magazines. The project began with a problem. A 14-year-old boy desperately wanted privacy from his sisters, who found it convenient to get to their own bedrooms through his. Paul, working with his Design Directions partner, Chris Stocker, responded with what could be called the ultimate closet—a 7½-foot cube, containing a built-in bed, night table, shelves and a dressing mirror. This room within a room could be split into two along the diagonal, and the triangular halves rolled about on recessed 3-inch casters. So, if the boy was feeling friendly towards his sisters, he could part the halves and incorporate the space of the larger room in any way he wanted to.

At first he didn't want to. The cube intimidated him. To help the boy understand how the cube could be manipulated, Paul drew him a floor plan of the bedroom showing the floor tiles as a grid and cut out two triangles corresponding to the cube halves. The boy could move the halves on the plan like chess pieces, until he found an arrangement he liked. Then, guided by the floor squares, he could repeat his moves with the cube.

The possibilities were many. Two of the bedroom walls have bay windows, and a cube half could be rolled up to a bay to make a tiny room with a view. Or, the mirror wall of the whole cube could be rolled up to a window for the same purpose because the mirror is actually a 4- by 4-foot sheet of one-way

By incorporating a light source in a shelf unit, Paul created what is in fact a showcase. The light is concealed at the top of the unit behind a Plexiglas back. The Plexiglas is scored in a precise grid, which is highlighted by the light, creating a high-tech counterpoint to the ancient artifacts on display.

glass. When it's dark in the cube, the boy could look out but the world (including his sisters) couldn't look in.

Paul built the cube himself, on site. The hardest step was joining the large plywood sheets at their vertical joints. "Everybody told me there was no way I could do that without leaving a visible joint," he recalls. But he mitered the panels, then glued and nailed a strip of 1 × 3 inside the entire length of the joint. After sanding and filing the plywood smooth, he put on three coats of a thick latex paint.

This was all several years ago, and the boy has since grown up and gone off to college. The cube is usually empty now, but occasionally the boy's father slips inside to read.

As Paul Pugliese gets more involved with design, he has less to do with the hands-on construction of his pieces. He began helping out in his grandfather's mill at the age of 12, and made his own bedroom furniture, but admits, "I don't like playing around with the equipment anymore." His respect for power tools has become more of a fear, and for a good reason—he has come close to seriously injuring himself. He tells this story: "Earlier this year when I was working on my house, a piece of wood came flying off the table saw and went right through my pants. It's unbelievable how fast it shoots. I was almost finished with the cut and had removed the one piece, but the other piece jumped up on the blade and it shot back and knocked me down. And I'm pretty careful, especially when I see the guys in the Westchester mill. There aren't too many of them with all their fingers."

So this designer-craftsman now prefers to manipulate space and light with a drafting pencil. Asked if he is developing an identifiable style, Paul says he doesn't know if he wants to. "There are repetitive elements I can identify, but it's mostly through the detailing and not an overall vocabulary or style that I adhere to. I like to see each project as a unique problem, to let the design solution evolve based on the parameters rather than on a preconceived style. It's fresher that way."

ROGER B. YEPSEN, JR.

Larry Golden

PLYWOOD CHEST OF DRAWERS

Some commissions can be too easy. Larry Golden's friends needed a built-in bureau for a closet they were turning into a small dressing room in their new condominium in Minneapolis. Their requirements were basic: "We'd like to own a piece of furniture you've made especially for us. Twelve drawers for our clothes. Make it nice. Don't go crazy." That was about it.

Since the piece was going into a small space, Larry wanted it to be lively. And, since it would be built-in, the liveliness would have to reside in the front. How to make 12 drawer fronts look lively? In this case, by the choice of woods. Cut the drawer fronts from one sheet of 4- by 8-foot oak plywood. Wrap a padauk border around each drawer. Fix a mahogany pull in the center of each. Divide each tier of drawers horizontally with an oak strip and vertically with a walnut strip. Then frame the

Three very different woods — oak, walnut, and padauk — come together in a collision of figure and color in Larry Golden's dresser. The contrasts are deliberate.

whole composition in walnut and fix it to an oak plywood case with birch strips joining the top corners. Pretty lively.

Unlike a lot of craftsmen, Larry Golden thinks plywood is nice. Not quite as nice as particle board, maybe, with which he frequently sculpts. But lively, and very stable. Material is secondary to him anyway. He will not talk long about grain patterns and moisture content.

"Sometimes woodworking can get so tight and pedestrian," he complains. "I *like* randomness. I *like* chance.

"I think of myself as a sculptor first. The design, form, and effect are of more importance to me than if it lasts 20 years or 2000 years. When I build with wood, I use woods that are of pretty similar densities. Therefore, if the wood is well dried and I use a good glue and match all the joints and do a careful glue-up job, there's no reason why the piece won't stay together."

While the case of his chest of drawers is basic box construction, the face frame is more subtly designed and intricately constructed than his words suggest. The exposed side and the top are oak plywood. The side that is against the wall and that does not show is particle board. Inside the case, the center upright is also particle board. Three 1 × 4 pine rails at the top, middle, and bottom of the back are screwed to the wall for more support.

Larry built the face frame first using 5/4 oak and walnut stock. He cut five oak rails and cut mitered half-laps on their ends. He then cut five pieces of walnut that compose the center upright. He cut half-laps on both ends of three of them, while cutting half-laps on one end and mitered half-laps on the other end of the remaining two pieces. He notched the oak rails to receive the walnut uprights. He then fit and glued the individual walnut center uprights to the oak rails and clamped the assembly together.

Next, he cut the top, bottom, and sides of the face frame from walnut and cut wedge-shaped notches in these pieces to receive the mitered oak rails and the center uprights. He made his cuts with a backsaw, then cleaned them with a chisel. He cut rabbeted miter joints at the ends of the top, bottom and sides so that when the face frame was assembled, the beautifully joined corners would hide the nails on the front of the case. The angles of these joints are echoed in the shaped drawer pulls. The widths vary considerably among all the elements of the face frame, each width being a decision arrived at arbitrarily. "I'm an eyeballer," Larry admits.

Larry glued the sides of the face frame to the rails and used bar clamps to squeeze them tight. Next, he glued the top and bottom onto the assembly, completing the face frame.

Once he had glued up the face frame, he used a hand-held router fitted with an edge guide to make a groove all around the face

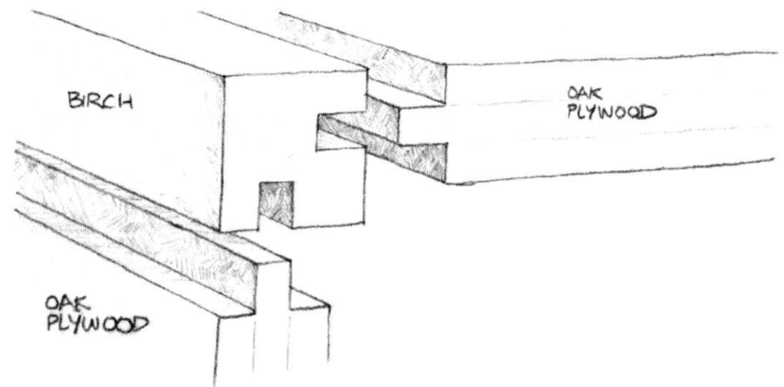

Detail of the case joinery. Tongues cut on the edges of the plywood case panels fit into corresponding grooves plowed in a strip of birch.

frame and the center uprights, in preparation for fitting it to the case later.

Case construction came next. The case measures 50 inches tall, 60¾ inches long, and 24 inches deep. First, Larry cut the oak plywood vertical member and used it as a template for the particle board center support and the particle board side. At the same time, he cut the oak plywood top.

He then used a table saw fitted with a dado blade to cut ¼- by ¼-inch tongues on the three verticals and the top. The tongues project from the front edge of all four case members to mate with the grooves in the face frame. He also cut tongues along both ends of the top of the case and along the top edges of the sides and center support. These mate with grooves in the birch strips, which he used later to create the corner joints of top and sides, as well as to add a decorative element to the case. The tongue on the center particle board support fits into a dado he cut in the center of the top.

Larry then notched out the back edge of the particle board center member at the top, the center, and the bottom to accommodate three 1 × 4 pine rails. To accommodate the ends of the rails in the sides of the case, he cut ¼-inch-deep stopped dadoes.

Next he used bar clamps to clamp the center vertical member and sides to each other so he could simultaneously cut notches in the bottom of each for a 3- by 3-inch toespace.

He then glued the face frame to the vertical members and held it in place with bar clamps. Next, he glued the 5/4 birch strips to each end of the top, first grooving each strip on two faces for the tongues that he'd cut on the top and the sides of the case. He then glued along the joints and fit the top in place.

To fill the toespace, he glued and nailed a strip of pine and a strip of mahogany at right angles to each other, with the strip of mahogany forming the visible piece.

To complete the case, Larry glued and nailed the three pine rails into the notches made for them at the back of the unit.

The drawers came next. He made the sides out of 5/8 Baltic birch plywood, a strong veneer-core plywood imported from Russia. The front, back, and bottom are ⅜-inch plywood. He cut vertical dado joints on the sides to receive the back and horizontal dado joints along the sides and back to receive the bottom. He assembled the parts with glue and nails. He joined the front to the sides with rabbet joints, which are also glued and nailed.

To make the decorative front of each drawer, Larry glued 2-inch-wide padauk stiles and ¾-inch padauk rails with mitered corners to the plywood panels. Both the plywood and padauk are ¾ inches thick. Using a band saw, he cut drawer pulls whose shapes echo that of sculpture pieces he was working on at the time. He then screwed each drawer pull in from the back and glued it to the plywood.

Finally, he added ball-bearing slides to the drawers, fitted them in place, and marked where the complementary slides for the insides of the case should go. He then fitted those, and slid in the drawers. Ball-bearing slides let the drawers roll in and out with great ease

The basic construction of the dresser is remarkably simple. Larry favors plywood for its strength, stability, and ease of use, so he made the case and drawers of plywood. The drawers are suspended on manufactured drawer glides.

and prevent them from ever sliding all the way out of the case.

Larry Golden is no fan of the grit and the rag. "I don't care for finishing at all," he says. In spite of this, he was thorough in finishing the chest of drawers. He worked with a Rockwell orbital sander first, in grits from 80 to 180, then cleaned the surface with a damp rag to raise the grain and hand sanded it to 220 grit. He then applied two coats of Watco Danish Oil with a brush, and a third coat with 4/0 steel wool. When the oil had dried, he rubbed it with 4/0 steel wool to give it a soft, deep finish. It is up to the owners now to apply paste wax occasionally.

When the chest of drawers was finished he delivered it to the site, and simply fixed it to a couple of studs in the wall by screwing through the middle 1 × 4 pine rails.

Throughout the design and construction process, Larry Golden worked alone. He showed his clients no sketches, and they did not see the piece until it was done. Realizing his major opportunity for creativity was in the front of the piece, he played with the number and kinds of wood he could use there. All the woods he used were from stock he had on hand. After assessing the range of his available wood, he chose to provide contrast. He explains, "Oak and walnut give you light and dark. Padauk needs special handling—it's weak and it splits apart—but I love the color. It's such a rich red. It darkens in time, almost to black, which is appealing against light oak."

Larry is self-taught in his craft. "It's all practice" he says. He lives in rural Wisconsin in a cedar-sided house he built himself and works in a large room above his garage. For wood, he drives 55 miles to Minneapolis. For inspiration, he goes even further afield. Oriental joinery is one important source. He admires Japanese woodworkers, who use hundreds of different joints and build their reputations on their skills as joiners. He is fond of *The Art of Japanese Joinery,* by Kiyosi Seike, which illustrates their imaginative techniques. His fascination with joints and, by extension, the concept of interlocking wooden parts also sustains his interest in the furniture of Wendell Castle and the sculpture of Ernst Trova.

Day after day, the din of his tools—band saw, table saw, radial arm saw, disc and belt sanders, drill press, and router—drowns out the surrounding quiet. He is always making something—doors or windows or furniture or sculpture in wood or wood by-products. Each commission is a chance to solve a problem with integrity and imagination.

Marilyn Hodges

John Vugrin

CABINET-MAKING IN THE ROUND

John Vugrin spent his twenty-fourth year creating the kitchen for a house in San Diego, California. He sculpted handles, inlaid decorative patterns, used glass in intricate ways, and laminated moldings, doors, and drawer fronts. He did everything but the tile work on the countertops and the floor.

Now, at the age of twenty-eight, when he looks back on the project, he shakes his head and says, "You're only young once."

There is certainly a lot of youthful exuberance in the complex design, the extravagant use of materials, and the extraordinary amount of detail. He used all his considerable skills as cabinetmaker and sculptor to create a space that moves far beyond function alone.

The kitchen is also a serious response to the needs of the owners' son, who is confined to a wheelchair. The kitchen's

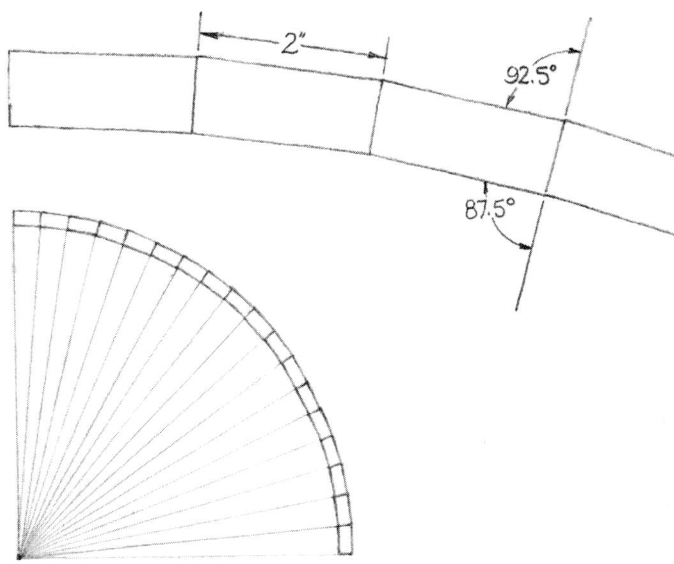

Calculating the bevel angles for the ribs of the curved doors. John first scribed the arc of the door, then broke the arc into 2-inch-wide segments. Using a protractor, he measured the bevel angles.

ample dimensions (15 by 20 feet) and curves give the boy space to maneuver his wheelchair. The toe space under the cabinets is high and recessed enough for him to pull up close to the counters, some of which dip down to a level at which he can work.

The house itself is redwood and poured concrete. It was designed by architect Ken Kellogg, who works in the tradition of Frank Lloyd Wright. Kellogg asked John to build the kitchen, specified the use of curved cabinetry, then let him work out the details on his own. John, who personally favors curvilinear forms, responded with a room rich with movement and energy.

John's shop is about 60 miles from San Diego. Because of the distance, it was important that he contrive a way to segment the cabinetry. He was able to divide the base cabinets into three sections and the wall cabinets into two. These he built in his shop, then trucked to the house for installation.

The complexity of the kitchen makes it necessary to limit the focus of this description to just one section of the dramatically horseshoe-curved base cabinet. That section forms the left tip of the horseshoe.

The face of the cabinet is teak. The drawers and all the structural members are maple and curly maple. The molding around the tile countertop is teak. The bottom of the cabinet is plywood.

John built the countertop molding first. It wraps around the countertop, which is 26 inches across. He began with a length of teak, which he ripped into ⅛- by 2-inch strips on his table saw. He ripped 16 strips, then planed them.

He then made a male mold by cutting three layers of plywood to the shape of the curve. He nailed the layers together, filed them, smoothed them, then waxed them well with Trewax, a floor wax, so glue wouldn't adhere.

To prepare the teak strips for gluing, he cleaned each strip with lacquer thinner to remove the teak oil it exuded. He then coated the strips with Urac, a waterproof urea formaldehyde glue that comes in the form of a powder and a resin that are mixed together. (He used Urac throughout the kitchen project.) Finally, he pressed the glue-coated strips together, forced them around the mold and clamped them to it.

Once the laminated molding had dried, he used it as a template, tracing its curve onto a sheet of ¾-inch fir plywood. He cut out the plywood and used it as the base of the cabinet. He created edge molding for the plywood base by laminating teak strips to follow its curve.

With the countertop molding and the base complete, he built his cabinet case. He made frame-and-panel structural supports to divide and back the two banks of drawers. He used maple for stiles and rails, and curly maple for the panels. These are beautiful and precious woods to lavish on interior construction, hidden from even the most discerning eyes.

There are few rectilinear surfaces in the kitchen "sculpted" by John Vugrin. The curved prow of the counter opens to reveal . . . curved-front, wedge-shaped drawers, mounted on hinges and lined with hammer-formed copper liners. Along the counter are hand-sculpted loops, not handles but moorings for hand towels. Each little element was just as involved to create as you might imagine. Many seemingly solid parts are actually fabrications—the drawer fronts, counter molding and towel loops are laminations of dozens of veneer-thin strips of wood; the doors were formed using dozens of individual ribs. Handwork abounds: the carved ebony drawer pulls, for example. Every element posed a new challenge, and John met them all. His year's labor is evident.

Stiles and rails of the frame-and-panel structural supports are mortised and tenoned together. At the bottom, they are screwed in place from beneath the plywood base. At the top, the stiles are joined to the counter molding.

The teak face frame covers the edges of the stiles on the cabinet front. In five places around the kitchen, including these horseshoe-curved base cabinets, John fitted teak towel holders into the face frame. As a handcrafted detail, they are characteristic of the care John expended to make this kitchen special.

To make the holders, he ripped teak into ⅛-inch strips and glued them together, selecting his strips carefully so that weak parts of the grain would be covered. He laminated the teak, then carved each handle and shaped it until it was smooth. He routed out a slot in the cabinet stile to receive the holder, and glued it in.

John's next task was to make the two banks of curved drawers, five in each tier, that are designed to store bread and other staples. Each drawer is triangular with a curved front,

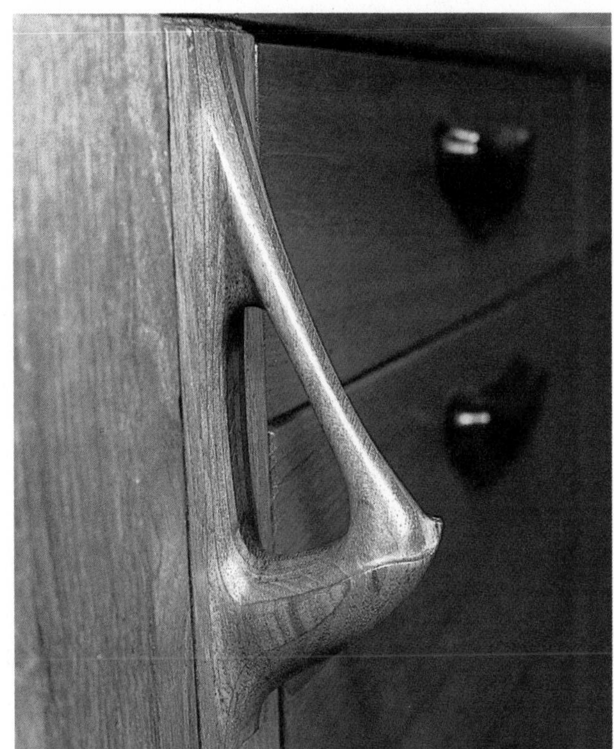

like a piece of pie. The drawer sides are maple, the bottoms are ¼-inch maple plywood, and all the fronts are curly maple, laminated out of the same board. Each drawer has a separate copper lining and lid.

John made the curved fronts first, using the same method he employed for the curved countertop molding. This time, however, he made male and female molds, rather than just a male mold. He fit the wood between the molds "like a sandwich with wood and glue as the filling." He put the mold into his veneer press until it dried. Since he had ten drawer fronts to laminate, and Urac takes 24 hours to dry, John came up with a shortcut to cut the drying time. He placed a space heater right next to the press and concentrated its heat by placing a piece of canvas over it. Three hours later he had his first drawer front.

He cut the drawer sides on his table saw, then made dovetails by hand with a chisel and a mallet to join the sides at the back. He cut the bottoms with a band saw and fit them into grooves in the drawer sides and face piece.

He screwed the drawer fronts and sides together because opposing angles made it impossible to cut usable dovetails. Never one to miss a decorative opportunity, he covered the screws with square ebony plugs.

He also made ebony pulls. Once he had drawn a shape that pleased him, he sculpted ten pulls, striving to make them look alike. He did not simply glue or screw the pulls to the drawer fronts. Instead, he recessed them into the face of the drawers. To create their exact shape on each drawer front, he used a router with a tracer bearing. He then gouged the recess to give it a texture that would help the glue grip the handle when he fixed it in place.

To make the copper liners, he started with a paper template. After transferring the shape of the template to the copper sheet, he cut out the parts with snips and silver soldered them together.

Each drawer has a removable copper lid, painstakingly hammered to shape and to dec-

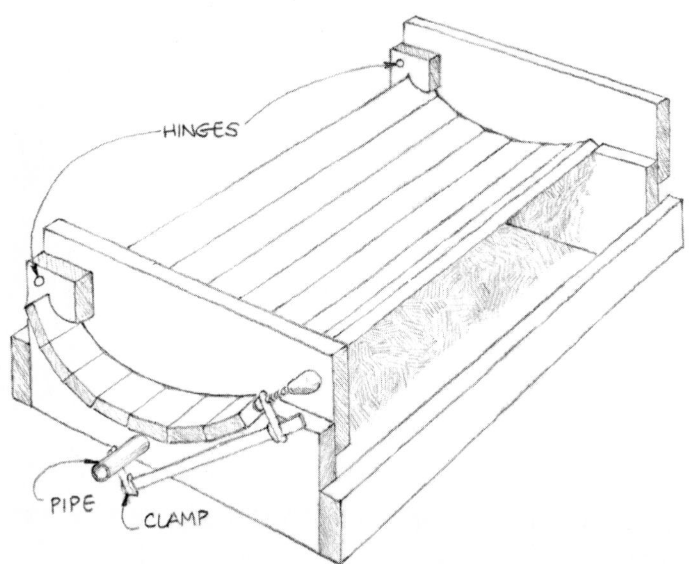

Gluing jig for the curved doors. The door ribs are laid in the concave arcs of the end pieces, then locked into place with hinged convex-arced end pieces. Using a pipe that extends the length of the jig as an anchor point, clamp pressure is applied to the outermost rib, pressing the ribs together and ultimately against the hinge block of the concave end piece.

orate it. Since hammering copper gradually hardens it and increases the possibility that it will fracture, John interrupted his labors periodically to anneal (soften) the piece he was working on. He did this by heating it with an oxyacetylene welding rig and allowing it to cool slowly. When the lids were finished, he attached an ebony pull to each.

John installed the drawers by mounting them on a piano hinge. The hinge leaf attached to the edge of the stile is solid, but the other leaf is broken in five places, creating in effect a separate leaf for each drawer.

The doors that close over these unusual drawers are teak. To make them, John ripped teak into 2-inch-wide strips, cut them to the right length, then calculated at what angle he had to bevel their sides in order to get the proper curve. To figure that angle, he drew the curve on paper, broke it into 2-inch-wide increments (one for each board), then used a protractor to take the measurement. He decided to bevel the edges of the boards on his joiner to an angle of 2½ degrees.

Once his boards were beveled he applied glue to their edges and assembled them in a plywood gluing jig of his own devising (see illustration). He rested the wood strips on the curved sides and held them in place with curved lids. With the strips sandwiched in place, they were ready to be clamped.

To accommodate clamps that would force the wood strips together, John drilled a hole in the curved side, just beneath the low point of the curve. He then threaded ¾-inch pipe through the mold. He clamped his strips against the pipe.

After releasing the door from its mold, John knocked off the excess and dried glue with a sander-grinder, a hand-held disc sander usually used on auto bodies, but quite effective on wood. He used an 18-inch hand plane to smooth the outside of the curve, and a spokeshave to smooth the inside of the curve. Cabi-

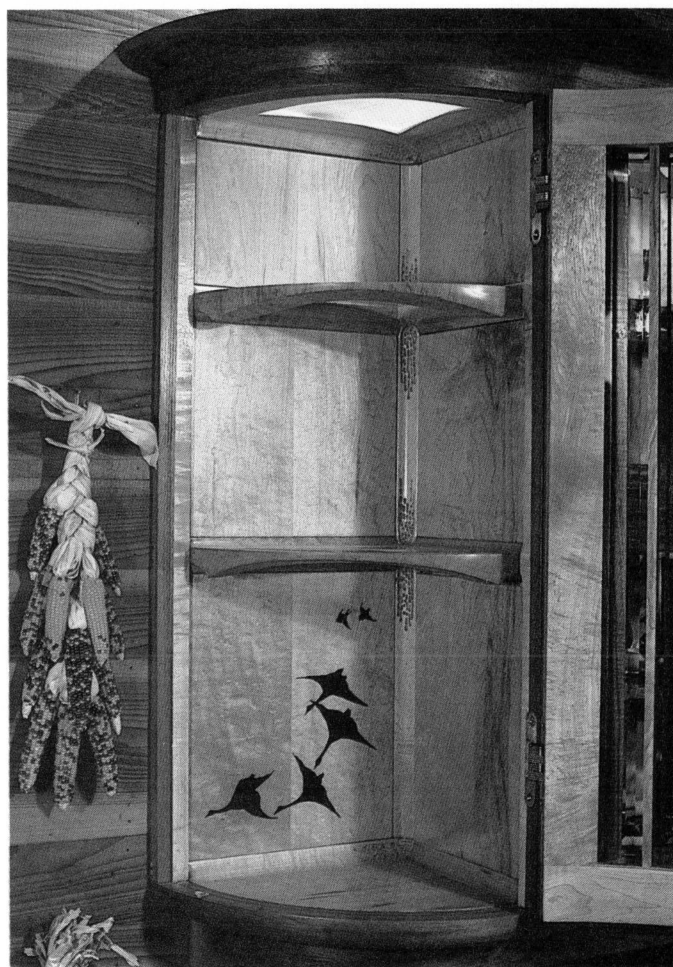

Surprises are everywhere. Open a drawer and discover an inlaid red maple leaf. Open a wall cabinet and discover a flight of swallows. The range of detailing is simply astonishing. Even the hidden areas are beautiful.

net scrapers helped him get the final shape he wanted.

To mount the doors, he used invisible hinges made of brass-plated steel, but he doesn't recommend using them on curved surfaces. They stuck out, and he had to grind them with his autobody grinder so they wouldn't show. He wishes he had used a butt hinge instead, which would have shown, but would certainly have been easier to install flush.

John constructed a separate, laminated teak base for his cabinets. He made it 8 inches high and recessed it 6 inches. He laminated it by the same method he used for the countertop molding and the maple drawer fronts. The cabinet is screwed to plywood support members within the base.

The cabinet is finished inside and out with two coats of oil, consisting of 1 part turpentine, 1 part unboiled linseed oil, and 1 part Verathane varnish. John applied the mixture with a rag, rubbing off each coat while it was still tacky.

John is not sorry he spent a year of his life lavishing a craftsman's attention on a custom kitchen, although he thinks it is unlikely he'll work on such a grand scale again. Between furnituremaking commissions, John is constructing his own house, up in the rugged mountains overlooking his shop. Not surprisingly, perhaps, the house will be wood, round, and embellished with many curvilinear forms. Though it won't have a large kitchen, it's sure to have a remarkable kitchen, one that will challenge his considerable skills as a designer and craftsman.

Marilyn Hodges

Stan Griskivich

PANTRY CLOSET

Stan and Toni Griskivich built their own house on Cousins Island, just off the coast from Yarmouth, Maine. Right on the property are Stan's woodworking shop and enough of a woodlot to fuel a Vigilant parlor stove in the living room and an old Princess Atlantic in the kitchen. Moored nearby is *Saturday Cove II*, the couple's 28-foot, wooden-hulled Down East cruiser.

Not so handy are customers for Stan's cabinetry. He fills in with rough finish carpentry, often guiding local owner-builders on their maiden projects. He especially enjoys outdoor construction jobs in Maine's fine summers. But he'd like to work full time as a cabinetmaker, yet finds this difficult because of Maine's economy.

Stan prefers to keep his own operation small, taking on a few helpers only when necessary. He'd rather be at his work-bench than at a desk managing other woodworkers.

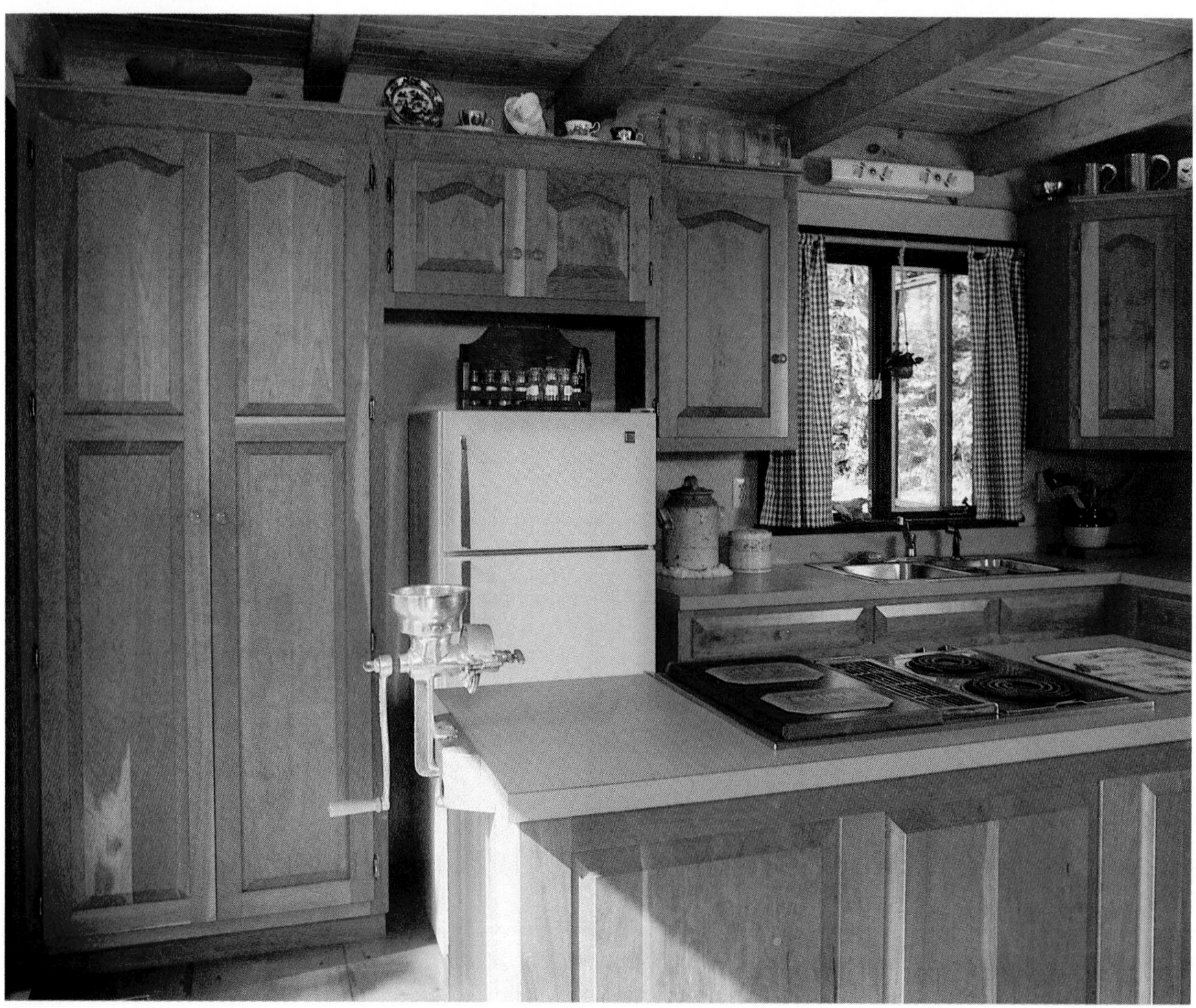

In talking about the kitchen cabinets shown here, he does not apologize for what he calls the appropriate use of nontraditional materials and methods: particle board, Masonite, plywood, staples, and dry wall screws.

The kitchen is his own. He put his money and his time where they show, in the solid cherry frame-and-panel doors. "Inside," he says, "there's no sense in using solid cherry. It'd be foolish. Plywood and particle board serve the purpose. They're a lot more stable than solid stock.

"And a lot of people think that staples connote a cheap product. It's not true. A staple gun, if it's handled by the right person, can produce a joint just as strong, if not stronger, than a regular finish nail. It's not quite as good as a screw, but then you have to look at where in the cabinet the joint is going before deciding what fastening to use." Stan used staples for attaching edge banding to the shelves, for example. On the exterior, however, he mounted the face frame with glue and conventional wood screws, and hid the screwheads with wood plugs.

If he were to build the same unit today, he'd probably use dry wall screws because they save time. "On some softer woods like pine, you don't have to drill a pilot hole. Just counterbore for the plug and drive the screw right in. Because the pitch of the thread of this screw is higher than that of a conventional woodworking screw, it drives a lot quicker and draws things up nice and snug. To drive them, I use a variable-speed electric drill with a screwdriver bit."

In talking with Stan Griskivich, it soon becomes obvious that he often has been over this topic of appropriateness of materials and methods. "If I'm doing a small piece of furniture," he says, "I may use mortise-and-tenon or dovetail joints. But it's very rare that I would on a kitchen. If the customer demands it, fine, but we've got to keep it affordable." And few of his neighbors can easily afford to pay for the time necessary to fashion traditional joints on a project as extensive as a kitchen with two dozen doors.

Materials, too, are chosen with responsibility to the client in mind. The top, bottom, and left case side of the tall cherry cabinet on these pages are ¾-inch Korepine, a high-density particle board. "When you say particle board, a lot of people turn sour," Stan admits, but he finds that Korepine finishes smooth and remains stable. In other words, it is appropriate to this application.

The right-hand case side, facing the refrigerator and exposed to view, is cherry plywood, and Stan says, "Again this is an appropriate use of material. The plywood is actually more expensive for me than the solid cherry per board foot, but you have to look at the savings in labor. You've got a big, wide case side that's 2 feet wide and over 7 feet high. To glue all that up from solid stock and sand it and square it up would take a lot of time, whereas you just cut the plywood out of 4 × 8 sheets and away you go."

Stan's tall cabinet is termed a pantry pack by the kitchen trade. This particular design is a hybrid of several pantry packs Stan studied.

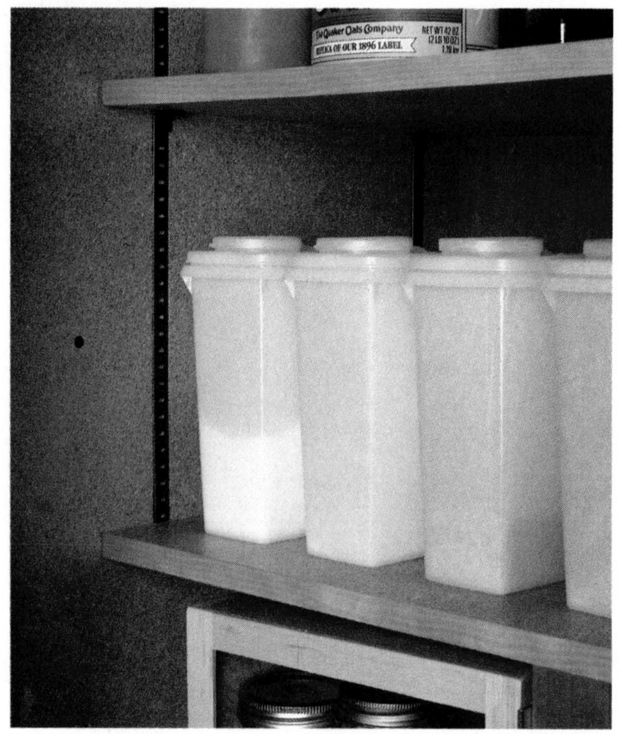

The use of nontraditional materials in Stan Griskivich's pantry cabinet is not immediately evident because they are only used where appropriate. Thus, the case is made of particle board held together with drywall screws and glue. The shelves are plywood with edgings stapled in place. But the doors and the face frame are solid cherry, made with traditional joinery.

"I just picked the best ideas from all the ones I'd done and built them into ours," he says. The cabinet's many shelves are a necessity in the home's modest-sized kitchen.

The cabinet's traditional exterior belies the very contemporary use of the storage space inside—three to four layers of shelves, with one layer swinging out on vertical piano hinges. As Stan describes it, the pantry pack "is basically just a big box, sized according to whatever width and height you want. There are two case sides, top and bottom, and a vertical partition up the center. The partition can run all the way to the top, but in the pantry pack I built for us, it goes only two-thirds of the way and stops where I placed a shelf across it. I've broken the inside of this box up into three compartments: left-hand and right-hand compartments to either side of the partition in the lower two-thirds, and one deep compartment in the upper third."

Stan used a table saw to build his home's pantry pack, but he cuts the plywood for built-ins made on site with a portable circular saw and a plywood blade. For an accurate cut, he clamps or nails a straightedge to the sheet and runs the saw along it. "You can cut edges just as straight and true as if they'd come off a table saw," he says, "but you have to guide your circular saw along a factory edge of a piece of plywood or particle board. The piece should be at least a foot wide so that it won't bow in the middle when under pressure from your saw."

The front of the pantry pack is solid cherry, and as with other cabinet fronts in the kitchen, it shows pronounced streaks of blond sapwood. "That's a natural characteristic of the wood," he explains. "Cherry is expensive and I didn't want to strip any pieces off just because a little sapwood was there. And I like the contrast between the cream color and the pinkish color." Stan builds drawers out of cherry boards that are mostly sapwood.

Stan purchased the cherry for these cabinets from a lumberyard, but he harvests much of his own wood: "It's great to go into the forest with a logger and pick out the trees when they're still standing. He'll drag them out for me and take them to the sawmill." Stan has most of the logs sawed into rough inch-thick boards, then takes them home and stacks them to air dry, outdoors but under cover. A month or so before he wants to use the lumber, he has it planed at a nearby mill and then stacks it in the shop so it can acclimate to the atmosphere in which it will be worked. Then he selects the boards which are most stable.

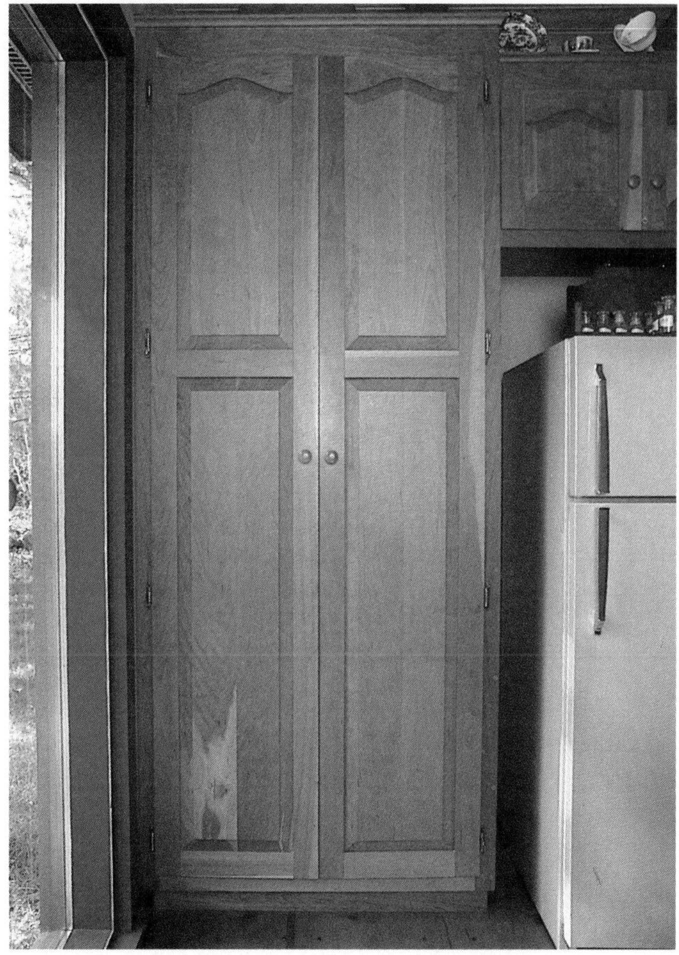

Since Stan was working with kiln-dried cherry, it wasn't necessary for him to put the wood through such a rigorous seasoning and selection process. Once he got the wood home from the lumberyard, he began constructing the pantry pack by cutting the major components. From ¾-inch Korepine came the concealed left case side, top, bottom, fixed shelf, and vertical partition running between case bottom and shelf. The case side that shows is of ¾-inch cherry plywood. The back is of ¼-inch lauan mahogany plywood.

Stan notched the sides for the kickplate, and routed the sides to take the top and bottom. He also routed vertical dadoes for the back and horizontal blind dadoes, two-thirds of the way up, for the fixed shelf. The bottom of the shelf was dadoed down the middle, front to back, to receive the vertical partition, which was also accommodated by a dado in the case bottom.

Once the basic pieces were cut and dadoed, Stan assembled them with glue and nails, starting with the sides and adding top, bottom shelf, and partition. He simply slid the thin plywood back into the dadoes made for it; no further fastening was necessary.

Next, Stan screwed on the 4-inch-wide kickplate, counterboring the holes and plugging them with dowels. He faced the front edge of the vertical partition with a 2-inch-wide piece of cherry, dadoed to fit the partition and glued in place. He mounted the swinging shelves on this plate.

Stan anchored the recessed back of the cabinet to wall studs with dry wall screws that are seated on washers and pass through shims that bridge the back and the house wall.

The elements of the pantry pack's face frame are of cherry and meet at doweled butt joints. Stan screwed the frame into the top, bottom, and sides of the cabinet, countersinking the holes and plugging them with dowels.

The rear-most shelves are of ¾-inch Korepine edged with an iron-on tape of birch veneer to cover up the raw edge of the particle board. Stan made the shelves adjustable by resting them on metal clips in tracks. These shelves run from top to bottom, but are less than full depth to allow room for both the shelves mounted on the door backs and, in the lower two-thirds of the cabinet, the swinging shelves.

Stan Griskivich's goal was to maximize the accessibility of the cabinet's storage space. He achieved his goal by attaching shelves to both doors and creating several hinged shelf units within the cabinet. The illustration, right, *shows this in cutaway and depicts, from top to bottom, the sequence for opening it.*

This middle layer of shelves pivots on brass-plated steel piano hinges anchored to the 2-inch central plate. Stan recalls that he had to situate the swinging shelves so that they wouldn't hit the face frame as they swung out. "It all depends on how deep you build the shelves and on how wide the doors are," he explains. "I drew the shelves out full scale on a piece of building paper, and just kept swinging arcs until I found the shelf size that would clear the face frame as it opened."

Stan refers to the shelf frames as backless boxes. He stapled them together of $\frac{1}{2}$-inch birch plywood. He lined them with $\frac{1}{2}$-inch particle board shelves resting on KD pins set in $\frac{1}{4}$-inch holes. (Note that the right-hand swinging unit is wide enough to house a second layer of shelves on the back side.)

Stan stapled a 1-inch lip of $\frac{1}{8}$-inch Baltic birch plywood to the shelf frame and shelf. This lip is an important feature on shelves that move about and threaten to throw heavy jars to the floor.

Stan constructed the outermost shelf boxes—those affixed to the insides of the doors—in much the same way. He attached them by screwing three fixed shelves to horizontal cleats on the doors. The other shelves rest on adjustable KD pins. The inside of each door serves as a shelf back.

The door frames were assembled with doweled and glued butt joints. Using his table saw, Stan cut a $\frac{1}{2}$- by $\frac{5}{16}$-inch groove in each frame member to receive the $\frac{1}{4}$- by $\frac{1}{2}$-inch tongue left on the panels. Thus, the panels are free to expand and contract over time.

He glued up each panel from two pieces of stock, using Franklin's Titebond glue and clamps. When making large panels of less-than-straight lumber, he sometimes dowels the pieces to get the surfaces flush.

The arched frame-and-panel area at the top of the doors took some doing. Stan cut out the curve for each arched rail with a band saw and then smoothed the cut with a little drum sander mounted on his drill press. Then he traced that curve onto the raised panel,

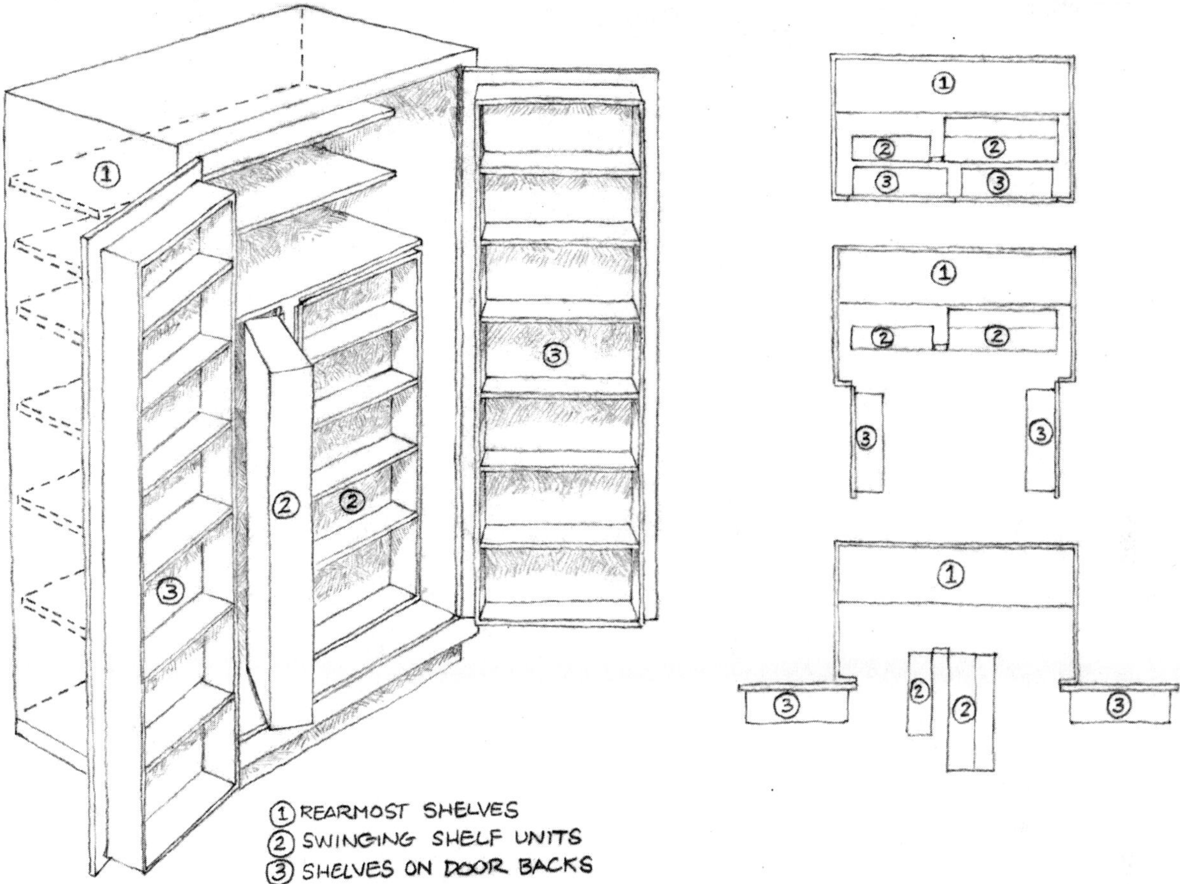

allowing an extra ¼ inch for the tongue that slides into the grooved frame. He cut the panel on the band saw and sanded it smooth, then used a shaper to bevel the panel edge.

Stan mounted the doors on Amerock cabinet hinges, four to a door. They're of a self-closing design employing a plastic cam that snaps the door shut when it comes within a few inches of closing. There's no need for a catch.

Stan ordered the turned maple knobs that dress the cabinet through Woodcraft Supply's catalog; they've darkened with tung oil and time to a color that looks at one with the cherry doors.

Since the pantry pack was assembled several years ago, Stan has improved his finishing method. Before final assembly of a piece, Stan goes over everything with a belt sander using an 80-grit belt. Once a piece is put together, he scrapes off any glue that may have come to the surface, then sands with 100-grit paper on an orbital sander. He applies two coats of his preferred finish, Southerland-Welles polymerized tung oil, to the exterior, and polyurethane to the interior for easy cleaning. He rubs down the exterior with 220-grit sandpaper and then applies a final coat of tung oil. When he uses this finish for cabinets installed in customer's homes, he advises them to renew the finish periodically.

How well does the pantry pack work? Stan's wife Toni says the unit offers more storage space than the entire pantry in their first house.

Roger B. Yepsen, Jr.

Roberta Katz

STAINED GLASS CABINET DOORS

Roberta Katz learned to do stained glass through experimentation. "I just waded in and never did stop," she says. "About a year after I started, I looked up and realized that I had found what I wanted to do."

What made her lift her head was a move from urban Denver to rural Arkansas. Like many who had grown up in the 60s, she wanted to go back to the land. When she won a major stained glass commission within three weeks of her arrival in Arkansas, she knew her dream was a reality. She was doing the kind of work she wanted to do where she wanted to do it. "I had a vague dream, and then somehow I walked right into it."

Now she feels quite comfortable with her life. She spends the days working at her craft. In the evenings, she sings in a band. In the cool hours of early morning and twilight, she gardens. This bal-

Roberta Katz's well-crafted leaded-glass panels lend a unique touch to these kitchen wall cabinets. Roberta's commission stipulated that the contents of the cabinets be kept visible. She met the stipulation by creating vividly colored wildflowers, each in a field of clear glass. The designs are graceful, subtle, elegant.

ance is good for her work. "I have to try to remember to keep the balance good," she says. "If I have myself straight and clear, not anxious or disorganized, then the work will be sound, too."

Roberta is very aware that for hundreds of years stained glass has been used to ornament cathedrals, so that its beauty would inspire religious awe. Her own work is secular, tailor-made for a particular site. But she does not forget the spirituality of her craft.

She does not sell her work at craft shows. For her, discrete panels, those made without reference to a particular client or site, "are like throwing seeds to the wind." She explains, "When I design for clients, I can plant seeds with care. It's a little magical if you can build something for someone that they can strongly identify with. I try to give my clients a good, healthy form of self-realization."

Sometimes, she knows, the point is lost. The symbolism eludes the client. Five years later, perhaps, time may reveal it. The stained glass panels she made for the cabinet doors in Kay Maris's kitchen met with instant recognition; nothing was lost.

Kay first got the idea of using stained glass in her kitchen cabinets from photos in a magazine. A word-of-mouth referral prompted Kay to visit Roberta's studio, and the visit led to the commission. In Arkansas, Roberta says, people tend to "stick with the home stuff," which is to say they patronize local craftsmen.

At Kay's request, Roberta traveled up from her house in Clinton (pop. 2,000) to Harrison (big enough to have a Holiday Inn). Kay showed Roberta a floorplan of the kitchen and the dimensions of the roughed-in cabinets that Kay's brother-in-law was building. Roberta made some thumbnail sketches on the spot.

She took her inspiration from the client rather than the kitchen. "I found Kay to be a pleasant and gracious woman," she explains. "I did something that was like her." The result was a wildflower theme for the cabinet doors.

Roberta headed home to draw up formal designs. For her, this phase is the most important and interesting part of any project—but it is also time-consuming. So, rather than designing and producing a different pattern for each of the 11 cabinet doors, she created three

patterns, used each on one door, and then its mirror image on another. For the remaining 5 doors, she used a single pattern of clear glass and "peepers," which are small, round, beveled glass ornaments that look like jewels.

To create some contrast to the kitchen's angularity, she designed all the glass panels with a curved border design. The flowers—a shooting star, a primrose, and a daisy—are also gently curved.

In accordance with Kay's request that the dishes and glasses stored in the cabinets be readily visible, Roberta used large areas of clear glass as background. For the flowers, she chose opalescent glass, which is milky and translucent. This type of glass has surface color and does not depend on light passing through it to reveal its color, as cathedral glass does. The curved pieces are seeded marine antique glass, which is the generic name for glass with a tiny, bubbly texture. Another glass possibility for the clear background areas would have been German antique glass, which she describes as "like looking through moving, shallow, clear water."

Roberta prepared a watercolor rendering (in itself pretty enough to frame) of her design and sent it to her client, along with glass samples. With Kay's approval, she set to work to make full-size patterns, called cartoons. First, she enlarged each of the three flower designs, using an opaque projector. Gridding is a good substitute for a projector.

She then inked in the enlargement of her drawings using a fat felt-tip pen to allow for the thickness of the lead lines around the glass. She also allowed for a ⅜-inch border around the panels (a structural support and cushioning device hidden by the oak frame of the cabinet doors). Roberta measured everything twice. "It's so easy to measure wrong," she admits. "Then, right at the end, when you're ready for triumph—disaster." She then traced each pattern in order to have a second one to use for leading.

When it comes to cutting glass, the next step, Roberta is on sure ground. "It seems the longer I do it, the slower I get. But when I have my tail on fire, I can probably cut faster than anyone in the whole state of Arkansas."

To cut each piece, she laid her cartoon on a light table that illuminated it from underneath. Then, with a piece of glass positioned on top, she scored the glass, following the lines of the pattern. Scoring glass along a pat-

To counteract the angularity of the cabinets, Roberta worked curved forms into her designs for the leaded-glass panels. All, whether they hold a wildflower or only cut-glass "peepers," have a crestlike border. The supple rise of the flower stems and the graceful display of the leaves dominate, suggesting gentle movement. The texture of the glass, the colors and the pewter gridwork of the leading also soften the overall effect.

tern that includes curved lines is difficult, because glass tends to break in straight lines.

But scoring the glass is just the first step. Like scoring a line on paper before folding it, the mark of the glass cutter simply creates a weakness. To actually break the glass requires firm pressure exerted along this line of weakness. By using the edge of her workbench as a fulcrum beneath the lines as she snapped off the waste glass, Roberta was able to shape most of the pieces she needed.

To cut curves and circles, she scored the glass in short arcs and gradually broke away the excess to create the desired shape. Cutting circles is the trickiest task of all, but with practice it becomes easy—and Roberta has been practicing for 14 years.

To the experienced stained glass artisan, the glass itself gives some clues as to the way in which it should be cut. Some of it scores and breaks easily. Some of it is brittle and unpredictable. In addition, some kinds of stained glass have a grain. Roberta took advantage of the grain in opalescent colored glass to create a midrib and veins on the leaves of the shooting stars. Taking good advantage of the glass's inherent pattern in her design is, for Roberta, "one of the big thrills of the material."

Ordinarily, the space between the top of a wall cabinet and the ceiling is enclosed with a soffit and thus wasted. In the Maris kitchen, that space has been turned into a showcase for the family's collection of beer steins. The showcase effect was created by extending the stiles of the face frame and adding stiles at the wall and rails along the ceiling, all to define the space without enclosing it.

Once each piece was cut, she prepared it for leading. To adjust for errors in cutting and to create smooth edges, she used glass pliers and grinder. The process is called grozing.

Next, she taped her traced leading pattern to her workbench and tacked a framework of wood strips around the perimeter. Then she put the glass pieces in place within its borders.

Though lead came is traditionally used to join pieces of stained glass, it is not the best materials choice for delicate work. It must be bent around each piece rather than wrapped around it, making a highly visible joint that is appropriate for large panels. Copper foil, in contrast, is easier to manipulate around small pieces. It comes rolled up like tape, in a variety of widths, and with an adhesive backing and paper to protect the adhesive.

Roberta chose 3/16-inch copper foil to assemble her wildflower panels. One by one, she carefully wrapped the edges of each piece. She put the sticky side on the edge of the glass and then folded down the overlapping edges to make a seal. To smooth the foil, she used her fingernail. Then she placed the piece back on the pattern.

Unaided, solder itself does not bond to the copper foil. It requires a catalyst, called flux, to produce bonding and to remove oxidation from the copper foil. Roberta brushed flux onto the copper foil first and then began applying 60-40 solder (60 percent tin, 40 percent lead). She tinned the tip of her Weller W100 temperature-controlled soldering iron by dipping it in flux, then melting solder onto it. (Her Weller is the Cadillac of soldering irons; it maintains a constant temperature of 800°F.)

Then she applied the solder to the copper foil, touching the solder to the hot tip of the iron so that it flowed onto the foil like hot candle wax. Solder in the molten state is like mercury, adhering to itself to produce a continuous, raised surface.

To create a smooth crown over the line of copper foil, Roberta simply continued applying the solder in a long, smooth bead. Her aim was to achieve a leadlike look. Once one side was beaded, she turned the panel over and soldered it on the other side.

She then took a roll of lead came, cut it, and stretched it to fit the four sides of each panel. Then she soldered the four pieces together at the corners. She used H-channel lead to create a surface that would later fit into the grooves routed in the back of the oak cabinet doors.

To remove excess flux, she washed off each panel with liquid glass cleaner and paper towels. Because solder left alone turns a dull and unattractive gray, she applied a copper sulphate patina to it to turn copper-colored. She then washed the residue off the glass.

With Roberta's task done, she delivered the panels to Bob Maris, who had constructed the kitchen cabinets. He made the cases of oak plywood and the face frames of solid oak. Each case was assembled using dado joints, glue and nails.

The rails and stiles of the face frames are joined with mortise-and-tenon joints. Each frame is glued and screwed to its cabinet, the screws concealed under oak pegs.

The frame-and-panel cabinet doors had to be strong, because the glass is heavy, but they also had to be narrow for aesthetic reasons. Each door frame member is only 1½ inches wide, but the joints are through tenons, pegged for maximum strength. Bob made each door frame with a rabbet around the back side for the glass to rest in. He added oak molding to hold the glass in place, using brads and dots of glue to secure it. The molding strips are butt jointed.

To hang the doors, he used unobtrusive, brass butt hinges. Oak knobs are stained to match the cabinets.

To create a space for the owner's beer stein collection, he extended the oak stiles to the ceiling and added rails of oak molding at the top. These rails and stiles were also joined with mortise-and-tenon joints.

All the cabinets were finished with Sherwin-Williams Danish Walnut stain, followed by three coats of spray lacquer.

The finished effect of the stained glass doors in the kitchen is uniformly pleasing. Roberta says, "I think this is one of my best jobs. The site was just great. The plain glass is the only reflective surface in the kitchen. And the color, which is subdued in photographs, is alive in the kitchen—the green especially—and very welcome. This was really fertile ground to throw my seeds on."

She thinks stained glass is best used where people congregate. That eliminates entryways, a traditional spot for stained glass but an illogical one because lights are not always on in hallways and people do not spend time in them. Kitchens and dining rooms, and even bathrooms, are good spots.

The wildflower panels in Kay's kitchen cabinet doors brought Roberta several other commissions, but she warned each new client to relinquish the preconceptions they garnered in the Maris kitchen. She persuaded each to start fresh, just as she begins again with each new client.

Marilyn Hodges

Steve Doriss

KITCHEN CABINET SCULPTURE

"I don't think I've done two doors the same," says Steve Doriss. "Each door is like a picture." Working alone in his small Fort Bragg, California shop, Steve has the time and flexibility to approach each cabinetry job as a fresh start. While larger shops may restrict themselves to several stock designs, he is free to create original designs for each new job. This is what he most enjoys about his work—talking with his clients, learning what look and functions they want, and then coming up with designs that make these ideas affordable.

Oddly, it was a surfeit of design work that led him to woodworking. "I gradually eased into woodworking. I went to architecture school, but I left after a year. It was too much of the desk, too design-oriented. I love to design, but my limit at the drafting board is about six hours, and then I start fidgeting."

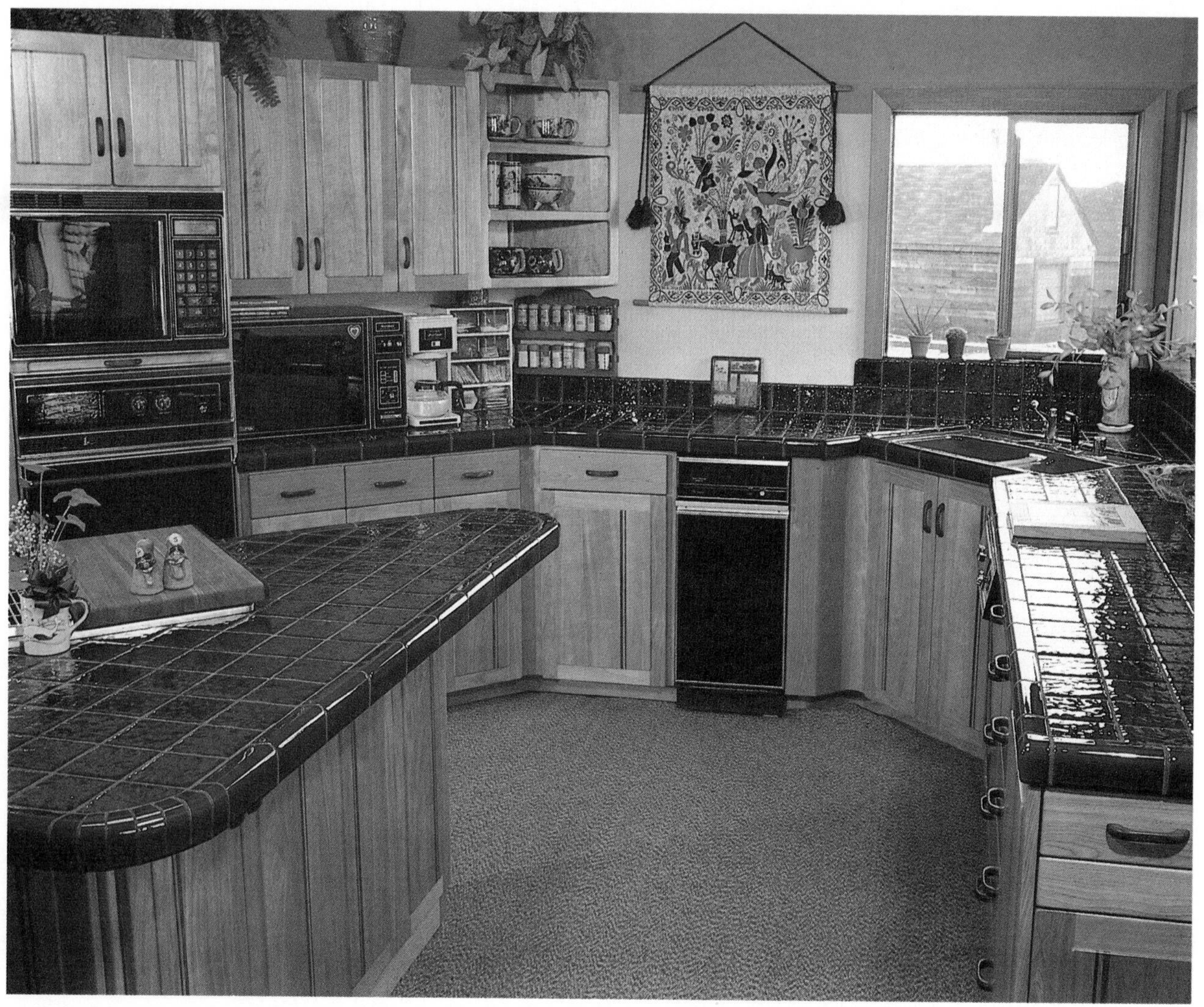

The pin-striped doors shown here were used in an Albion, California, kitchen. The cabinet fronts are almost entirely made up of doors, with a face frame visible only as a horizontal band just below the countertop. Steve was able to dispense with vertical elements of the face frame by using Grass side-mounted hinges. This German-made line of hardware is fairly expensive, but Steve figures using it actually saved the clients' money in the long run: space was spared by devoting the fronts entirely to doors, and labor was spared by not constructing a full face frame. To keep costs for hardware down, Steve used one self-closing hinge and one free-swinging (and less expensive) hinge on each cabinet door.

One of the chief advantages of the Grass side-mounted hinges is that they are easily adjusted. Should any of the cabinet doors ever come out of alignment, Steve's clients can adjust the door up or down, right or left, in or out, merely by turning one of the three screws that attach the hinge to the door. They need not call the cabinetmaker back.

Steve made the cabinets of ¾-inch birch plywood faced with ¾-inch strips of solid birch. The assembly was quite straightforward. He cut ¾-inch dadoes with a router to join case bottom to case sides, vertical dividers to case bottom and so on. The joints were glued and nailed for the most part, but if he expected a piece to experience greater-than-usual stress, as with wall cabinets, he used screws instead of nails. He made the kickplate of solid red birch, and fit it into a notch in the case sides. He countersunk the screws and covered the heads with wood plugs.

He cut the core for the countertop of ¾-inch fir plywood, screwed it down into the frame, and protected it with waterproof paper so that the tile grout wouldn't harm the wood. He left the tiling to professional tilers. Although he could have done the work, as he has in the past, he doesn't take much pleasure in it.

Steve cut boards for panels, stiles and rails for his cabinet doors from ¾-inch-thick birch lumber. He assembled the frame with doweled butt joints. He glued up the panels to form a wood slab and then rabbeted the inner edge of the panels so that they sit down into the frame but rise a bit above it. Then he glued the panels in place.

The panels feature pinstriping of a contrasting wood—dark lines of rosewood glued into the birch. So that the dramatic effect of the strips wouldn't seem contrived or forced, Steve searched his wood pile for birch that had a grain which would flow through the stripes in a pleasing way. He used his jointer to give the wood he'd selected for the panels and stripes a good, glasslike edge for gluing. In fact, he used the jointer to surface the broad sides of panels as well.

Because his jointer has an 8-inch capacity, Steve often builds up panels for his cabinet doors from boards no wider than that. He glues them up using yellow glue and pipe clamps. "When I get rich, I'll buy myself bar clamps," he says. Try as he will, the boards never produce a perfectly smooth surface, so he goes over each panel with a Record smoothing plane. "I use that plane to hit just about everything that comes off the machines, for one reason or another," he says.

The D-shaped door handles are walnut. Steve marked the pattern on ¾-inch stock, cut out the rough forms with a band saw, then gave each handle a smooth curve, using a belt sander for the outside and a sanding drum on his drill press for the inside. Next, he used a rounding-off bit in his router, which is table-mounted, to give each handle a uniform edge. Finally he put each handle in a vise and finished up with a rasp, Nicholson's #49 (ordered through Woodcraft Supply's catalog) and sandpaper.

One of the base cabinets in the Albion kitchen has a pull-out writing table. The surface is 24 inches deep, but the depth available for it was just 19 inches. Fitting the 24-inch surface into the 19-inch space was made possible by a mechanism sold by Hafele America, consisting of telescopic slides with plates that screw both to the cabinet and to the table pieces. This is not an inexpensive item, but Steve says the cost was compensated for by the time it would have taken him to design and construct such an elaborate extension table from scratch. "The table is made in two pieces," Steve explains, "and they're hooked in with this hardware in such a way that as you push the nearest piece, it gets halfway in and the rear piece kicks up to allow the front piece to continue sliding underneath. It's amazing. And it's sturdy. You can really press on it and get very little flex."

Steve made the shelving inside the cabinets adjustable by drilling holes in the case sides and resting the shelves on common plastic Amerock pins. He installed Grant side-mounted ball-bearing roller guides to support the drawers.

Quite different from the Albion job is the monochromatic and sculptural cabinetry of a maple kitchen Steve recently built for an older Glendale, California, home. "My personal tastes run closer to the Glendale kitchen," he says, "to a simpler, understated design." The couple who commissioned the kitchen were fond of the warmth and variable hues of red birch, but agreed with Steve that maple would play up the sculptural drawer faces and asymmetrical cabinet handles.

The case construction Steve used was similar to that used in Albion: ¾-inch plywood joined with dadoes. Case sides are of maple plywood, face frame of solid maple. To add structural strength to the cabinet, Steve installed a horizontal plywood sheet as a dust panel between drawers and cabinet doors. This sheet is dadoed into case sides and back, and vertical partitions between cabinet doors are dadoed into it. The maple rail that's glued along its edge reconciles the differences in the profiles of the drawers and cabinet doors.

Beneath the dark green countertop tiles is a ¾-inch plywood core. Rather than screw the edge molding to this core, Steve came up with an alternative that left the molding unmarked by plugs. He rabbeted the back of the molding, glued a ½-inch mahogany spline into the rabbets, and anchored the spline with screws into a ¼-inch recess running along the front top edge of the core.

The routed drawer handles repeat the prominent horizontal of the counter edge, and in fact, both the drawer faces and edge were taken from the same piece of maple "so that they would seem to grow together."

Steve made each drawer face of two pieces of wood. The lower piece is simple ¾-inch stock. The upper piece, which incorporates

The color scheme is the first thing that hits you, but the centerpiece of this kitchen in Albion, California, is the battery of Steve Doriss cabinets. The low-key design makes quality workmanship essential: there's no way to hide flaws. The cabinets have few drawers but lots of doors. They're made of red birch with rosewood accent stripes and hand-sculpted walnut handles.

These simple cabinets, which Steve Doriss made for a Glendale, California, kitchen, reflect his personal taste. The doors grossly understate the workmanship that has gone into them. Though they appear to be simple slab doors, their construction is frame and panel (see illustration, p. 162). The handle similarly understates its origins.

the handle, was worked from stock 1½ inches high and 1¾ inches wide. To make the recess for fingers, Steve first lopped off one edge of this piece on a table saw, with the blade set at approximately 45 degrees. He slid this beveled face over a router table, using a ¾-inch bull-nose bit to rout out a hollow. He rounded the sharp edges and made them comfortable for fingers with a block plane, rasp and sandpaper. Then he glued and clamped top and bottom pieces together.

Steve used a clever trick to align the drawer faces. This was a sensitive job because there were no horizontal elements in the face frame to play down poor alignment. He attached each drawer face to the front of an already complete drawer box of ½-inch Baltic birch plywood, in the following procedure. He drilled two ½-inch holes in the front of each box, then installed the boxes on Grant drawer guides. Then he went down the row, positioning the maple faces against the drawer boxes as accurately as he could by hand. He marked their places with a pencil through the holes. He drilled pilot holes at the marks and screwed the faces on through the inside of each drawer box. Because the diameter of the screws he used was much less than ½ inch (in fact, large fender washers had to be used to support the heads over the holes), he was able to adjust the drawer faces right or left and up or down. The screws were driven only far enough to make the face fairly snug, and then the fine tuning began, shifting each face so that it lined up with its neighboring drawers. When all was well, Steve secured the faces to the box fronts with two more screws.

The Glendale clients wanted the simple and plain effect of a slab door, but, as Steve says, "You don't just glue up a solid slab door of two or three pieces and leave it at that. It contracts and moves, which is why you need frame-and-panel construction." His answer was to build a conventional frame door with a difference: the stiles are so substantial that they appear to be pieces of vertical molding, and the rails are concealed by an overlapping panel.

By looking closely at the top of the cabinet door, you can see the 1/16-inch gap Steve allowed between the tongue and the groove of the stile. He came up with this distance as the maximum needed by an expanding panel, given the size of the panel, the moisture content of the wood while he worked it, and the likely humidity of its new environment in the Glendale home. He allowed 1/16-inch gap for expansion on either side and encouraged even, bilateral expansion by pinning the middle of the panel top and bottom rails with a spot of glue. The glue also serves to pull the frame and panel together for a joint that is *visually* tight. To allow the panel to expand and contract freely, he rubbed wax on the panel where it touches the rails.

The handles are part of a ¾-inch wide strip that runs the height of the panel. The handle profile was roughed out of the strip on a band saw and then shaped after the strip was glued between the boards making up the panel. Steve used a die grinder and a rasp to work the handles of paired doors into asymmetrical twists that mirror each other. He let the wood suggest the ultimate shape of the

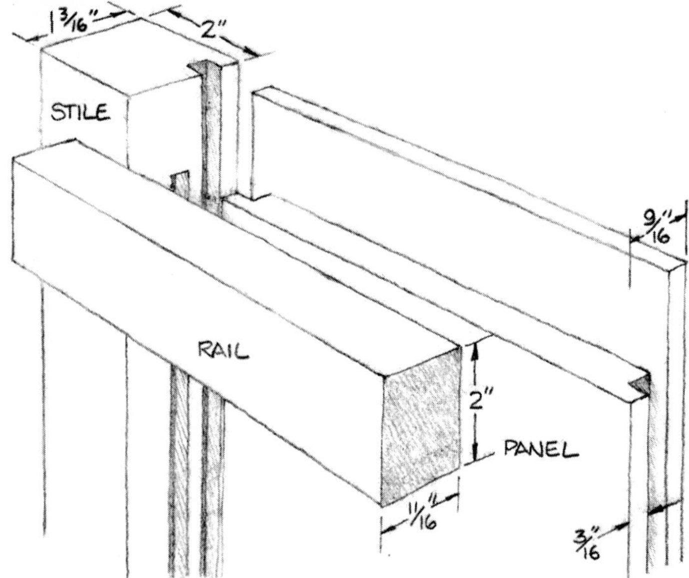

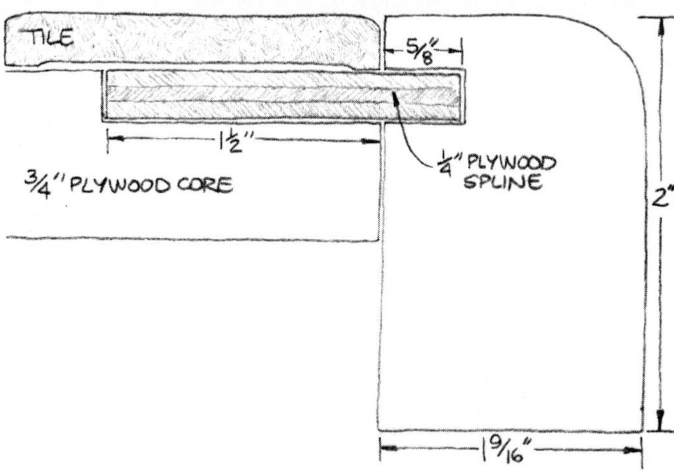

Detail of the joinery, top, *of the cabinet door shown on page 160. The finished door is clean and simple, the joinery is deceptively complex. A preferred technique for edging a countertop is shown in cross section,* bottom. *The birch edging of this type of countertop is seen in the photo on the facing page.*

handle: "A fascinating thing is that as soon as you start cutting away wood, the grain will do things for you. And very often it's a surprise." Finally, he made a recess into the door behind each handle using the grinder and a curved scraper. He finish-sanded the doors and hung them on Grass hinges.

As a general rule, Steve uses a Swedish steel scraper to finish panels then goes over all parts of the cabinet with an orbital sander at 80 or 100 grit. He gives a final pass with 150. At least once in the process he dampens the wood to raise the grain. To protect the wood surface, he uses Zipguard urethane wood finish. He brushes one coat inside and out for ease of cleaning then follows up with another coat or two on the outside.

Once, he finished an oak kitchen with hand-rubbed linseed oil and feared the worst because the household had a lot of young children. With this job, as with other jobs, he sent out a questionnaire some months after completing the kitchen. "The clients just check boxes and comment if they want," he explains. "It completes the job, really, because it gives them the opportunity to tell me that, for example, there's a little something that needs to be adjusted. Well, with this oak kitchen I was scared. I couldn't stand thinking about it because I had this vision of grime everywhere. But, according to the client, the finish worked out fine." He mixed up 1 part linseed oil to 2 parts marine gloss varnish and 3 parts turpentine. He had heard that the linseed oil could work up to the surface and yellow the finish, but so far this hasn't been a problem.

Steve works a 40- to 50-hour week of billable time. He'll spend an additional 10 or 11 hours at the desk or maintaining tools. With experience he has learned to pace himself.

A few years ago he had a run-in with a radial arm saw and lost the tip of an index finger. "Like 99.99 percent of the injured woodworkers you talk to, I was tired, hassled and rushed," he says. "I was doing repeat compound miter cuts and getting into this fast rhythm. I now have very strict guidelines for myself. I don't use a tool if I'm in a bad frame of mind. If I'm too tired, it's just no good. Built into me is the sense of my fingers slipping through the knives or the cutters or the blades. It's not a morbid thing. I'm just highly aware at all times of what could happen."

Steve says that he has all but given up working on Sundays: "For a long time I tried to get work done on Sundays and I found all I could do was make mistakes. I came in one Sunday afternoon to do some finishing, and it was one of those rare times I brought a beer into the shop—as a rule I won't touch a beer until I'm done working. I put the can down and then inadvertently picked up the jar of tinted stain and took a swig."

Steve's shop is just yards from his home. He says his three young daughters "have a clear sense of what I do for a living. They pop into the shop all the time and I love it."

What is his own kitchen like? "A total mess. It's awful. It was an old kitchen with cabinets of green plywood, and one day I got just totally sick of it and literally ripped the doors off. I guess we have the cobbler's kids' shoes syndrome. My wife is a designer of quilted clothes, and it takes me months to get a patch sewn on my pants."

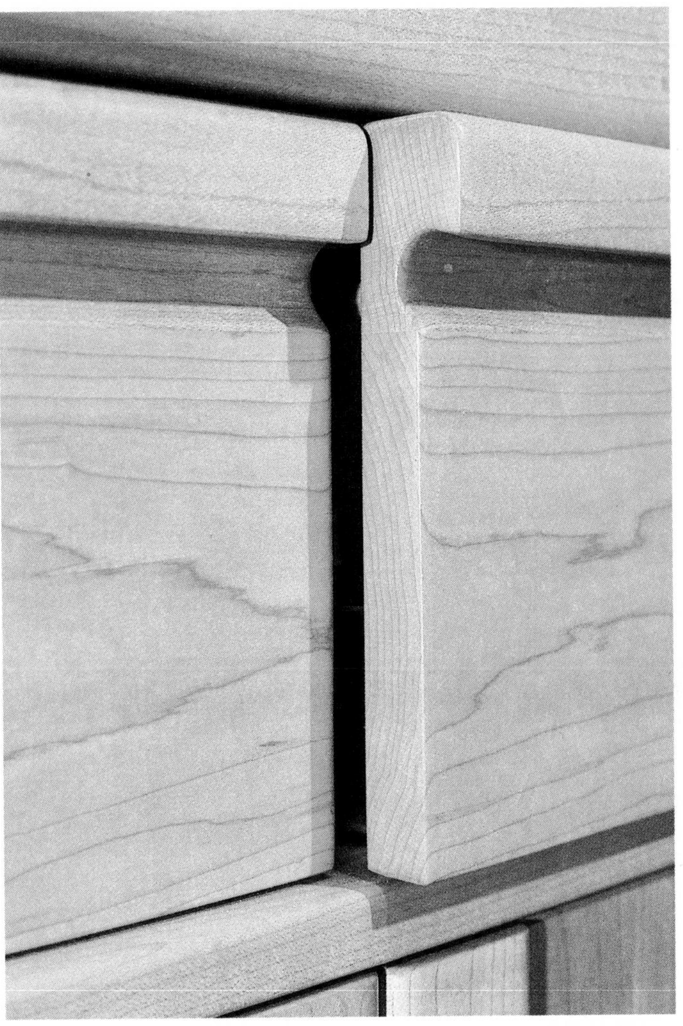

The integral pulls of these drawers appear to be sculpted into the drawer fronts themselves until you study the grain. A peek at the endgrain reveals the cabinetmaker's trick. The groove for the fingers was routed into a separate strip of maple, then the strip edge-glued to the drawer front.

Roger B. Yepsen, Jr.

Nelson Denny

OLD WOOD, NEW KITCHEN

Sean and Karen Kernan were not house hunting when they heard that a Cape Cod house, circa 1748, was up for sale in Stony Creek, Connecticut. "We never thought of buying a house," Karen says, "but we looked at it one day and the next week it was ours." Their enthusiasm was sparked by the fact that no substantial changes had ever been made to the interior. It did not even have a kitchen, just a large stainless steel sink set into a metal cabinet, Sears circa 1920.

The Kernans asked Nelson Denny of Stony Creek Construction Company to act as their designer and contractor. Sean Kernan wanted the feeling of "a Japanese house in a forest," apparently half a design-world away from the house he had just bought. Nelson brought this Oriental simplicity home by revealing and emphasizing the uncluttered lines of the early American house.

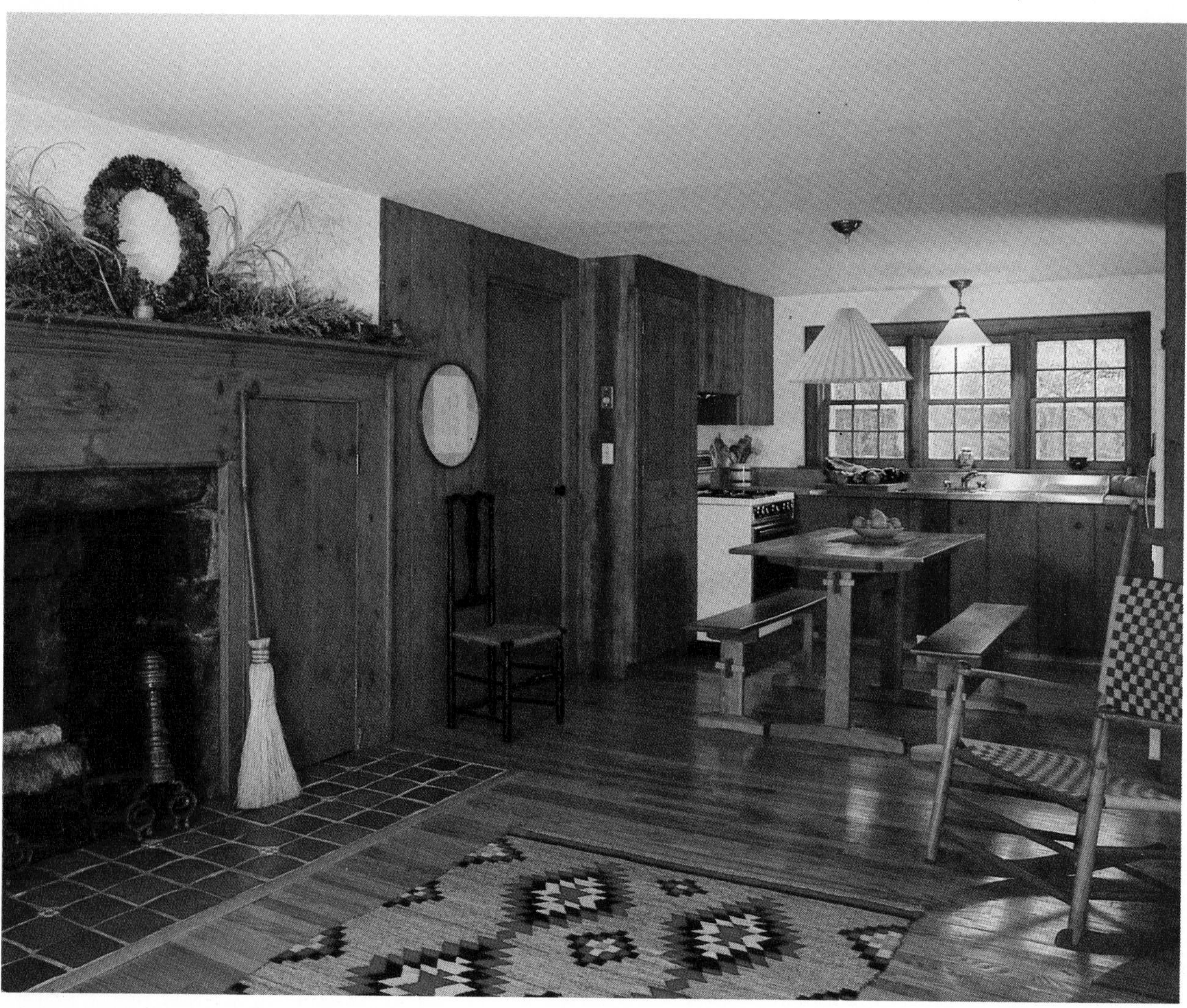

The Kernans took on the preliminary work that plagues all do-it-yourself restorers: paint scraping. They began with the "kitchen," a small space divided by a partition wall into a pantry and a room with a walk-in fireplace. The paint was so thick on the pantry and fireplace walls that the Kernans did not realize there was wood paneling underneath until weeks after the work had begun.

"For a solid month we scraped the walls, windows and doors," Karen says. "Evenings and weekends we scraped and sanded."

Nelson remembers, "After the first week they were totally aghast at the size of the project. But they're an unusual couple and they got into the Zen of doing it."

The pantry wall required the most arduous cleanup—chemical strippers and a Master heat gun to take off innumerable layers of oil-based paint, then scrapers and a Makita hand-held orbital finishing sander to remove the oldest layers. The original finish was finally revealed as an ochre-colored, water-based stain.

The wood itself looked like tulip, although the Kernans had to make an educated guess as to the species because of the age of the wood. It is straight-grained, and about the same density as boxwood, harder than pine, but not as hard as maple or oak. It is very stable for milling and as "dry as dust," that is, well-cured. Though they call it tulip, the wood of the tulip tree (or tulip poplar) is also called yellow poplar, whitewood, tulipwood, tulip poplar, hickory poplar, white poplar, popple, and ironwood. Whichever, it is a local wood, probably plentiful when the house was built, but less so now.

The pantry wall was load bearing and composed entirely of 1½-inch-thick tulipwood boards nailed to the floor and ceiling beams. It had no stud frame at all. The wall around the fireplace, though paneled in the same wood, had plaster lath on the other side. All the tulip boards had been hand-planed and had beaded edges where they were butted together. Though they were all floor to ceiling length, they were various widths, extremely thick and thin, very warped, and, as none could fail to notice, beautiful.

The boards became the solution to the problem of adding on to the house an element it never had, a kitchen the original builder could not have conceived. The original kitchen area had been handcrafted in a rude way by a man working only with a handsaw and a plane. Nelson suggested that that anonymous builder's materials simply be recycled into a new kitchen. By taking down the pantry wall, they could create one big space where there had been two and use the old boards to make kitchen cabinets.

Unfortunately, the pantry boards alone did not yield nearly enough material with which to build the cabinets. When the carpenters discovered the attic floor looked like tulip, they pulled it up and added those boards to their stock. Altogether, their stockpile was less than a hundred square feet, just barely enough to make all the cabinet faces out of tulip. Even then, they had to fill in with old boards that Nelson found in a shed up the road.

The attic floor boards, unlike the pantry boards, had been rough-sawn and never finished. Lighter and finer grained than the

pantry boards, they may actually be beech. Once raised, they were put through a planer in order to remove black coal soot and 200 years' worth of dust. The pantry boards could not go through a planer because they were slightly cupped, a desirable feature that a planer would have obliterated. The attic boards were later hand-planed to give them the same arc.

To color match the planed attic floor boards with the ochre-stained pantry wall boards, the Kernans experimented first with dried pigments mixed with water. When that didn't work, they bought up the whole range of ready-mixed, linseed oil-based Minwax stains and tested them on scraps of tulip until they found the right shade.

Since there was no way to match the grain patterns of the quartersawn attic boards to the plainsawn pantry boards, the attic boards became the top cabinet faces and the pantry boards became the lower cabinet faces.

Nelson Denny decided to tuck the kitchen unobtrusively into the U-shaped alcove where the pantry used to be and reserve the space in front of the fireplace for easy chairs. He then laid out the essential appliances so they would not be conspicuous from other parts of the room. He specified that the kitchen sink should go at the far end of the room, and the side of the refrigerator facing the room should be hidden by the remainder of the original tulip pantry wall. He had the range fan mounted above the stove in a cabinet with a false bottom, which keeps the stainless steel appliance out of sight.

While the Kernans scraped paint and ripped away plaster lath far into the night, three carpenters went to work by day, to carry out Nelson Denny's design. George Ghyssels, Michael Houde, and Louis Riccio made and installed rough frames for the cabinets. The carpentry they used was basic: simple lap joints, small nails, and yellow glue. Though the kitchen was far from square, they tried to stick to conventional kitchen cabinet dimensions (24 inches deep by 36 inches high for the bottom cabinets). They used ¾-inch birch plywood for the uprights and shelving and inserted push-pin shelf clips to make the shelving adjustable.

They made the drawers of ½-inch lauan plywood with ¼-inch birch bottoms and installed them with K.V. side-mounted, nylon glide rollers to keep them from binding.

The Kernans, who wanted the kitchen to look primitive but be functional, then sanded, primed and painted the framework and drawers with two coats of oil-based enamel—good protection for the wood in a kitchen's erratic climate.

In a project where everyone is happy with the results, credit is willingly given. Louis Riccio, 30 years a carpenter and by all accounts a very cheerful fellow, gets the credit for making the most efficient use of the recycled tulipwood. Once the framework was fully installed, he spent a week making the door and drawer fronts that completely overlay the framework and eliminate the need for a face frame. When he was finished there was 4 feet of waste wood left.

Working right in the kitchen, he first rough-sanded all the boards. Then he decided where each board would go and penciled its destination on the wood. For three of the four tiers of

Old, old wood dominates here, not razzle-dazzle joinery. The stockpile was carefully parceled out so none of it would be wasted. Where possible, adjacent drawer fronts, left, *were cut from single boards. But the basic casework and joinery for the cabinets is straightforward to the point that cabinet doors are a rudimentary batten design.*

drawers, he chose ¾-inch-thick boards long enough so that the grain would run across the tier. With the top tier this was not possible.

He allowed board widths to determine the size of the cabinet doors. The doors on the wall cabinets are either one or two boards wide, and backed with a cleat. The doors under the sink are each three boards wide. The center board in each door retains its rustically uneven dimensions in order to echo the unevenness of the paneling around the fireplace.

Having designated where each board should go, Louis cut them to size with a table saw. Because every one of them was warped, he then braced each across the grain with a 1- by 4-inch piece of wood, screwed in from behind with six screws.

The fronts are now as flush as possible, though far from uniform. Their only decoration is the beading that runs along the top of each drawer. It closely resembles the hand-planed, 5/16-inch beading on the paneled fireplace wall. Louis copied the original beading with the help of a custom-made molding cutter on his table saw.

The wood ran out before Louis could build the doors of the large closet to the left of the stove. As a substitute, he used the original pine pantry door that was stained the same ochre as the tulip boards. He cut it down the middle to make two narrow doors and hinged it on either side with the same Stanley recessed pivot hinges he used to hang all the cabinet doors.

Although Louis was able to groove the bottom of each wall cabinet door for easy opening, making the drawer pulls similarly unobtrusive was a problem. Since no one wanted to make a mistake with this irreplaceable wood, they vacillated for more than a year among tulip knobs, leather tabs and other kinds of natural hardware. Finally, Karen says, "We got tired of using knives to get the drawers open! We settled on round, wooden Shaker knobs for the drawers and undersink cabinets and ordered them from the Shaker Workshop catalog."

Choosing the right countertop was easier. Nelson Denny found kiln-dried bird's-eye maple at a specialty lumber supply. Its stability was a point in its favor because it was destined to be edge-glued and doweled. So was its appearance. It was a good complement to the old and mellow tulip boards.

Louis Riccio squared up the 5/4 maple boards on a joiner, then grooved the edge of each with a saw. He inserted a spline in the grooves, applied glue, and joined the boards. He clamped them until dry, then cut his countertop to size.

Once the drawer and door fronts and the countertop were installed, the Kernans sanded them again and applied two coats of Watco tung oil. They varnished the insides of the drawers with polyurethane. With that the job was done.

Why go to so much trouble for old wood? Louis Riccio, who has worked with wood for three decades, finds it a pleasure to handle. "If you have an old house, there may be wonderful old wood on the staircase wall, in the attic floors or the attic ceiling—heavy cedar and

There's subtle variety in the Kernan's kitchen, but no clashing contrasts. It's primarily a three-part harmony—the old flatsawn tulip boards from the house itself, used in the base cabinets, and the old quartersawn tulip boards from the shed up the street, used in the wall cabinets, together with the lighter accent of the new bird's-eye maple countertop. It strikes a warm, appealing chord.

pine, old chestnut, maybe. Use it," he says. "It's good to work with the house you've got."

On the other hand, the people who sold the Kernans their house, moved across the street into a prefab that arrived in two trucks. From the vantage point of their lawn chairs, they watched the Kernans' industrious renovation efforts. But Karen Kernan now believes her kitchen was well worth the effort. "We wouldn't have undertaken it if we had thought too much about what it would take, but it's been a very exciting thing to make something beautiful. The wood has a feeling of life to it. It's a very dark, honey-colored wood and there is a touch of honey color in the ceiling paint. Most of the time, the room itself feels golden.

"I think this kitchen reflects pretty much how we live our lives. It's our first house and I can't believe our incredible good fortune in living here."

Marilyn Hodges

Alex MacLean

BEDROOM WALL UNIT

Scottish-born Alex MacLean works out of a cabinetry shop in Marin County, but his voice has neither a burr nor the laid-back cadences of California. His accent is that of a New Yorker, and it was in this city that he grew up and began woodworking some ten years ago, collaborating with an architect-builder.

In his straightforward manner of talking, Alex explains his approach to woodworking: "I'm a table saw cabinetmaker. That's about all I use. The guy I worked with taught me that you can do about anything on a table saw. I don't consider myself an artist. Most of my stuff is edged ply. It's very conceptual because the look and the finish are what's important to me. The stuff holds together structurally, but I'm not into dovetail joints. I like to see something happen quickly.

"I worked six months for a guy who was the most unbeliev-

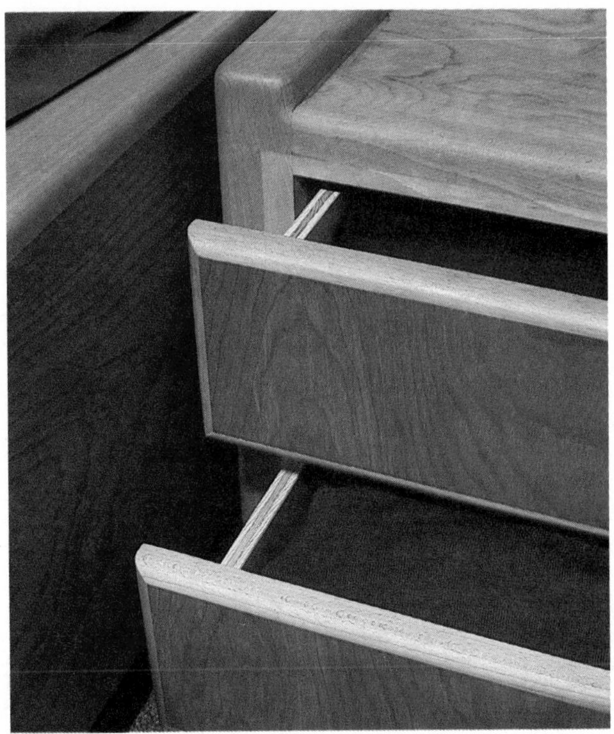

This bedroom wall unit looks good, yet it is quite a simple structure, and it was built relatively quickly. As can be seen in the drawers especially, right, *the unit was constructed of hardwood plywood edged with contrasting solid woods.*

able woodworker. Everything was from solid wood. He was excellent, his things were beautiful, but he was the most frustrated being I've ever met. He just couldn't get the right price for his art.

"I'm basically self-taught, so a lot of the things I do are not necessarily according to Hoyle"—things like nailing cabinets together instead of using traditional joinery. The bedroom wall unit shown here uses finishing nails as well as dry wall and woodworking screws. Both the bed frame and the three cases that provide shelving and storage space are made of birch plywood, edged with strips of solid wood.

The couple who commissioned Alex to build the wall unit liked their water bed and didn't want to give it up. So he designed the bed frame to slip right over the bed and attach to a headboard in the central case, making the bed an integral part of the design. In case of problems with the water bed or the electrical connections that feed the outlets in the headboard shelf, the bed frame can be easily removed. Running around the ¾-inch red birch bed frame is a 3-inch-wide ledge. It is of solid beech, a wood whose pale golden tones provide a pretty contrast to the warmer hues of the birch.

The central case of open-backed shelves is attached with screws to the side cases, which are backed with birch plywood and screwed to the studs. Because Alex wanted the unit to fit tightly against the sidewalls of the room, he made the face oversized in his shop so he could trim it on site. Similarly, he made both the wall unit and the bed frame with 3-inch-high kickplates so that he could trim them to accommodate the less-than-level floor of poured concrete.

The side cases contain not only shelves and cabinets, but built-in night tables about 20 inches deep and 24 inches wide. The night table drawers are all of ⅜-inch red birch plywood mitered to take ⅜- by ¾-inch edge bands of solid beech. The beech edges are rounded over with a router. Since Alex will spend time on traditional joinery only at the client's request, the drawers are put together with only nails and glue. They travel in and out of their openings on Grant slides with nylon rollers, standard hardware items. The pulls are simply recesses routed out of the top of the drawer faces and the bottom of the cabinet doors. The cabinet doors above the night tables are mounted on Stanley 335 hinges concealed in a kerf sawed into the door with a table saw. Since completing this project, Alex has discovered European hinges that are so greatly adjustable as to make proper alignment a far easier job than it is with more traditional hard-

In hanging the cabinet doors, left, *MacLean struck a balance between design and cost. The pivot hinges,* right, *are discreetly visible when the doors are closed, but they were readily available and inexpensive.*

ware. "There's no way you can screw up," he says. "Your case construction could be an obtuse scalene and you could still hang the door."

The shelves in all three cases appear to be 2 inches thick, but in fact are ¾-inch red birch plywood faced with a frame of beech. The frame is screwed together and the screwheads hidden by plugs. Then the edges are softened with a ⅜-inch rounding-off bit on a shaper. The shelves are fastened in place with screws; the screwheads are hidden by plugs. Alex says of this design, "I like the substantial look to it. People like to put those 1⅛-inch fluorescent lights underneath shelves, and this gives them that option." The face piece creates a 1¾-inch recess beneath the shelves.

To visually connect the shelves with the night tables, Alex continued the vertical line of 2-inch-wide shelf-facing by using a piece of the same width as a ledge on either side of the night table.

Alex carries his plywood pragmatism through to finishing. He suggests that some woodworkers border on fanaticism with their finishing rituals. His pieces are sanded to 100 grit, then oiled with clear Watco and rubbed with 000 steel wool. On top goes a layer of clear Trewax and more work with the steel wool. Alex hand-rubs the wax and gives his clients a can of it to encourage them to maintain the finish.

Alex says sanding is " . . . the most unpleasant work for me. I find it tedious." Why, then, hasn't he taken on a helper to relieve him of this drudgery? "I guess because I went through what it's like to be a helper. I might find it hard to make somebody sand forever, and yet that's essentially what I'd want them to do. And then I realize that sanding is essential to the end product, so that I'd end up wanting to do everything."

Asked if working alone is ever lonely for him, Alex MacLean says no. "Oh, I am absolutely lost in"—and he searches for the right word—"bliss. You can imagine. When you're doing something you enjoy and there's really no thought, you're just floating in this very nice state of doing. I'm a very social being, and I've got plenty of friends, but this shop is where I come to be alone. It's great coming into the shop. It makes everything right for me."

Alex says that many of his clients seem to envy him. "They realize what a good thing I've got." He laughs, and adds, "Too bad there's not more money in it. I figure all I can do is make a wage. I work out an hourly wage for myself, but I give a bid and stick to it whether I lose it or not. I don't lose it that often."

As do a number of craftsmen, Alex finds himself increasingly preoccupied with the design aspect of his work. Function still counts, of course, but he builds certain pieces simply because he wants to, rather than to match the needs of a client. "If you like them, buy them,"

he says to those who come to look at his work. "If you don't, don't." For the present, he is concentrating on pieces composed of torsion boxes—plywood sandwiches edged with solid wood. As with the shelves in the bedroom wall unit, the boxes look sturdy, like a solid mass; but the boxes have superior strength and resist the tendency wood has to torque, or twist, with time. He makes lacquered tables of three torsion boxes, placing one box on a pair of plinthlike uprights. The boxes are sprayed with many coats of lacquer by a neighboring auto body shop, starting with color and ending up with clear.

The trio of self-supporting shelves shown here is nothing more than backless torsion boxes, slipped snugly over 1½-inch-high hanging rails lag bolted to the wall studs. Each box is of ½-inch plywood, top and bottom, nailed and glued into a ½- by ⅜-inch rabbet in an edge piece of solid stock. If the shelves are to be painted, Alex chooses alder, poplar, or another close-grained wood that takes paint well. To make certain the box won't twist, Alex runs ½-inch-wide plywood struts from front to back, spaced every 18 to 24 inches, depending on the length of the shelf. The hanging rail affixed to the wall is made up of two laminated layers of ¾-inch plywood. The thicker the shelf and its rail, the stronger the shelf and the wider it can be.

Alex is still experimenting with these torsion box shelves and says he has yet to come up with a rule of thumb on the proper proportion between the width of a shelf and its thickness. "I just completed one that was 27 feet long. That's pretty darn long. It was 4 inches thick, so the rail inside was 3 inches wide and 2¼ inches deep, and it held solid."

Alex places a lag bolt in every stud and tries not to have a shelf end come just short of a stud so that it hangs unsupported. When he can't reach a stud he uses a heavy-duty Molly bolt. The box shelves are painted in the same color as the surrounding wall to play up their sculptural mass.

For now, Alex MacLean continues to support himself with journeyman cabinetry. "I'll do anything," he says. "I do a lot of stuff that some cabinetmakers wouldn't, like tear down walls and put in windows." But his heart is in his lacquer pieces. "They're taking me closer to art, to the sculptural part of making furniture. That's what I really want to do."

ROGER B. YEPSEN, JR.

Tom Bender

STORAGE BENEATH THE STAIRS

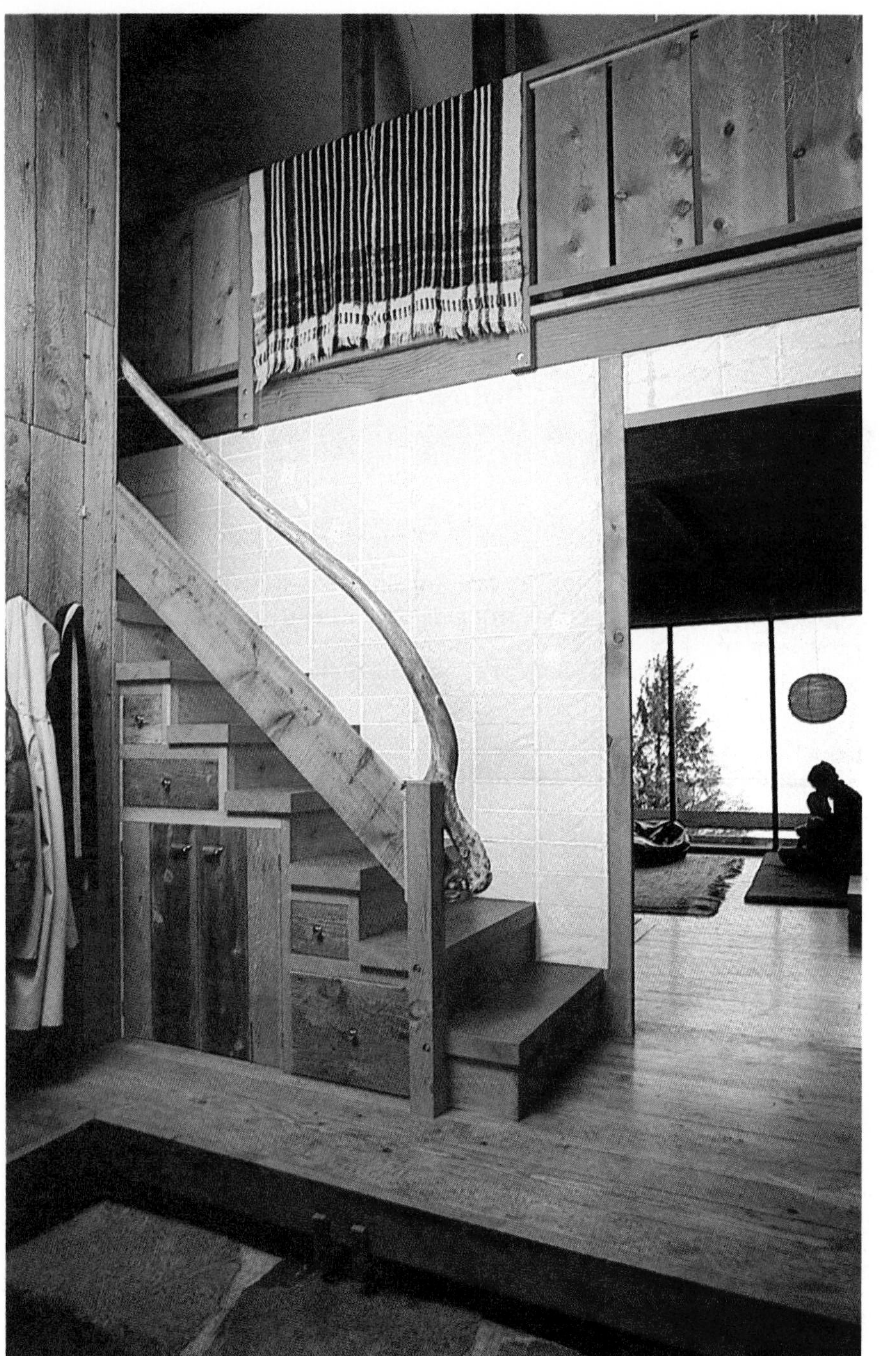

Tom Bender and Lane deMoll built their house on a mountain cliff 300 feet above the Pacific Ocean. Built with wood indigenous to their fishing and logging community, it is crafted to reflect their admiration for Japanese design. The stairs that link the first and second floors, and the shoji screens that form one wall of the stairwell are evidence of their success in carrying out this intention.

Ten years ago, Tom and Lane visited the home of the famous Japanese potter, Kuwai Konjiro, in Kyoto. The staircase in that house lingered in their memories. It was a series of boxes and chests assembled for climbing, and it made the act of climbing a more conscious experience. It also somehow redefined the second floor as a subtle balancing act of matter suspended over space.

Tom flattered Konjiro in the sincerest way by using his idea. He claims his efforts are

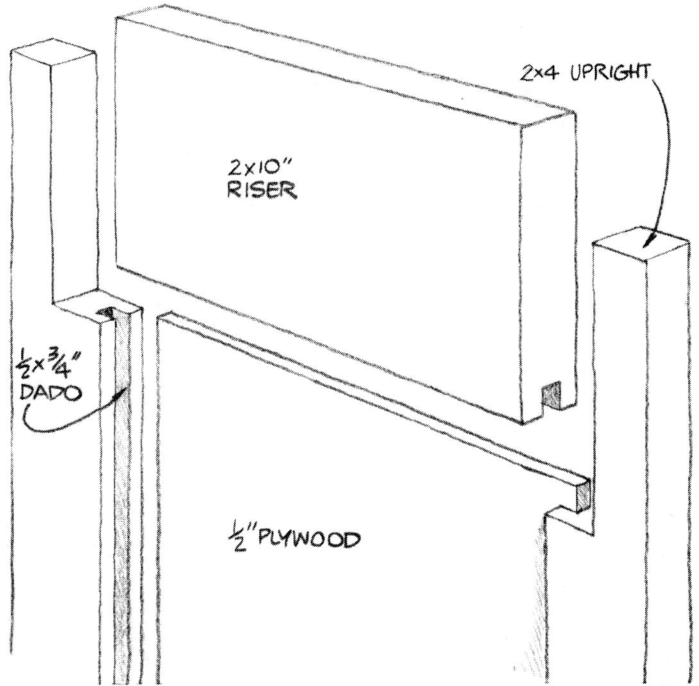

Construction drawing of the vertical partitions in the Bender staircase. There are four of these units in the staircase, each of a different height.

crude by comparison, and for several reasons. First, Tom had never built a staircase before. Second, his old Sears table saw, Skilsaw, belt sander, and motley collection of hand tools did not lend themselves to Japanese joinery. Third, the budget only allowed for construction-grade fir. And last, the tiny Bender children would have been hard on fine woods and meticulous craftsmanship anyway.

Tom built his whole house of local softwoods, mainly fir. In Oregon, softwoods are plentiful. There is spruce along the ocean, and hemlock, cedar and Douglas fir a couple of miles inland. Ponderosa pines grow east of the mountains. Tom enjoys using such woods because they are light, easy to cut and sand, and don't split easily.

He bought the fir to be used for his staircase from a local lumberyard. His shopping list included two sheets of plywood and a dozen 2 × 4s for the framework. He also bought 30 lineal feet of 3 × 12 stock for the stair treads. For the drawer and door fronts, he used 100 square feet of recycled shiplap boards left over from paneling the living room and entry. (Shiplap boards have rabbeted edges, so each board laps over a neighboring board. When shrinkage occurs, it doesn't show.)

Tom piled his staircase wood in the living room and gave it several months to acclimate. Meanwhile he did some careful planning. His project was more complicated than just building stairs since it also included 15 drawers, 7 cupboards and 6 shelves. Designing the stairs was at least as difficult as constructing them.

Usually, stair treads are supported by two or three stringers that extend from floor to floor. But Tom's stair treads would be supported by a stepped-top cabinet. The casework of this cabinet would have to be particularly sturdy to support the loads to which stairs are routinely subjected.

He began by measuring the vertical distance from floor to floor and dividing the sum by 11, the number of risers he planned to have, to determine the height of each. He then multiplied the width of each tread by 10, the number of treads, to arrive at the horizontal length of the stair cabinet.

Next, he designed the framework for the cabinet. The four main vertical supports are modified frame-and-panel assemblies; the stiles are 2 × 4s and the single rail is a 2 × 10, the panel ½-inch plywood. The top end of each stile is notched to accommodate the rail-riser, and the inner edges of the stiles and rail are grooved to accommodate the panel. Wherever a horizontal member intersects the stiles, there is a ⅛-inch-deep dado for it. All the horizontal members are 2 × 2s.

Tom Bender's remarkable under-stair storage could be realized only by departing completely from the traditional stair construction. Instead of stringers, he used a stepped framework, allowing all the space under the treads to be used for an assortment of drawers, cupboards and open shelves.

Because every partition has a tread sitting right on top of it, and another tread fixed to its side, most of the weight is transferred directly to the floor. This allows for the frame to be relatively lightweight. The floor it rests on is 2 × 6 tongue and groove. The high end of the stairs rests against a plywood wall.

Because he had so many framing members to cut, Tom made a long checklist, grouping members by stock size and length. He hung the list near his workplace, a cramped corner of the woodshed. He ripped the stock to size, cut it to rough length with a Skilsaw, then cut it to its final length with his table saw, fitted with a carbide-tipped blade that gave the wood a very smooth surface. He cut extra pieces as well, just in case of error. He then cut all the horizontal support members on his table saw at one time.

Once all the pieces were cut to size, Tom cut the notches, grooves and dadoes. Using a cardboard template, he laid out holes for the dowel joinery that would link all the framing members together. After drilling the holes, he carefully sanded all the pieces with a belt sander.

The four vertical supports were assembled using 1½-inch lengths of ½-inch dowel and yellow glue.

The work of assembling the multitude of framing members began with these vertical supports. First, Tom fastened the tallest one to the wall. He laid out chalk lines on the floor, then set up the next-tallest support and tied it to the first support with the horizontal members. He used yellow glue and dowels and clamped the assembly with bar clamps. After checking

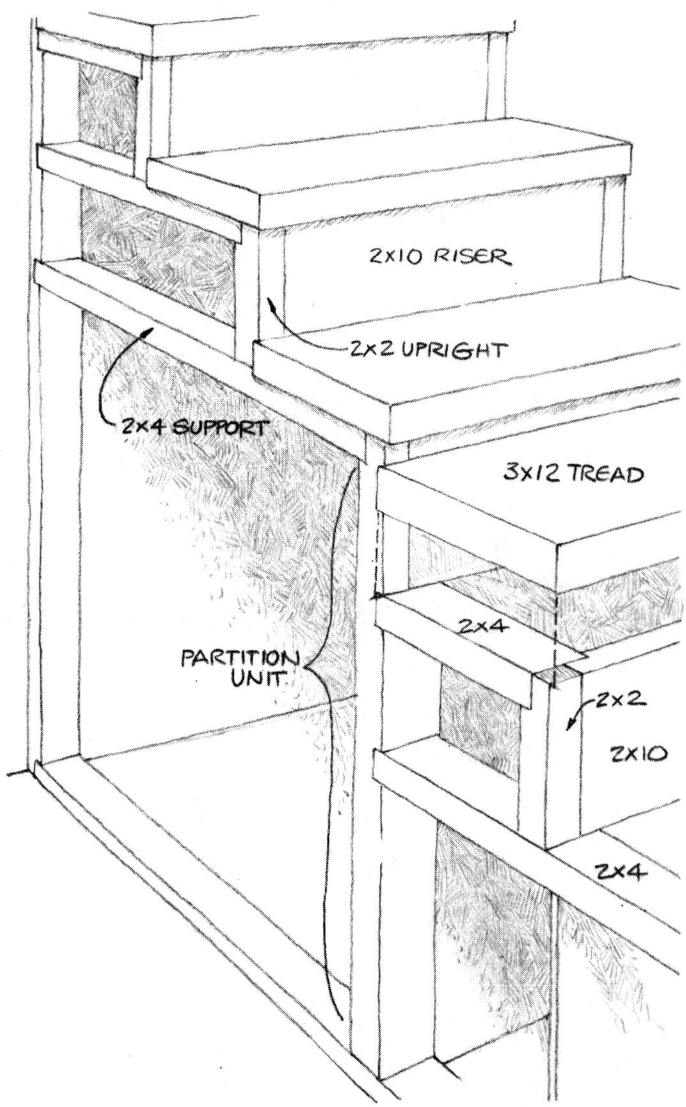

Framing detail of a section of the Bender staircase. Supports made of 2 × 4s extend between vertical partitions to bear the weight of steps not directly supported by the partitions. Tread supports are 2 × 4s, risers are 2 × 10s, and uprights flanking the risers are 2 × 2s.

the alignment, he toenailed the vertical supports to the floor. He repeated the procedure with the other partitions, linking them with horizontals, and then left the whole framework to dry overnight.

Next came the treads. Fixing the treads to the framework took a combination of clamps and nails. Tom glued the first tread in place and clamped it. Then he drilled pilot holes for nails. He nailed through the riser into the tread with 16d finishing nails. Where possible, he drove 10d finishing nails through horizontal members into the treads. With the nails in place, he could remove his clamps and use them on the next tread.

With the framework and treads assembled, Tom lightly hand-sanded the joints. He sanded the treads just to 80 grit, not wanting them too slippery-smooth. He chose linseed oil to give the wood an aged, gold brown color that was a mellow improvement on its initial, raw-sanded look.

Tom built the stairs first because he needed them. Storage doors came next and drawers last. He did not edge-glue the doors for fear they might bow. Instead, he assembled his shiplap boards and cleated them top and bottom. The door hinges are brass.

Each of the 15 drawers is a different size. Drawers on both the living room and the entryway side meet in the middle. A drawer under the bottom step holds socks and slippers. Under the second and third steps, what appears to be a drawer is actually a toy box on casters.

Drawer fronts are nominal 1-inch shiplap stock. Sides and backs are ½-inch plywood. The bottoms are ⅛-inch Masonite, which Tom likes because it is smooth, easy to clean, and inexpensive.

Each drawer bottom slips into a saw kerf cut around all four drawer sides. Drawer sides are dadoed to receive the back, then glued and nailed together. Fronts are rabbeted to receive the sides. The drawers move on runners of

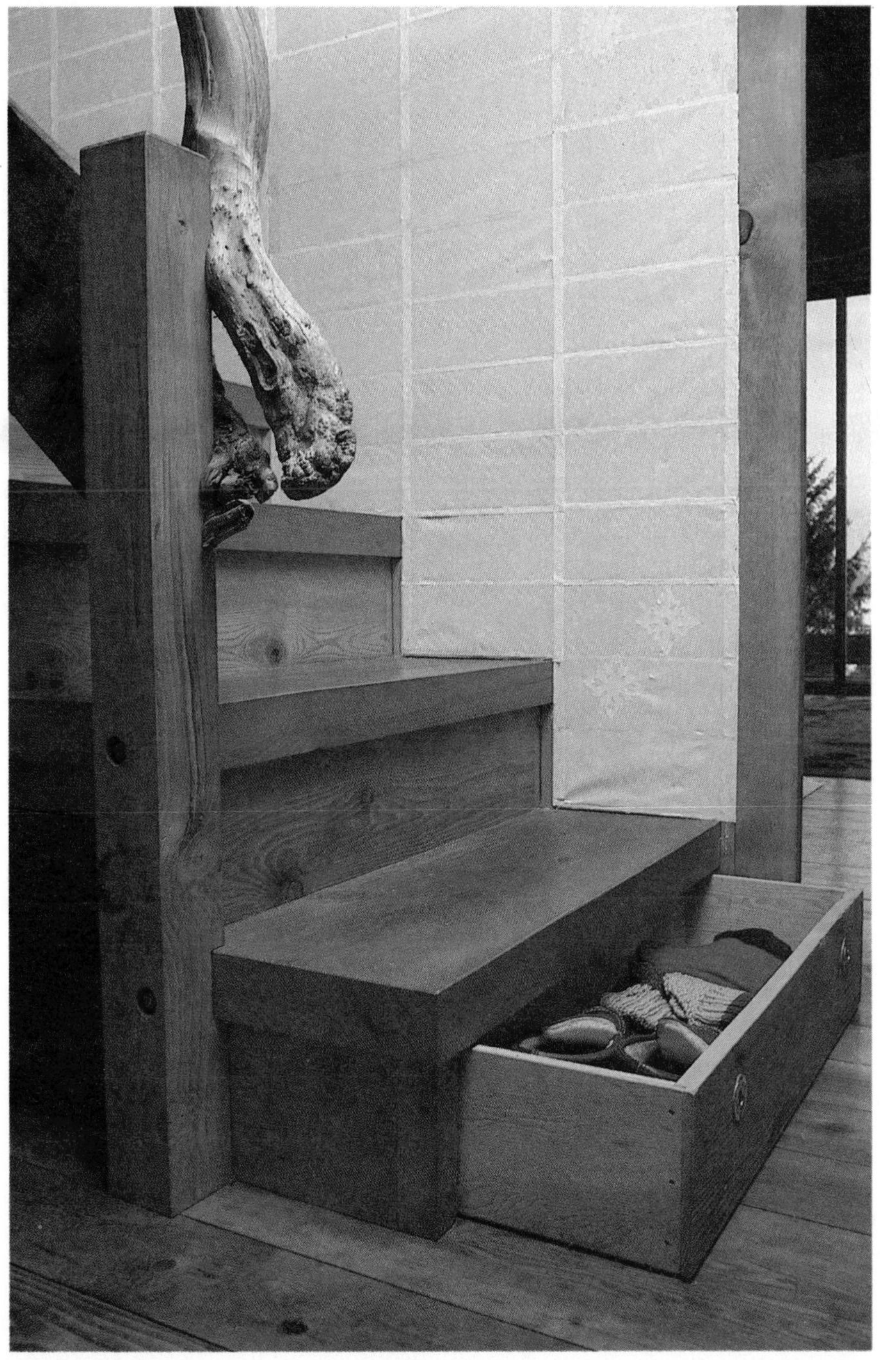

The treads, far left, *are bulky 3 × 12s, finished with linseed oil and polished daily with lots of foot action. Each tread caps some interesting storage compartment. The lowest one,* left, *is a broad drawer whose front acts visually as the riser. A shoji screen along the stairway divides the downstairs space into two rooms.*

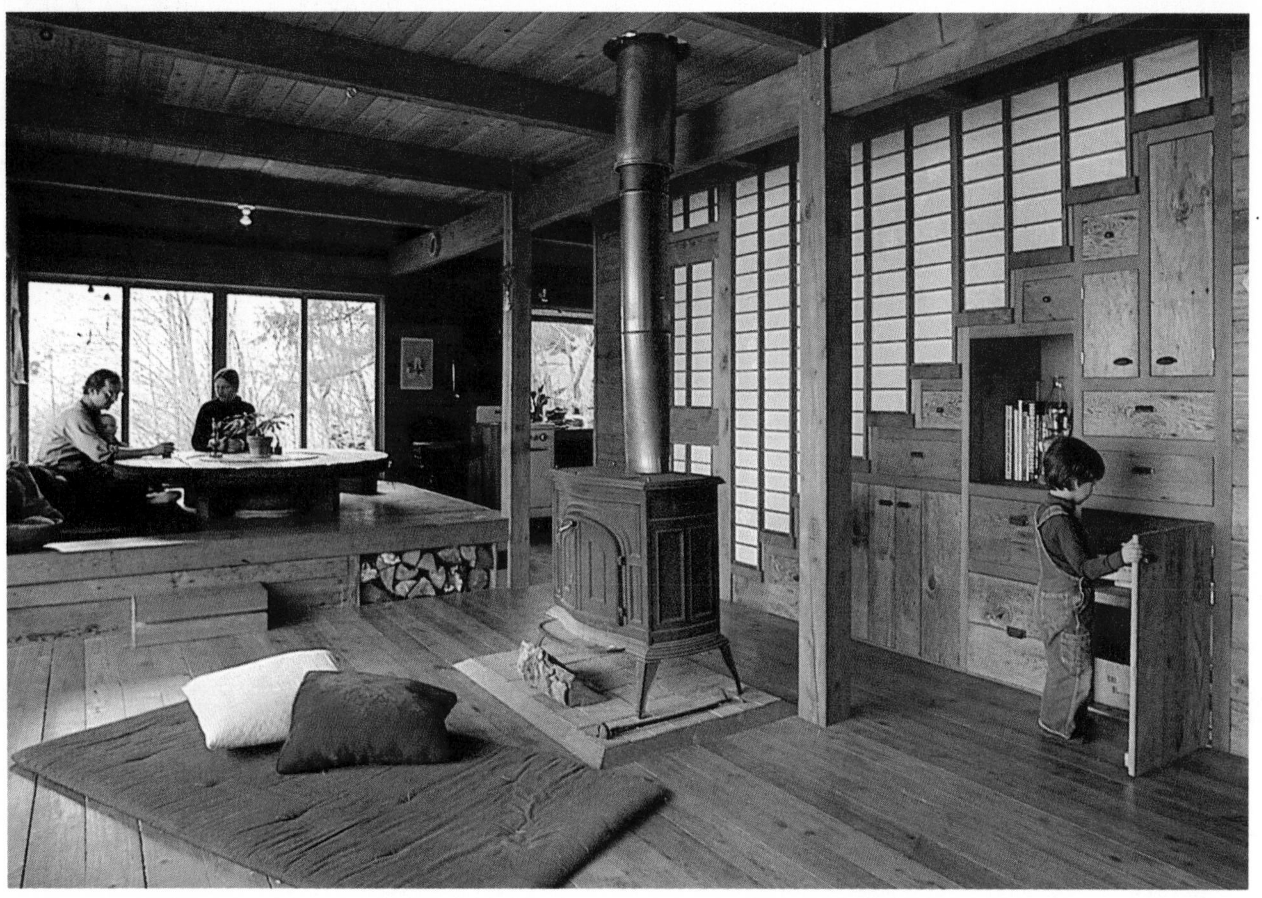

Many American craftsmen are influenced by Japanese woodworkers, Tom more overtly by their style than most. Even the model for his stairs was found in a Japanese home.

softwood that Tom concedes are likely to wear. He has coated them with beeswax. Weathered shiplap doors and drawers were left unfinished, to match the surrounding walls.

On the entry side, all the pulls are brass. Those on the living room side are a mixture of used finds. Some are from an old cabinet owned by Tom's grandfather, and others are from a cabinet Tom rescued from a pile of throwaways about to be carted to the dump.

Form followed function in this project, right down to the banister. A piece of spruce driftwood found lying on the beach below the house had just the right form to function as the Benders' handrail. Tom notched and screwed his freeform handrail to a 3 × 3 vertical post at the bottom of the stairs. At night, light from the living room filters through the shoji screen and casts the gnarled railing in silhouette.

Shoji screens are the Japanese way of softening and warming light. They create private spaces in a gentle way and contribute to household serenity. In the Bender household, they carry light into the entryway and create privacy in the living room. They also keep heat from traveling up the stairs and children from tumbling off the stairs.

Tom made the screen in separate panels, each three steps wide so he could take it down in the summer. But it is so pleasant to live with he has never removed it. To make the vertical members of the frame, he ripped

2 × 4s into ¾- by 1½-inch strips. For horizontal members, he ripped ⅜- by 1-inch strips.

He used the longest vertical strip and the longest horizontal strip to mark off the lengths for the other strips. He wanted to space the horizontals half a riser apart. On the vertical members, he marked the height and the midpoint of each riser. On the horizontal members, he marked the width of each tread.

He cut all the strips to length, then cut dadoes on them using the dado blade on his table saw. In assembly, the dadoes mate to form half-lap and cross-lap joints.

He mounted the verticals on the stairs. Each is notched at the top into an edge piece that he screwed into the framing of the floor above. He screwed the bottom of each vertical to the front projecting edge of a tread.

"I was real worried about alignment since I was using such long, thin members," Tom recalls. So he did a trial assembly and found that everything fit. Using a cotton swab as an applicator, he applied yellow glue to the dadoes and began the final assembly. The verticals proved strong, and as C-clamps eased the joints together, the horizontals were pulled into line. Tom was relieved. He wiped the frame with linseed oil on the side where rice paper would not be applied and let it dry.

All that remained was to apply the rice paper to the entryway side of the framework, wallpaper fashion. Tom mixed up a strippable paste of white flour and water, though any wallpaper paste would have worked. He applied it to the frame with a watercolor brush, covering about 2½ feet at a time. Then he applied the rice paper and pressed it to the frame with his fingers before the paste had a chance to dry. Tom's rice paper came in rolls about 11 inches wide. He went on until the end —pasting, papering, stretching it into place, smoothing out the wrinkles, trimming with a razor, and overlapping old and new rows at the verticals.

A swinging shoji door completed the stairway wall. The door eases busy household traffic by moving on double-swinging spring hinges. When the rice paper on the door and the screens succumbs to a direct blow, it is easily patched with a little butterfly or snowflake. It costs only about four dollars a roll so no one minds.

Tom's shoji screen is very much an adaptation, departing in many details from traditional Japanese shoji craftsmanship. His screens do not slide. The wood strips are not partially woven or left unfinished. Nor does Lane apply new paper to them at the start of a new year, as the Japanese women of the house would. Tom likes the yellowed look of his screens, and just keeps patching.

His concern is less with authenticity than with what makes sense for his household. His goal when designing the staircase was to put normally wasted space to good use, to provide easy access to everyday items, and to make the journey from one floor to another a pleasure. He is an architect, and what he has built looks good and makes sense to him. What more could you ask of a design?

MARILYN HODGES

Al Garvey

BUILT-IN DRESSER

Seen from the outside, the addition to the Swanson residence in northern California looks just like a conventional ranch house. From the inside it is something else again. Rich woods and stained glass color the ceilings and walls of the bedroom and dressing room. A waterfall splashes over Mexican river stones into the Jacuzzi. And a hundred canaries sing in an aviary, their wings catching light as they fly behind the glass wall of the addition.

Al Garvey, who designs and builds such suites of rooms as "environmental sculptures," says that the starting point for such splendor is his client's fantasies. He found Roy and Louise Swanson easy to work with and was able to draw from their rich store of experiences and dreams.

The cabinets and drawers shown at left are part of this addition—a small element that reflects the line, color and richness of the whole. The cabinet

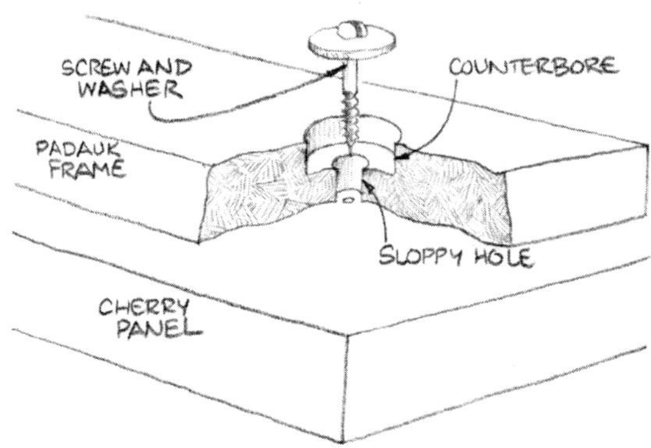

stores clothes in the dressing room area, between bedroom and bath. Made of Finnish birch plywood, American black cherry and padauk from Sri Lanka, it fits into an alcove 5 feet 2 inches wide and 2 feet deep.

The storage unit strongly echoes the details of its surroundings. The arch on the doors, especially, is a reminder of the arch on the door to the suite.

Al built the whole cabinet in his shop, forming it of two independent cases. Their installation required only that he screw both to the alcove.

The top case is 2 feet 4 inches high. Three sets of cherry and padauk doors conceal dead storage. Behind them adjustable plywood shelves, faced with cherry molding, rest on L brackets.

The bottom case is 4 feet 6 inches high. In it, cupboards flank a bank of drawers. The cupboard on the left provides a space exactly long enough for Roy Swanson to hang his shirts. Beneath this shirt closet are two large drawers for blanket storage. To the right of the bank of drawers is a shoe cabinet that is 4 feet tall and fitted with nine Elfa baskets, each holding two pairs of shoes. The baskets are epoxy-coated steel wire construction and slide in and out on runners.

Al regrets not having installed the baskets in the dead storage—the upper case—as well. He could have fit three in each cupboard and avoided the deep reach into the back that now exists. But then he's a long-time fan of the Elfa system. "It's the best possible storage system I've ever run into," he says, "and it comes in a huge range of shapes and sizes."

Rather than fabricate conventional frame-and-panel doors with all the tedious cutting and fitting of parts that's necessary, Al Garvey simply attached a padauk frame to each solid cherry slab door. Beneath each plug in the padauk is a screw, which fastens frame to panel. Oversized, or sloppy holes in the frame (see illustration), allow the two woods to move at their own pace without damaging the structure.

Because only the front of the cabinet can be seen, the case itself could be constructed of plywood. To simplify the construction and eliminate the need for a face frame, Al edge-glued 2-inch-wide strips of cherry to pieces of ¾-inch birch plywood that had been roughly cut to the sizes needed for the tops, bottoms, sides and vertical partitions of the two cases. Then the pieces were cut to finished size and assembled. The cherry strips are the only parts of the case that show, resembling a face frame surrounding doors and drawers.

Sculptural qualities dominate Garvey's contemporary armoire. The shapes of the door frames are most obviously sculptural, but even the details are subtly so. For example, as the overhead light strikes the cabinet, it highlights the top edges of the drawers, attracting the eye, then the hand, to the half-moon cutouts that serve as drawer pulls. The light's glint on the metal door pulls does the same.

A variety of joints were used in assembling the case. The joint used in a day's work "depends on what I have for breakfast," Al jokes. Among the repertoire displayed in the cabinets are stopped dado joints and tongue-and-groove joints.

The dadoes and grooves for these joints were cut either with a router or a table saw. All the tongues, however, were cut with a router. By using washers to space two ¼-inch slotting cutters ¼ inch apart, Al is able to create a bit that cuts a tongue in one pass.

To create a toespace in the bottom case, Al cut a notch 4 inches high and 3¾ inches deep in the two side panels and the two upright partitions. After assembling the case, he attached a cherry board in the space with glue and screws. The screws are in counterbored holes and are hidden with cherry plugs.

The doors are not frame and panel, though at first glance they look it. To make them, Al glued up panels of ¾-inch-thick cherry boards. He dressed each panel, cut it to finished size, and fitted it with a decorative padauk molding. The padauk acts like a cleat to keep the cherry from warping.

Al created the padauk decoration by first making a template out of Masonite. He then doweled and glued three pieces of padauk together in a C-shape. He clamped the shape together, and when it had dried, he put the template on top and traced the curves. He cut to the lines on a band saw, rounded over the edges and sanded it carefully.

Each padauk section is attached to its cherry door with screws. To allow for the seasonal movement of the two woods, Al drilled what he calls "sloppy holes" through the padauk. He first drilled a counterbore in the padauk, then an oversized pilot hole—the sloppy hole. Positioning the padauk on the cherry, he then drilled a proper-sized pilot hole in it, centering it in the oversized hole. He used roundhead screws and washers to fasten the padauk to the cherry, filling the counterbore with a padauk plug.

Grass invisible German hinges are used on all the doors. They are self-closing. Brass ring pulls are recessed into a round plate that is mounted flush on the cherry door.

The drawer back and sides are ½-inch-thick white oak, a wood that is both very strong and easy to finish. The drawer bottoms are ⅜-inch-thick birch plywood. The drawer fronts are ¾-inch padauk.

Building the drawers was an exercise in precision. Al cut dovetails to join front, back and sides using a router with a dovetail template.

He cut a dado ¼ inch up from the bottom of the front, sides, and back, and then slid in the bottom and glued it in place. The sides of the drawers taper ⅜ inch from top to bottom creating sufficient play at the back of the drawers to allow for the tight squeeze between drawer fronts, which are a scant ⅟16 inch apart. To make the tiny half-moon slots that serve as pulls, he made a template, traced the shape onto each drawer front, cut it out and sanded it smooth rounding over the edges in the process.

The drawers are suspended on Grant No. 329 heavy-duty slides, which Al prefers for their strength—they can carry up to 100 pounds at full extension—and their quiet and effortless operation. As a consequence of this hardware choice, the drawer bodies are 1 inch narrower than the opening in the case, the ball-bearing slides taking up ½ inch on each side. The drawer fronts are sized to conceal the hardware.

Both cabinets were finished with two coats of Watco Danish Oil, with each coat allowed a day's drying time. On the third day, Al applied Penofin, another penetrating oil, using three coats and sanding each with progressively finer grits while the wood was still soaking wet. This wet sanding forces the oil deeper into the wood as well as creating a smoother finish, Al says.

Al never fills or stains wood. He uses Watco because it gives wood a warmer, yellow color. It does bleed to the surface for a considerable length of time, he believes, so he completes the finishing process with Penofin. In his opinion, Penofin stops bleeding to the surface within 20 minutes and builds up a harder surface than Watco.

Al's pleasure in this commission was primarily in the idea-gathering. He enjoyed the studio work most, designing every detail to relate to every other detail, the whole forming "a sculptural environment."

Execution of his designs is of secondary interest to him, and he would be quite happy to leave it to others. "I use the simplest joinery possible that will do the best job," he says. "I never let the joinery dictate the form. For me the sculptural form is everything, and I create it however I can."

As a high school boy in Chicago, he set up a shop in his basement, but in those days design was secondary to learning basic woodworking skills. Luckily, a retired cabinetmaker in his neighborhood looked in on him regularly and offered advice. Art school followed, then work as a professional printmaker. During this time he supported himself by doing carpentry on the side. He developed a strong sense of design backed up by solid shop skills. Now Al considers every part of a house fitting territory for his imagination. His environmental sculptures—whole rooms of handcrafted details—express his excitement with design, and materials, and life.

Marilyn Hodges

Ellis Walentine and Michael Gorchov

BUILT-IN SEWING CABINET

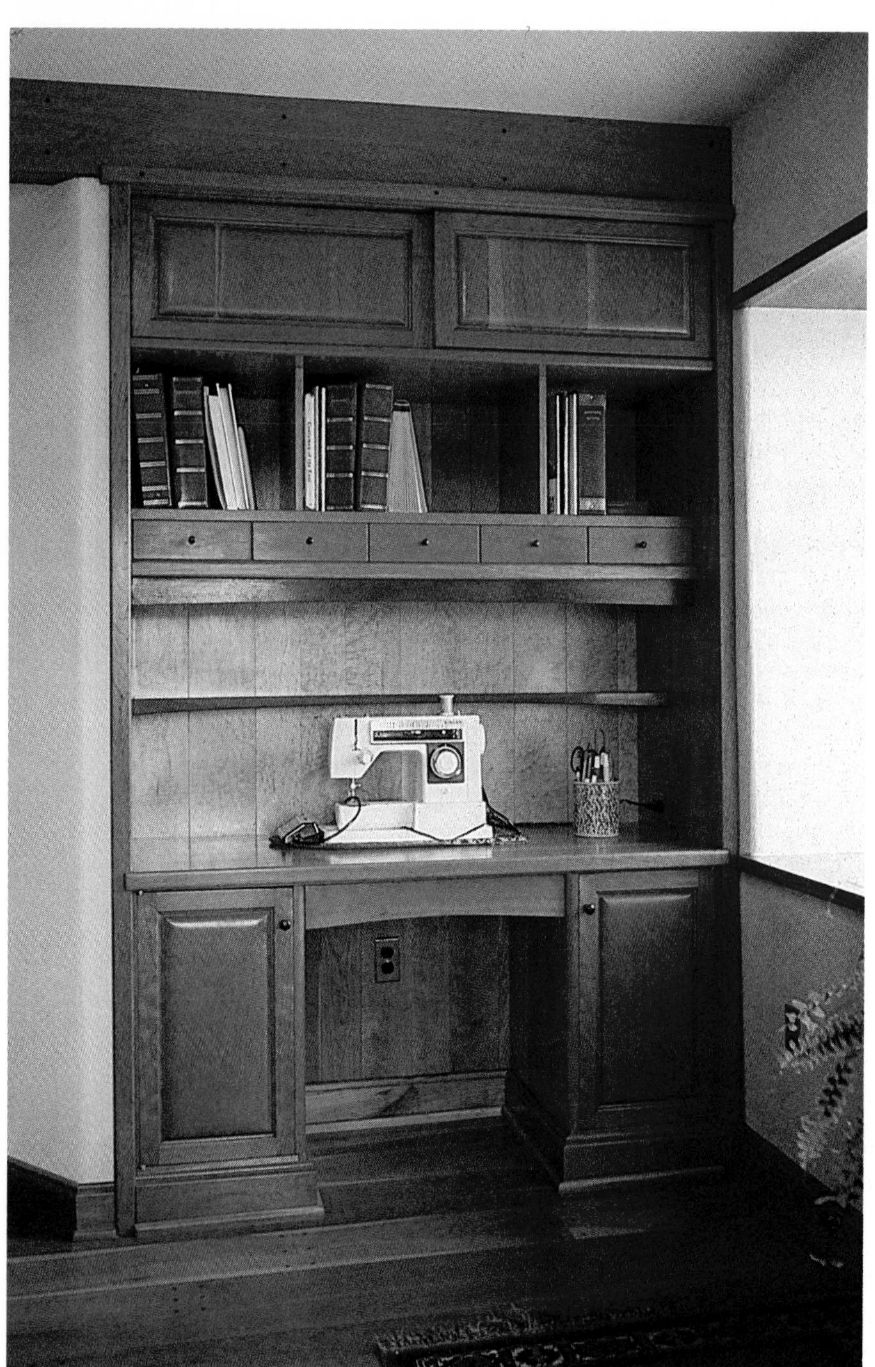

A few miles from the Bucks County woodworking studio where brothers Ellis and Craig Walentine work, there is a house whose renovation exemplifies the high level of design and craftsmanship favored locally. For Ellis, the house became the ideal commission, an opportunity to exercise design control over all the interior architectural work. For almost two years he worked at transforming its hollowed-out interior for a client who wanted all the accoutrements of the good life and wanted them beautifully handcrafted and finished.

Ellis designed the built-in, solid cherry sewing cabinet in the upstairs hallway to quietly echo other parts of the house. He specified frame-and-panel construction for the cabinet doors, just as he did for passage doors throughout the house. The double-stepped roundover detail on the frames also appears on all the baseboards, including the baseboard that wraps around the bottom of the cabinet. The panels, all so softly rounded that they go by the name of pillow panels, also appear prominently in the 6-foot-wide pocket door right beside the cabinet.

The cabinet is 87 inches high, 55 inches wide, and 24 inches deep. Because of its size, Ellis designed it in modules that would fit up the stairs. Each base pedestal is a module, the desktop is another, and the top half is a fourth.

Ellis used American black cherry in the cabinet and in the house as a whole (10,000 board feet of it altogether!), with other woods for contrast. "Cherry is a laid-back wood," he says. "It doesn't have a lot of character of its own and so I've punctuated it with rosewood, ebony, and African padauk."

The punctuation is more on the order of periods than exclamation points. For example, all the floors, some of the room paneling, and the sewing cabinet have screws that are plugged in a contrasting wood—evidence of the influence of architects Greene and Greene, who handcrafted many of the interior details of the bungalows they popularized in California at the turn of the century. The sewing cabinet is further embellished with knobs and a tapered shelf of padauk and is partly backed with curly bird's-eye maple.

The knobs and padauk shelf are, in fact, the only elements of the cabinet design that Ellis actually made. So extensive was the work involved in designing and constructing an interior of this size and standard that Ellis augmented his team of two woodworkers with several others, including Michael Gorchov, who built the sewing cabinet.

"Ellis took a leap of faith, asking me to build this cabinet," admits Michael, who was at the time of the commission a woodworker with only three years experience. Still, Michael is a meticulous craftsman with standards so high some would call them old-fashioned. He works with great care, taking particular pleasure in hand planing wood to perfect smoothness and hand cutting joints of great intricacy.

Michael, who also designs furniture, did not mind working from another craftsman's drawings and constructing a piece that was part of the interior architecture of a house. He saw the work as an opportunity to do what he enjoys most.

With Ellis's drawing in hand and a shop full of cherry to contend with, he set to work. He began with rough-sawn boards in several thicknesses: 4/4 for the most part, but also 5/4, 6/4 and 8/4. He milled the wood to the proper thicknesses, glued up solid wood slabs for case sides, shelves and panels, then planed and sanded the lumber.

To glue up the panels he used yellow glue. To cope with the problem of shifting boards, he inserted dowels ⅛ inch in diameter and 1 inch in length into holes ⅝ inch deep (long enough to allow for glue and breathing space), made with a horizontal boring machine. Choosing to emphasize that the boards were glued up, he chamfered the edges of each with a router fitted with a V-groove bit. All 11 cabinet panels have these articulated joints.

To smooth the glued-up boards he used a sequence of bench planes. First he worked diagonally with a 14-inch jack plane. Then he worked with a 25-inch jointer plane, first diagonally, then with the grain. Finally he used

The sewing cabinet's details reflect excellence of craftsmanship more than emphasis on design. Solid wood construction, harmoniously matched elements, and tightly fitted joints highlight the piece. The kneewell, left, *and the drawerbacks,* right, *are as well-fitted and -finished as the completely exposed surfaces.*

a 9-inch smoothing plane. Preparing the wood by hand was a long and exhausting task. In the "If I knew then . . ." department, he now sees that he could have saved himself weeks of work by having it milled at a good cabinet shop.

With that lesson belatedly learned, he then equipped himself with a true timesaver: a storypole. Working from Ellis's scale drawing, he marked off all the points where horizontal elements met the vertical on a 2-inch-wide strip of plywood cut to the height of the cabinet. He made marks with a try square for each door, drawer and shelf and then notched them with a knife. Then he used the storypole to transfer the cutting lengths of all the pieces without having to measure them.

Michael carefully considered how to place the boards so that grain direction would contribute to the dimensional stability of the finished piece. He knew the cabinet would expand and contract considerably with the seasons, as well as move with the house. To allow for this movement, he built the cabinet so that the grain moves around it in a big circle, just as it moves around each drawer in a smaller circle.

Since it was left to Michael to decide which board went where, he used the opportunity to display a little virtuoso showmanship. He decided to cut all the small drawer fronts out of a single board so that the grain would flow from one to another without interruption. One goof with the drawers would have sent the whole project back to square one, but he managed it without a hitch.

The grain of the drawer between the pedestals echoes the curve along the bottom edge of the drawer front. On the padauk shelf, too, which tapers in width and thickness from the ends to the center, the grain at the front of the shelf arches upward so that the shelf does not look like it is sagging.

The drawers involved a great deal of handwork, and Michael is particularly proud of them. He rabbeted the back of each drawer front to create a lip. He then hand-cut lap (or half-blind) dovetails to join the sides of each drawer to the front, and cut through dovetails to join the sides of each drawer to the back. He cut the dovetails in a 8:1 ratio (making the angle of the pins as narrow as he could) to make them beautiful. He cut more pins than most craftsmen would, to make the joints stronger.

Each drawer has a solid wood bottom that slides in a groove. Drawers have ½-inch-

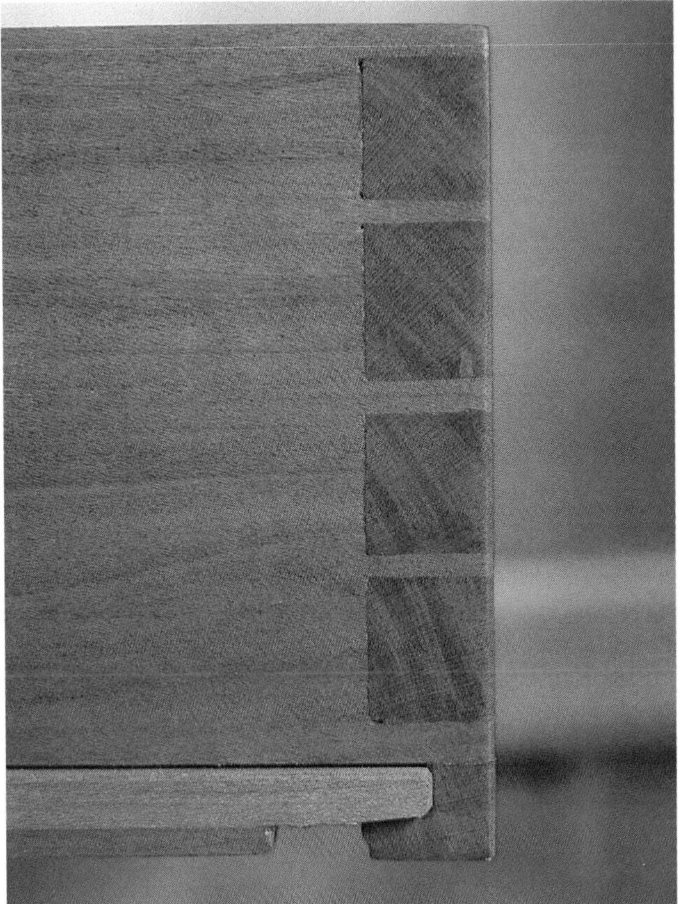

thick backs and sides, and ⅜-inch bottoms. The drawers are each $1/32$ inch narrower in the front than in the back—a tiny nuance that makes them travel in and out better. The tops of the drawer sides are sloped toward the back with a plane and each back is shorter than the front. The large desk drawer is side-hung, gliding on rosewood runners, which are dimensionally stable and long wearing. The small drawers are each made to fit their own space to tolerances of $1/32$ inch and slide perfectly without any hardware.

Michael cut the dividers between the drawers so their grain runs vertically for dimensional stability. After he checked them for fit, he cut grooves in their top and bottom edges, stopping them ⅝ inch short of the front edges. Then he cut matching grooves in the shelves above and below the drawers. After positioning the dividers, he slid ¼-inch-thick splines into the grooves from the rear.

Michael made all the cabinet doors with frame-and-panel construction. He dressed the stiles and rails to be 2 inches wide and 1⅛ inches thick, cut integral molding on them with a router fitted with a rounding-off bit, and grooved them to receive the panels. He chiseled mortises in the stiles and shaped haunched tenons on the rails. After he had cut rabbets all around the inside edges of the ¾-inch-thick panels, he raised the panels with a molding head fixed on his table saw. Then he assembled the frames, floating the raised panels in the grooves, so that their gentle curves would be visible on the face, and their level surfaces flush with the frames on the interior. Finally, he used a router to round off the outer edges of the doors.

Knife hinges engage the doors on the bottom pedestals at top and bottom so they do not show. A removable shelf inside each pedestal base is recessed to avoid the deep pockets that hinder accessibility. The sewing machine can be stored inside either pedestal. Each shelf rests on pieces of dowel projecting from holes drilled into the cabinet sides. To align the holes on either inner side of the pedestal so that the shelves can be moved, Michael drilled holes into a piece of Masonite cut to the same dimensions as a side of the pedestal and used it as a template.

The cabinet is in two separate cases. Everything from the drawers on up is part of the top case. Everything below the drawers is part

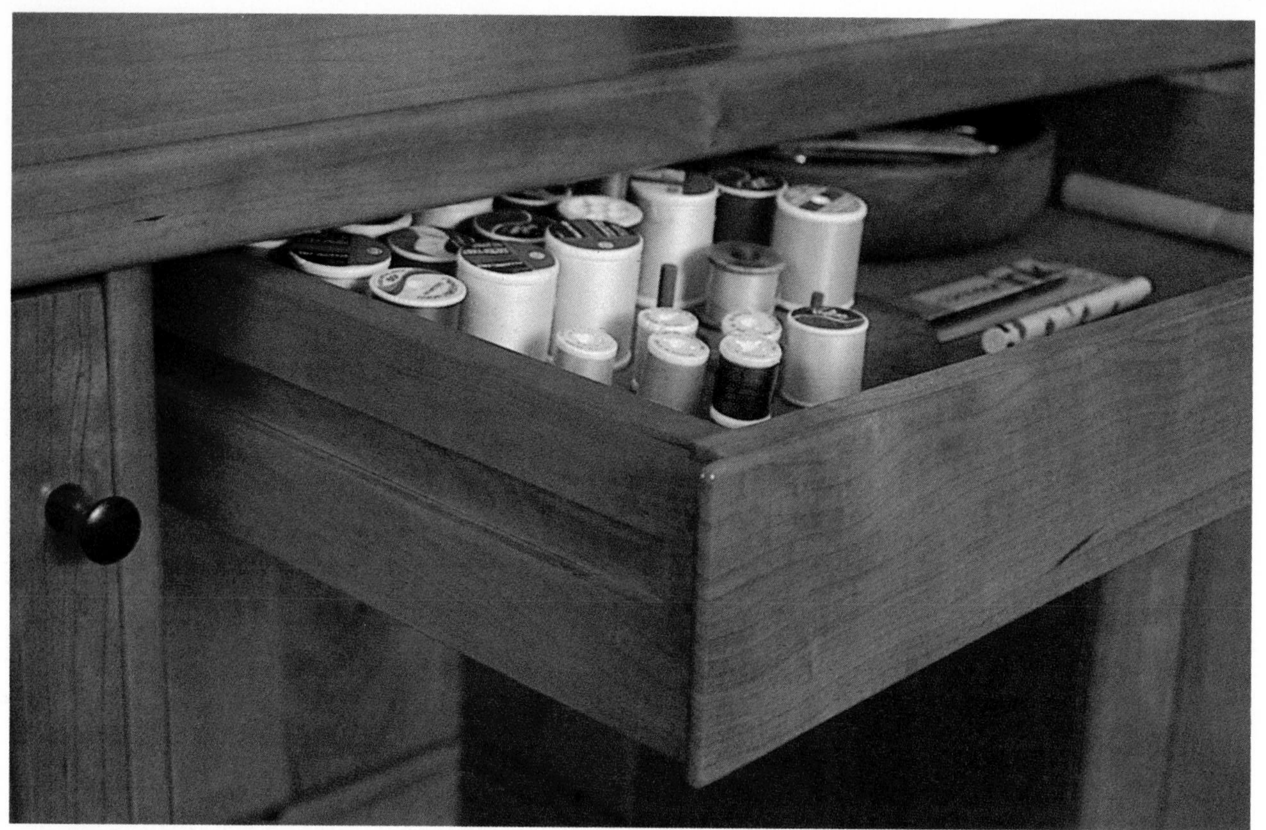

Solid wood construction is used exclusively, so good workmanship was essential. The drawers, above, *glide not on nylon wheels, but on wooden runners. The doors,* right, *do pivot on metal hinges. But given the relative instability of wood, great care was needed to find that perfect balance between snug fit and easy operation.*

of the bottom case. In both cases, all the horizontal shelving members are fitted into full dadoes in the case sides and secured from the outside with screws. The back panels, cherry behind the top case and between the pedestals, and curly bird's-eye maple above the desk surface, were attached to the cases before installation.

Because a strip of bullnose molding runs along the front of the bottom of the top case, the top case had to go into the alcove first, elevated slightly, so that the bottom case could slide in under it. To accomplish this, Michael required a little help from his friends. Together they hoisted the top case in place and wedged it to secure it temporarily. Then they slid the bottom case into the alcove, removed the wedges, and lowered the top case over the bottom case.

Michael screwed the top and bottom cases to the walls in three places on each side. He screwed the panels in place at top and bottom. All screws are countersunk, counterbored and covered with ebony plugs.

The final addition was Ellis's padauk shelf, left for last so he could best decide its optimal position. He grooved it on three sides and slid it into position on cleats of wood that he had screwed to the sides and back of the cabinet.

A good deal of the pleasure in all this hard work came from the use of well-made hand tools. Michael cut all those many dovetails with a Japanese dovetail saw, called a Dozuki saw. Japanese tools, though newly appreciated in America, have an ancient and honored place in woodworking. Both craftsmen are enthusiastic about them.

To understand the virtue of a Japanese saw, Ellis suggests imagining a blade of grass held between your fingers. You can push it only with difficulty because it is so thin, but you can pull it easily. Japanese saws, in deference to this principle, cut on the pull stroke. They can therefore be made of much thinner steel than Western saws, which cut on the push stroke.

Ellis also has high praise for Japanese chisels. American chisels take many hours to turn into equivalent first-rate tools, including removing the milling machine marks from the flat side.

Michael and Ellis order Japanese tools from *Woodline, The Japan Woodworker,* and the *Hida* catalog. The latter carries tools made in small quantities and imported into this country by Makoto Imai, a Master Temple carpenter, in San Rafael, California, and by Robert Meadow, a luthier working in Saugerties, New York. "Half a woodworker's work is finding sources," Michael notes.

The other half, many craftsmen jest, may well be finishing. Michael finished the inside of the cabinet before the outside. He did not oil the insides of the drawers, anticipating they might smell like tung oil in summer. Instead, he mixed one-third of a pint of 3-pound cut shellac with 3 pints of alcohol. He let the mixture sit for two days, poured off the clear, amber liquid and discarded the bottom residue. Then he added an equal quantity of denatured alcohol to the amber liquid. He used a rag to apply five coats of this mixture to the cabinet surface. Each coat took five minutes to

dry. Finally, he sanded the surfaces with 280-grit paper.

Michael began sanding the outside of the cabinet with garnet paper in his orbital sander and finished by hand to remove swirls left by the sander. He held the sandpaper under his middle three fingers, gripping it in place between pinky and thumb.

Michael then applied three coats of Waterlox "transparent," which contains tung oil, sanding lightly between each coat with 220- and 280-grit Carborundum Dri-lube Paper (striated blue and white silicon carbide paper). For hand rubbing, after the third coat, he used 4/0 steel wool. The cabinet now has the kind of luster that only a great deal of hand rubbing can achieve.

Michael spent two months building the cabinet to the exacting standards he and Ellis believe in. It all seems like serious hard work, and it was. But, as Michael explains, he tries to do the best job he can so that, simply enough, he will get the chance to do it again. It's that rewarding.

MARILYN HODGES

Mike and Dianne Radcliffe

BEDROOM STORAGE WALL

Mike Radcliffe quit teaching school to apprentice with a cabinetmaker, but he couldn't find a cabinetmaker who needed an apprentice, so he ended up designing jewelry. His interest in woodworking did not die, however. Eventually it led him and his wife Dianne to build a house on one of British Columbia's Gulf Islands.

The bedroom reflects their intention to keep the house as simple and uncluttered as possible. The Radcliffes didn't want to spend their lives moving heavy objects just to dust under them, so they built a cantilevered bed that hovers a foot above the floor. And rather than litter the bedroom with dressers and night tables, they provided for a variety of storage needs by building cupboards and closets into the cedar wall behind the bed. The result is a highly functional room that requires little maintenance.

The storage wall makes use of the crawl space under the eaves

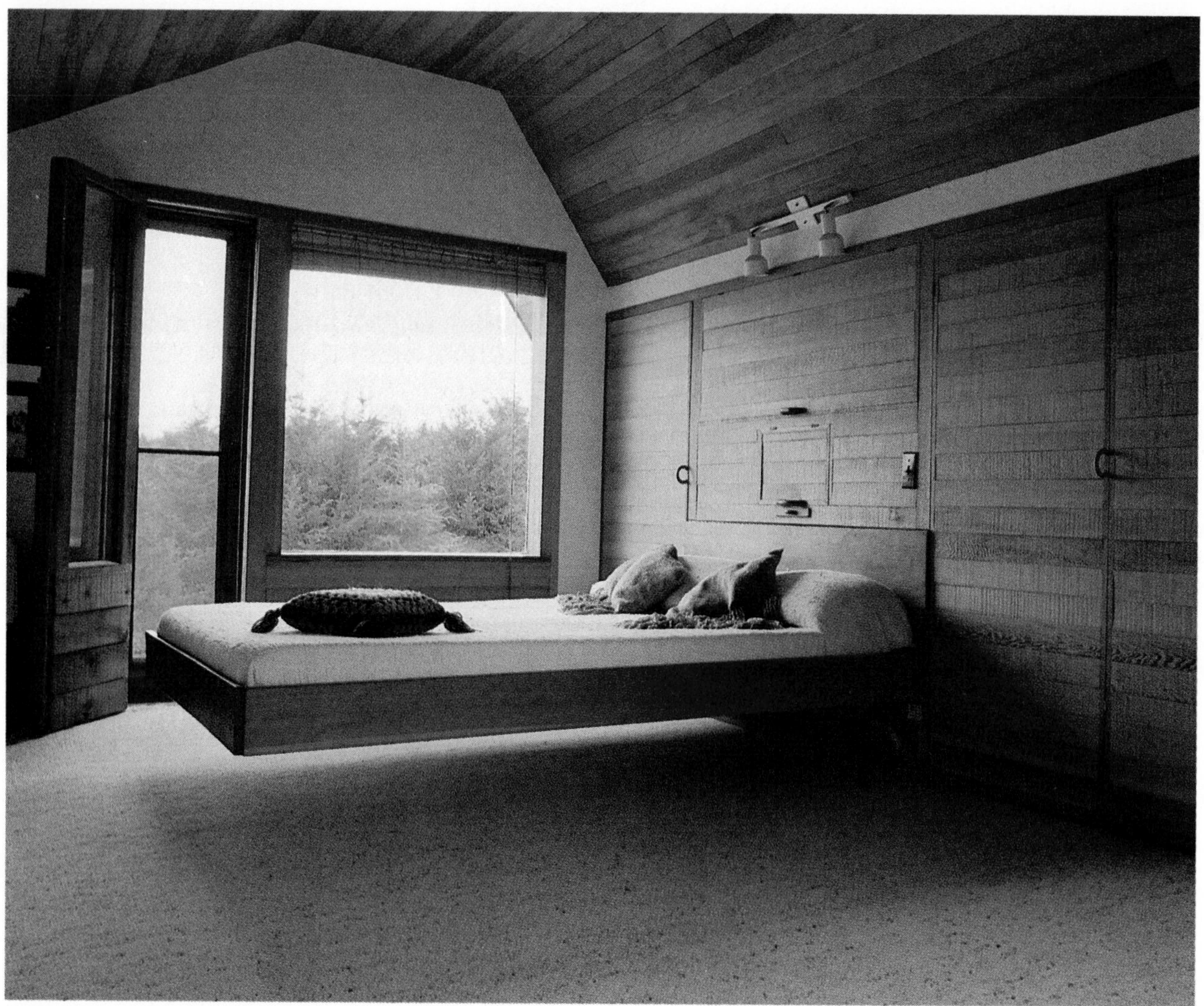

of the steep roof. The cabinets to the right of the bed hold shelves and hangers for clothes. Above the bed are three handles. The uppermost pulls up the top-hinged door of a quilt cupboard. The space within is triangular in section because of the roof line, but there's room for a plump eiderdown. The quilt cupboard door runs the width of the bed and is about 2 feet high. Beneath this is another top-hinged cupboard that holds a clock, books, and other items that would otherwise collect dust on a night table. Pull the maple half-ring handle just above the headboard and a little cedar shelf slides out of its snug pocket. It's a foot deep, half that wide, and holds drinks and snacks while the Radcliffes read or watch television.

Nowhere are there drawers, you'll notice. That's because drawers take longer to make than cabinets and shelves. As elsewhere in this house, Mike chose an efficient alternative to save time. He and Dianne do not consider the house their life's work.

The Radcliffes designed and built the story-and-a-half, stud-frame house themselves. It measures just 24 feet square and is sheathed with western red cedar 1 × 4s. Inside, they also nailed cedar to the studs for ceilings and storage walls. The wood was suited to their needs because it is both visually striking and inexpensive. "I think we got the whole 4,000 board feet of cedar mill ends for around $150," recalls Mike. These were tongue-and-groove boards that had left the planer with flaws on the finished side. The Radcliffes used the boards rough side out, still bearing the marks of resawing. In recent years the rough look has become fashionable. "West Coast Contemporary is the rage in B.C.," says Mike, "and they use that wood everywhere." In fact, the look is now intentionally approximated by an expensive textured plywood.

The mill ends have a highly variable color, running from nearly white to nearly black. The Radcliffes wanted to avoid placing contrasting cedar boards side by side because this zebra effect would have been out of keeping with the couple's less-is-more aesthetic. "It might have looked artsy, but it would have been extremely busy," says Mike. (He has unkind words for woodworkers who use riotous combinations of planking patterns, grain, and color under the guise of "the natural look.") Dianne spent days sorting the boards by color.

Originally the Radcliffes nailed an unbroken expanse of cedar to the studs and rafters, from floor to ceiling, but they found this oppressive, "like living inside a rolltop desk." They remedied the problem simply by replacing a few courses of cedar with a strip of white drywall where wall meets ceiling. "As we finished it took some juggling to find exactly where those visual lines should be," Mike recalls. The white strip now seems to both stretch the bedroom and elevate the roof.

The Radcliffes used a radial arm saw to cut the cedar paneling because that's the saw they used to frame and sheathe the house. They found that the saw was accurate enough for finish work if kept properly adjusted.

Mike used a router to trim the cedar wall at both ends of the room, then nailed a ¾-inch-square strip of cedar into the resulting reveal. He dispensed with more elaborate molding in the interests of time and simplicity of line.

Mike made the closet and cupboard doors out of tongue-and-groove mill ends. He cut the tongue off the top board, fitted the boards together horizontally without glue or nails, and then clamped them from top and bottom. He kept the boards in place with stiles at either end. (Mike intentionally picked darker tongue-and-groove stock for the stiles in order to define the doors in the great expanse of lighter wood.) He ripped the stiles down to a width of 1½ inches and glued and nailed them on the door edges with the wide dimension perpendicular to the door face. He used 6d finishing nails for a firm anchor in the endgrain of the horizontal boards and made sure the stiles stayed put by clamping them until the glue dried.

The result is a sturdy door that was quick and easy to fabricate. Mike has heard of others who back tongue-and-groove doors with plywood for strength, but he believes this is unnecessary.

Mike hung some cabinet doors with customized hinges. Starting with an ordinary padlock hasp, he bent the leaf that fits over the staple at right angles, drilled screwholes in it, and mounted it on a concealed vertical support so that the barrel would project out. This allows the door to swing in a far greater arc than if the barrels were directly on the support. He hung the other flush doors with conventional cabinet hinges.

Mike made cupboard handles from old 3½-inch curtain rings of blond maple. He sawed off a section to provide a flat surface for installation. He cut the D-shaped closet handles out of cedar with a coping saw. He screwed on both kinds of handles from the backs of the doors.

The cedar is treated with one coat of regional brand wax-type finish. "You paint it on and it doesn't appear to make any change at all," Mike says. "If you rub your finger on

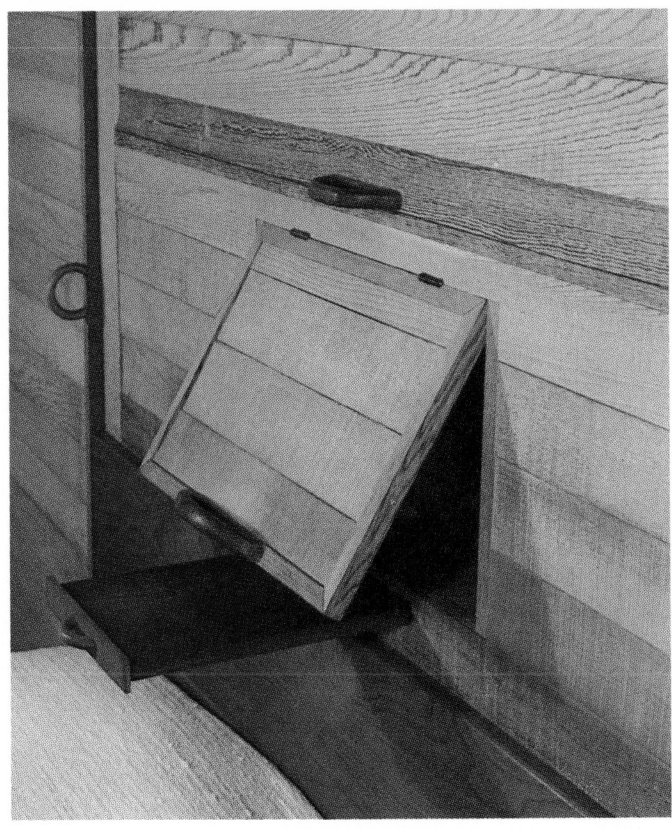

The Radcliffes' bedroom is remarkably free of clutter, thanks to the huge storage area beneath the eaves, which flank the room. Behind a battery of vertical and horizontal doors—drawers are too difficult to make, so there are none—are storage bins, shelves, and closets. Above the bed is a quilt cupboard, far left, *hiding a bulky eiderdown, and a similar bin for a clock, books and other commonplace bedside items, even a pull-out shelf for bedtime snacks,* left. *There's nothing to clutter the room or gather dust.*

it, you get a waxy feel like you would from a piece of teak. The finish doesn't have a sheen, but stops the wood from darkening. That's important—otherwise, the cedar will go black when exposed to light, in 10 or 15 years."

Mike installed ½-inch plywood shelves in some of the cupboards and closets, and hanger rods (cut from lengths of galvanized-steel electrical conduit) in others. To support the shelves, he screwed ¾-inch cedar cleats into the framing behind the drywall. All the shelves are faced with strips of cedar ripped from mill ends.

Of course the most striking feature of the room is not the storage wall but the floating bed. In working out its design, Mike kept to ordinary materials and methods. The mattress rests on a cantilevered platform of kiln-dried, clear spruce 2 × 3s. These pass through the wall and extend another 5 feet or so and are firmly anchored to rafters. The platform rests on a little 1-foot-high stud wall of it own, which is flush with the room wall and ties into floor-to-ceiling studs on either side of the bed. (Downstairs, the focal point of the living room is a fireplace with a cantilevered hearth of slate.)

The platform can be thought of as a laminated grid of 2 × 3s, run on edge and 2 inches apart. Between each of the boards are 6-inch-long spacers, placed every 2 feet or so. Because he thought nails would weaken the platform, Mike glued and clamped the whole grid. The spruce was surfaced smooth enough for gluing just as it came from the lumberyard and needed no further attention.

Concealing the grid of 2 × 3s and containing the mattress is a box frame of smooth cedar 1 × 6s glued to the edge of the grid. The sides and foot of the frame are simply butted and held together with angle brackets. The sides overlap the foot a bit in an effect

The storage wall doors blend into the room. Cedar boards—the same as those paneling the room—were lined up and secured together with stiles glued and nailed to their butt ends. The approach is clean, simple and functional.

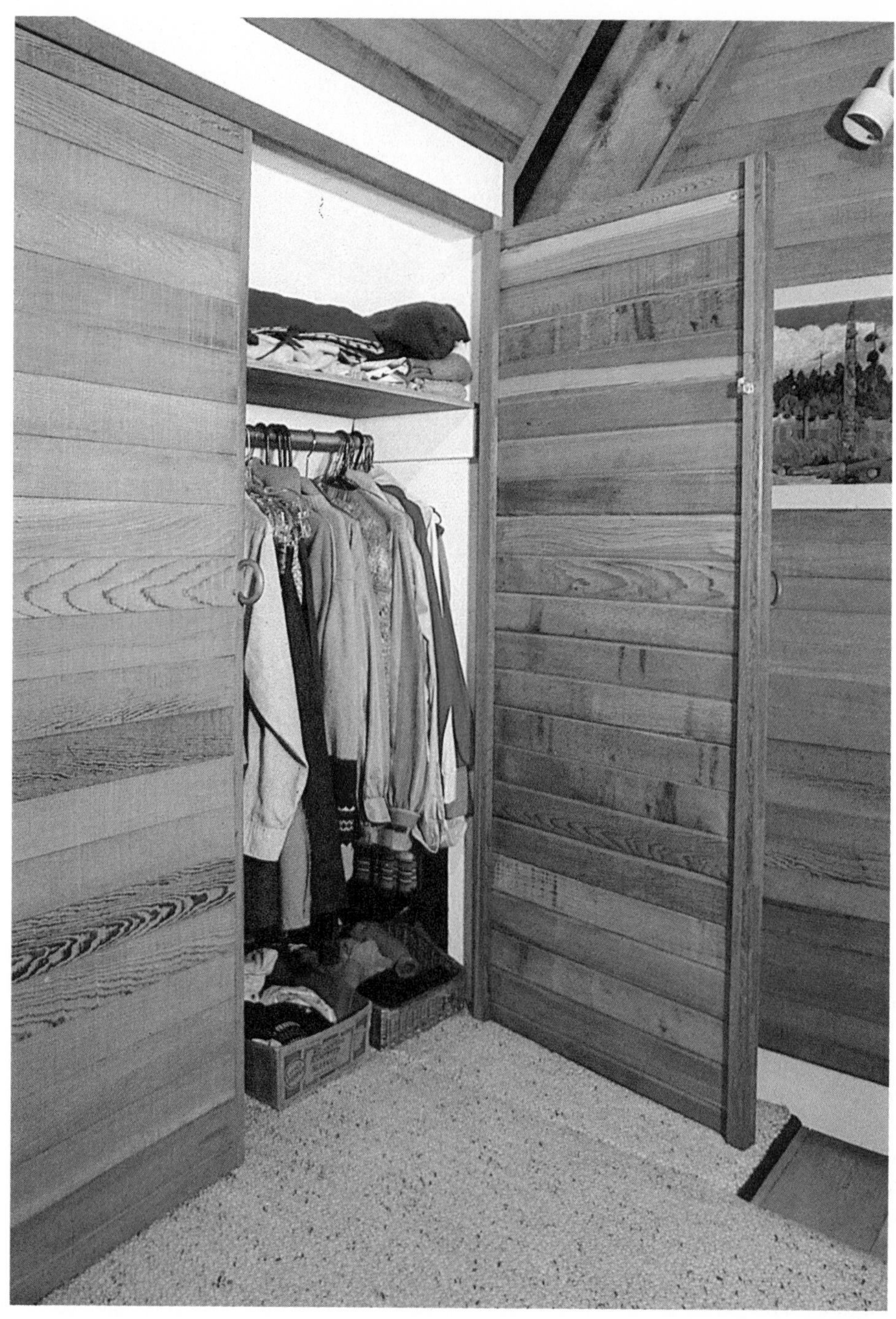

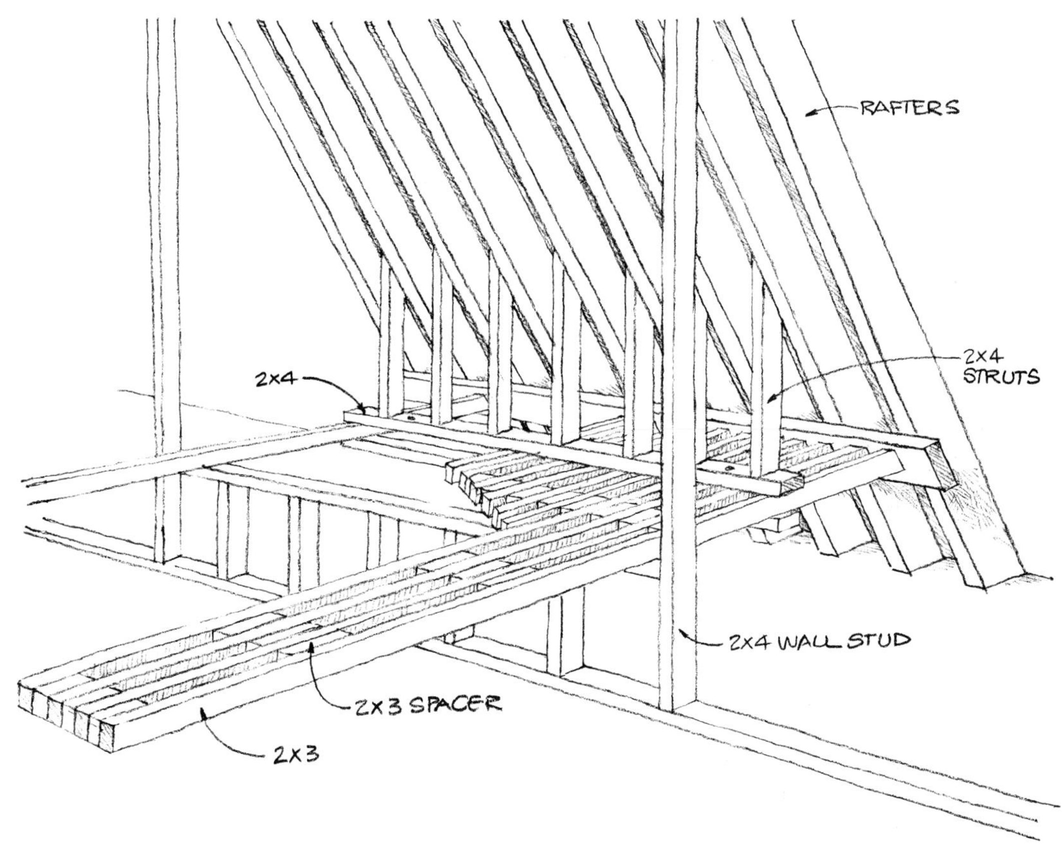

Cutaway view of the cantilevered bed's framing. The bed platform is constructed of full-length 2 × 3s alternated with 6-inch 2 × 3 spacers. The platform rests on a foot-high section of the storage-wall framing and is butted against the rafters. Struts extending from the rafters to the platform anchor it in place.

reminiscent—to Mike at least—of Japanese joinery. The Radcliffes finished the frame with Watco Danish floor oil, as they did the home's windowsills and oak floors.

The bed is both flexible and strong. "It'll drop 3 or 4 inches if two people sit at the foot end," Mike has found. "But when you lie down in the bed it doesn't move at all because the weight is distributed more toward the middle."

This house is the work of two jewelry designers, and you might expect it would reflect the thought that goes into their work each day. Was there indeed a carryover?

"Yes," answers Mike without pause. "Simplicity. Simplicity of design, and my wife's sense of proportion and scale. Without that sense, anything you make is apt to be awkward." Handcrafted projects are no exception, he adds. That a closet or cabinet is made by hand isn't a guarantee of success.

Roger B. Yepsen, Jr.

APPENDICES

There are several resources you need to make your own shelves and cabinets — tools, materials, technical information and inspiration. Using the resources listed in these appendices, you should be able to take your project from planning stages through completion.

You may already have the tools and materials you want to use in your workshop, or you may want to seek out those that are more unusual. The manufacturers and suppliers listed below will be able to provide you with both standard and special items.

Under "Tools," you will find manufacturers of some of the most popular brand name hand and power tools, as well as mail-order companies that will ship anything from a try square to a table saw right to your door. The list of "Materials" suppliers gives you access to fine hardwoods from all over the world, as well as veneer and inlay, wood moldings and decorative medallions, paints, stains and finishes, and hardware manufactured specifically for shelves, chests of drawers and cabinets.

If you would like to browse through some design books or read more about particular construction techniques, you'll find the books and magazines listed here helpful reference works.

If you have no ambitions to try to make your own shelves and cabinets, but admire the sure-handed touch and imagination of the craftsmen whose work is pictured on the pages of this book, you might want to commission a craftsman to build some shelves or cabinets for you. Locate a craftsman near you by referring to the list of "Makers of Handcrafted Shelves and Cabinets," or make your selection on the basis of work photographed for this book by referring to the "Photo and Design Credits." Although some craftsmen are unknown, most are named and are willing to receive queries about commissions at their studio or home address.

TOOLS

Chances are that many woodworkers, when asked where they found their favorite hand tool, will tell you about the good buys they made at a country auction or farmer's market. As for power tools and floor equipment, they may cite a mail-order catalog as their source.

Of course, if you want specialty tools or particular brands of tools, you may have to look farther afield. Contact the manufacturer for the name of the distributor nearest you. If the distributor is hundreds of miles away, the manufacturer may be willing to sell and ship his products directly to you.

Another alternative is to order through a mail-order company. The companies listed generally offer a choice of brand names. In addition, they may also retail their own brand.

Their catalogs are "wish books" for woodworkers. Not only do they advertise quality hand and power tools, but they frequently also offer veneer and inlay, finishing supplies, and hardware. A few mail-order companies charge for their catalog, but they invest so much time in assembling tips on proper woodworking techniques to accompany their advertisements that most woodworkers find the catalog very worthwhile.

Black & Decker Mfg. Co.
Towson, MD 21204

Brookstone Co.
126 Vose Farm Rd.
Peterborough, NH 03458
(mail order)

Albert Constantine & Son, Inc.
2050 Eastchester Rd.
Bronx, NY 10461
(mail order)

Craftsman Wood Service Co.
1735 W. Cortland Ct.
Addison, IL 60608

The Cutting Edge
3871 Grand View Blvd.
West Los Angeles, CA 90066
(mail order)

Frog Tool Co., Ltd.
700 W. Jackson Blvd.
Chicago, IL 60606
(mail order)

Garrett Wade
161 Ave. of the Americas
New York, NY 10013
(mail order)

The Japan Woodworker
1004 Central Ave.
Alameda, CA 94501
(mail order)

Lee Valley Tools, Ltd.
P.O. Box 6295
Station J
Ottawa, ON K2A 1T4
Canada
(mail order)

Skil Corp.
5033 N. Elston Ave.
Chicago, IL 60630

Stanley Tools Ltd.
600 Myrtle St.
New Britain, CT 06050

Universal Clamp Corp.
6905 Cedars Ave.
Van Nuys, CA 91450
(mail order)

Woodcraft Supply Corp.
313 Montvale Ave.
Woburn, MA 01801
(mail order)

The Woodworkers' Store
21801 Industrial Blvd.
Rogers, MN 55374
(mail order)

MATERIALS

Native and Exotic Woods

Although your local lumber supplier may not be able to sell you purple heart or padauk, the companies listed below retail hardwoods from all over the United States and the world. You may want to visit one near you to see just what woods they have available and to hand select the wood you want to work, or you may be content to have them ship you your order sight unseen. If you do the latter, inquire about the possibility of a minimum order.

Maurice L. Condon, Inc.
250 Ferres Ave.
White Plains, NY 10603

Croy Marietta Hardwoods
P.O. Box 643
121 Pike St.
Marietta, OH 45750

General Woodcraft
100 Blinman St.
New London, CT 06320

Hallelujah Redwood Products
P.O. Box 669
Mendocino, CA 95460

Leonard Lumber Co.
P.O. Box 2396
Branford, CT 06405

Mountain Lumber Co.
P.O. Box 285
1327 Carlton Ave.
Charlottesville, VA 22902

The Sawmill
The C. F. Martin Co., Inc.
P.O. Box 329
Nazareth, PA 18064

Sterling Hardwoods, Inc.
412 Pine St.
Burlington, VT 05401

TECH Plywood & Hardwood Lumber Co.
110 Webb St.
Hamden, CT 06511

Unicorn Universal Woods, Ltd.
137 John St.
Toronto, ON M5V 2E4
Canada

Weird Wood
Box 190 FW
Chester, VT 05143

Willard Bros. Woodcutters
300 Basin Rd.
Trenton, NJ 08619

Wood Shed
1807 Elmwood Ave.
Buffalo, NY 14207

Wood World
1719 Chestnut
Glenview, IL 60025

Veneer and Inlay

All the suppliers listed below will ship veneer to you directly, as will some of the mail-order companies listed under "Tools" (especially Albert Constantine & Son, Inc. and The Woodworkers' Store).

However, it is in your best interest to inspect the veneer flitch if you possibly can so that you can make sure the figure of the wood is pleasing to you, and the veneer sheets will make a good match.

J. H. Monteath sells veneer skins, which are thicker and more stable than veneer sheets because they are two-ply. Most people find them easier to apply than veneer sheets.

Homecraft Veneer
901 West Way
Latrobe, PA 15650

J. H. Monteath Co.
2500 Park Ave.
Bronx, NY 10451

Bob Morgan Woodworking Supplies
1123 Bardstown Rd.
Louisville, KY 40204

Wood Moldings and Decorative Medallions

To obtain the look of hand-carved moldings and wood ornaments, you can do the knife work yourself or contact one of the mail-order suppliers listed below.

Cumberland Woodcraft Co., Inc.
2500 Walnut Bottom Rd.
Carlisle, PA 17013

Driwood Mouldings Co.
P.O. Box 1729
Florence, SC 29503

Focal Point, Inc.
2005 Marietta Rd. NW
Atlanta, GA 30318
(mail order)

Fypon, Inc.
P.O. Box 365
Stewartstown, PA 17363

Klise Mfg. Co.
601 Maryland Ave. NE
Grand Rapids, MI 49505

Old World Mouldings & Finishings Co., Inc.
115 Allen Blvd.
Farmingdale, NY 11735

Paint, Stains and Finishes

Most hardware stores carry the brand name products of the manufacturers listed below. Building materials suppliers and paint stores also make some of them available. If an easy tour of your town doesn't reveal the product you want tucked away on some store shelves, contact the manufacturer directly for the name of the nearest distributor.

Samuel Cabot, Inc.
1 Union St.
Boston, MA 02108

Daly's Woodfinishing Products
1121 N. 36th St.
Seattle, WA 98103

Deft, Inc.
17451 Von Karmen Ave.
Irvine, CA 92714

The Flecto Co., Inc.
Flecto International, Ltd.
1000-02 45th St.
Oakland, CA 94608

Formby's, Inc.
P.O. Box 667
Olive Branch, MS 38654

Glidden Coatings & Resins
Div. of SCM Corp.
900 Union Commerce Bldg.
Cleveland, OH 44115

Hope Co., Inc.
2052 Congressional Dr.
St. Louis, MO 63141

McCloskey Varnish Co.
7600 State Rd.
Philadelphia, PA 19136

Minwax Co., Inc.
102 Chestnut Ridge Plaza
Montvale, NJ 07645

Benjamin Moore & Co.
Chestnut Ridge Rd.
Montvale, NJ 07645

Watco Dennis Corp.
1756 22nd St.
Santa Monica, CA 90404

Manufactured Hardware for Shelves, Chests of Drawers and Cabinets

The manufacturers listed below distribute shelf, drawer and door hardware to hardware stores. The mail-order companies retail the products of several manufacturers.

Of particular interest to cabinetmakers, Knape & Vogt make several styles of drawer runners. Grass America, Inc. and Hafele America, Inc. make the German hinges so popular with craftsmen who build custom kitchens.

Amerock Corp.
Rockford, IL 61101

Ball & Ball
463 W. Lincoln Hwy.
Exton, PA 19341
(mail order)

Grass America, Inc.
P.O. Box 1019
1377 South Park Dr.
Kernersville, NC 27284

Hafele America, Inc.
P.O. Box 1590
High Point, NC 27261

Knape & Vogt Manufacturing Co.
2700 Oak Industrial Dr. NE
Grand Rapids, MI 49505

McKinney Forged Iron Hardware
820 Davis St.
Scranton, PA 18505

Omnia Industries, Inc.
P.O. Box 263
49 Park St.
Montclair, NJ 07042

Renovator's Supply Co., Inc.
135 Northfield Rd.
Millers Falls, MA 01349
(mail order)

Ritter & Son Hardware
46901 Fish Rock Rd.
Gualala, CA 95445
(mail order)

Selby Furniture Hardware Co., Inc.
17 E. 22nd St.
New York, NY 10010
(mail order)

Stanley Hardware
Division of the Stanley Works
New Britain, CT 06050

Glass and Glassworking Materials

Should you choose to make stained glass panels for your cabinet doors, you will require glass and a glass cutter, lead came, flux and a soldering gun and possibly other tools and materials to carry out your project. The companies listed below will sell and ship stock items directly to the customer.

S. A. Bendheim Co., Inc.
122 Hudson St.
New York, NY 10013

Boulder Art Glass Co., Inc.
1920 Arapahoe Ave.
Boulder, CO 80302

Delphi Stained Glass
2116 E. Michigan Ave.
Lansing, MI 48912

Franklin Art Glass Studios, Inc.
222 E. Sycamore St.
Columbus, OH 43206

Jennifer's Glassworks, Inc.
1200 Foster
P.O. Box 20447
Atlanta, GA 30325

C. R. Laurence Co., Inc.
P.O. Box 21345
Los Angeles, CA 90021

Occidental Art Glass
410 Occidental St.
Seattle, WA 98104

Whittemore-Durgin Glass Co.
P.O. Box 2065
Hanover, MA 02339

READING RESOURCES

Books

Adams, Jeanette T. *Arco's New Complete Woodworking Handbook,* rev. ed. New York: Arco Publishing Co., 1978.

Adding Storage Space. Los Angeles: Peterson Publishing Co., 1978.

Bealer, Alex W. *The Tools That Built America.* New York: Bonanza Books, 1976.

Better Homes and Gardens New Decorating Book. Des Moines, Iowa: Meredith Corp., 1981.

Boericke, Art, and Shapiro, Barry. *Handmade Houses: A Guide to the Woodbutcher's Art.* San Francisco: Scrimshaw Press, 1973.

———. *The Craftsman Builder.* New York: Simon & Schuster, 1977.

Brann, Donald R. *How to Build Kitchen Cabinets, Room Dividers and Cabinet Furniture.* Briarcliff Manor, NY: Directions Simplified, 1974.

———. *How to Build Storage Units.* Briarcliff Manor, NY: Directions Simplified, 1973.

Built-Ins. Alexandria, Va.: Time-Life Books, 1979.

Burch, Monte. *The Home Cabinetmaker: Woodworking Techniques, Furniture Building, and Installing Millwork.* New York: Popular Science Books, 1981.

Conran, Terence. *The House Book.* New York: Crown, 1974.

Daniels, George, and Philbin, Tom, eds. *Black & Decker Power Tool Carpentry.* New York: Van Nostrand Reinhold Co., 1978.

Davidson, Marshall B. *The American Heritage History of Notable American Houses.* New York: American Heritage, 1971.

Dennis, Ben, and Case, Betsy. *Houseboat: Reflections of North America's Floating Homes . . . History, Architecture, and Lifestyles.* Seattle, Wash.: Smuggler's Cove, 1977.

Dittrick, Mark, and Dittrick, Diane Kender. *Decorative Hardware.* New York: Hearst Books, 1982.

Duncan, S. Blackwell. *The Complete Plywood Handbook.* Blue Ridge Summit, Pa.: TAB Books, 1981.

Feirer, J. L. *Cabinetmaking & Millwork,* rev. ed. New York: Charles Scribner's Sons, 1977.

Fine Woodworking Biennial Design Book. Newtown, Conn.: The Taunton Press, 1977.

Fine Woodworking Design Book Two. Newtown, Conn.: The Taunton Press, 1979.

Fine Woodworking Techniques, No. 1. Newtown, Conn.: The Taunton Press, 1978.

Fine Woodworking Techniques, No. 2. Newtown, Conn.: The Taunton Press, 1980.

Frank, George. *88 Rue de Charonne: Adventures in Wood Finishing.* Newtown, Conn.: The Taunton Press, 1981.

Frankel, Virginia. *The Incredible, Wonderful, Flexible World of Built-Ins.* New York: Charles Scribner's Sons, 1977.

French, Jennie. *Glass-Works: The Copper Foil Technique of Stained Glass.* London: Litton, 1974.

Frid, Tage. *Tage Frid Teaches Woodworking: Joinery.* Newton, Conn.: The Taunton Press, 1979.

———. *Tage Frid Teaches Woodworking: Shaping, Veneering, Finishing.* Newtown, Conn.: The Taunton Press, 1981.

Gault, Lila, and Weiss, Jeffrey. *Small Houses.* New York: Warner, 1980.

Geary, Don. *How to Build Kitchen Cabinets, Counters and Vanities.* Reston, Va.: Reston Publishing Co., 1979.

Gibbia, S. W. *Wood Finishing and Refinishing,* rev. ed. New York: Van Nostrand Reinhold Co., 1971.

Gick, James. *Creating with Stained Glass.* Laguna Hills, Calif.: Gick, 1976.

Hand, Jackson. *How to Do Your Own Wood Finishing.* New York: Popular Science/Harper & Row, 1976.

Haney, Robert, and Ballantine, David. *Woodstock Handmade Houses.* New York: Random House, 1974.

Hedden, Jay. *Successful Shelves & Built-ins.* Farmington, Mich.: Structures Publishing Co., 1979.

Hoadley, R. Bruce. *Understanding Wood: A Craftsman's Guide to Wood Technology.* Newtown, Conn.: The Taunton Press, 1980.

The Home Workshop. Alexandria, Va.: Time-Life Books, 1980.

Hylton, William H., ed. *Build Your Harvest Kitchen.* Emmaus, Pa.: Rodale Press, 1980.

Jackson, Albert, and Day, David. *Tools and How to Use Them: An Illustrated Encyclopedia.* New York: Alfred A. Knopf, 1978.

Jones, Peter. *Shelves, Closets and Cabinets.* New York: Van Nostrand Reinhold Co., 1977.

Joyce, Ernest. *The Encyclopedia of Furniture Making.* New York: Drake Publishers, 1978.

Kornblum, Mary. *Shelves, Closets & Cabinets: From A-Frames to Z-Outs.* New York: Van Nostrand Reinhold Co., 1977.

Krenov, James. *A Cabinetmaker's Notebook.* New York: Van Nostrand Reinhold Co., 1976.

———. *The Fine Art of Cabinetmaking.* New York: Van Nostrand Reinhold Co., 1977.

———. *The Impractical Cabinetmaker.* New York: Van Nostrand Reinhold Co., 1979.

Lidz, Jane. *Rolling Homes: Handmade Houses on Wheels.* New York: A & W Visual Library, 1979.

Lucie-Smith, Edward. *The Story of Craft: The Craftsman's Role in Society.* Ithaca, N.Y.: Cornell University Press, 1981.

McCarthy, Bridget Beattie. *Architectural Crafts: A Handbook and a Catalog.* Seattle, Wash.: Madrona Publishers, 1982. © Western States Art Foundation.

Mulligan, Charles, and Higgs, Jim. *The Wizard's Eye: Visions of American Resourcefulness.* San Francisco: Chronicle, 1978.

Nakashima, George. *The Soul of a Tree.* San Francisco: Kodansha International, 1981.

Pile, John F. *Design: Purpose, Form and Meaning.* Amherst, Mass.: University of Massachusetts Press, 1979.

Practical Wood Finishing Methods. Pittsburgh, Pa.: Rockwell International Tool Group, 1978.

Pye, David. *The Nature and Art of Workmanship.* New York: Cambridge University Press, 1968.

Rigan, Otto B. *New Glass.* Westminster, Md.: Ballantine, 1977.

Scharff, Robert. *Complete Book of Wood Finishing,* 2d ed. New York: McGraw-Hill Book Co., 1974.

Schoen, Elin. *The Closet Book.* New York: Harmony Books, 1982.

Scott, Ernest. *Working in Wood: The Illustrated Manual of Tools, Methods, Materials and Classic Constructions.* New York: G. P. Putnam's Sons, 1980.

Seike, Kiyosi. *The Art of Japanese Joinery.* New York: John Weatherhill, 1977.

Stamberg, Peter. *Build Your Own Furniture: 20 Designs.* New York: Ballantine Books, 1981.

Stevenson, Robert P. *How to Build and Buy Cabinets for the Modern Kitchen.* New York: Arco Publishing Co., 1974.

Wade, Alex. *A Design and Construction Handbook for Energy-Saving Houses.* Emmaus, Pa.: Rodale Press, 1980.

———. *Thirty Energy-Efficient Houses . . . You Can Build.* Emmaus, Pa.: Rodale Press, 1977.

Wampler, Jan. *All Their Own: People and the Places They Build.* New York: Oxford University Press, 1978.

Weills, Christopher. *The Goodfellow Catalog of Wonderful Things, Traditional & Contemporary Crafts.* New York: Paragon Books, 1977.

Weiss, Jeffrey, and Wise, Herbert H. *Good Lives.* New York: Quick Fox, 1977.

Wise, Herbert H. *Attention to Detail.* New York: Quick Fox, 1979.

———. *Rooms with a View.* New York: Quick Fox, 1978.

Wise, Herbert H., and Weiss, Jeffrey. *Living Places.* New York: Quick Fox, 1976.

———. *Made with Oak.* New York: Quick Fox, 1975.

Magazines

Fine Homebuilding
The Taunton Press, Inc.
52 Church Hill Rd.
P.O. Box 355
Newtown, CT 06470

Fine Woodworking
The Taunton Press, Inc.
52 Church Hill Rd.
P.O. Box 355
Newtown, CT 06470

New Shelter
Rodale Press, Inc.
33 E. Minor St.
Emmaus, PA 18049

The Old-House Journal
The Old-House Journal Corp.
69A Seventh Ave.
Brooklyn, NY 11217

Pacific Woodworker
P.O. Box 4881
Santa Rosa, CA 95402

Woodsmith
Woodsmith Publishing Co.
2200 Grand Ave.
Des Moines, IA 50312

MAKERS OF HANDCRAFTED SHELVES AND CABINETS

The men and women whose names and addresses are listed below have many skills and talents. Some are architects and custom builders as well as occasional cabinetmakers. Others are full-time craftsmen, working within the tradition of cabinetmaking or exploring the boundary between craft and art. Most work principally in wood; a few work in glass.

Most of these individuals have work pictured in this book. If you like the shelves or chest of drawers or cabinets in a particular photograph, you can look up the name of the craftsman who made the furniture in the "Photo and Design Credits," and then find his or her address below. Others, whose work does not appear, are listed because they do good work, but limitations on the number of photographs we could use prevented us from including them.

Contact individual craftsmen for more information about their work and to inquire about their willingness to undertake commissions.

Fred Atwood
Brother Wood
1636½ Laburnum
Chico, CA 95926

James Bacigalupi
118 University Ave.
Los Gatos, CA 95030

Tom Bender, architect
Neahkahnie Mountain
38755 Reed Rd.
Nehalem, OR 97131

Barbara Boughton
Barbara Boughton Interiors
P.O. Box 65
Glendale, MA 01229

Robert D. Brady
Box 523
La Honda, CA 94020

Michael Bullard
Steve Ball
Bullard & Ball Fine Woodworking
Rt. 7 MLC-1
Tallahassee, FL 32308

John Calella
80 Murray Ave.
Kentfield, CA 94904

Arthur Espenet Carpenter
Star Route
Bolinas, CA 94924

The Cascades Woodwrights
1319½ E. Tennessee St.
Tallahassee, FL 32303

Gary Church
Spring Grove Design
Box 314
Albion, CA 95410

Ed Colin
General Delivery
Hornby Island, B.C. V0R 1Z0
Canada

James T. Connelly
2528 Huntingdon Pike
Huntingdon Valley, PA 19006

James Cottey
Rt. 4, Box 311
Clinton, AR 72031

William Davidson
Apache Canyon Woodworks
Rt. 3, Box 95-I
Santa Fe, NM 87501

Volker de la Harpe
Box 641
Santa Fe, NM 87501

Nelson Denny, architect
Stony Creek Construction Corp.
P.O. Box 3169
Stony Creek, CT 06405

Rhonda L. Dixon
General Delivery
La Rue, AR 72743

Steve Doriss
Doriss & Fox, Ltd.
3095 Kerner Blvd.
P.O. Box 2223
San Rafael, CA 94912

Al Garvey
281 Scenic Rd.
Fairfax, CA 94930

Larry Golden
475 Cambridge Ave.
Claremont, CA 91711

David Goldfarb
53 River St.
Great Barrington, MA 01230

Michael Ivan Gorchov
Jamison, PA 18929

Stan Griskivich
Energy Efficient Hand Made
Houses
153B Cousins Island RR #1
Yarmouth, ME 04096

David Haust
RD Box 205-N
Chatham, NY 12037

Stephen Heckeroth
30151 Navarro Ridge Rd.
Albion, CA 95410

Kim Hicks
345 Camino Del Canyon
Mill Valley, CA 94941

Victor Hiles
Box 1109
Homer, AK 99603

Gary Michael Jones
200 Coopers St.
Camdentown, NJ 08102

Roberta Katz
Pentacle Studio
P.O. Box 202
Clinton, AR 72031

Kel Kelly
General Delivery
Denman Island, B.C. V0R 1T0
Canada

Des Kennedy
General Delivery
Denman Island, B.C. V0R 1T0
Canada

Peter Kerekgyarto
1126 Richmond Rd.
Lancaster, PA 17603

Jack Larimore
325 Gaskill St.
Philadelphia, PA 19147

Tom Larsen
General Delivery
Denman Island, B.C. V0R 1T0
Canada

George Light
107 Lea Ave.
Longwood, FL 32750

Nelson Lindley
32000 N. Highway One
Fort Bragg, CA 95437

Earl McFarland
Standing Rock Designery
Stained Glass Studio
972 Gardenview Dr.
Kent, OH 44240

Alexander K. MacLean
14 Mt. Foraker Dr.
San Rafael, CA 94903

Bruce McQuilkin
50 Deluca Pl.
San Rafael, CA 94901

Don McVay
Skyhill Construction
P.O. Box 656
Felton, CA 95018

Alan Marks
Alan Marks Design
1204 Lincoln Ave.
Pacific Grove, CA 93950

Richard Marks
Box 193
Carbondale, CO 81623

Paul Moser
Moser Bros., Inc.
Architectural Woodwork
Third & Green Sts.
Bridgeport, PA 19405

Simon Newby
Cabinet Maker & Joiner
18th Century Architectural Woodwork
Box C-414
Westport, MA 02790

Douglas Pinney
Bartlett Rd.
Nantucket, MA 02554

Keith Pollari
PZA, Inc.
530 Selby
St. Paul, MN 55102

Paul Pugliese
64 Binney Ln.
Old Greenwich, CT 06870

Rick Redden, AIA
Allison Moses Redden
217 W. Second St.
Suite 200, Gans Bldg.
Little Rock, AR 72201

Bob Richardson
Wood Design
Box 775
Santa Fe, NM 87501

Stephen J. Ripper II
The Haycock Village Woodworks
RD #4 Box 197
Quakertown, PA 18951

Illka Salo
General Delivery
Hornby Island, B.C. V0R 1Z0
Canada

Dean Santner
4210 Holden St.
Box 88185
Emeryville, CA 94662

Stan Saran
Saran Glassworks, Inc.
P.O. Box 50
Claryville, NY 12725

Ted Scherrer
Fairhaven Woodworks Co.
500 Larrabee Ave.
Bellingham, WA 98225

James Schriber
Box 1145
New Milford, CT 06776

Vic Schulman
Pickles Rd.
Denman Island, B.C. V0R 1T0
Canada

Richard Silvera
9063 Lasell Ln.
Durham, CA 95938

Mark Simon, AIA
Moor Grover Harper, architects
Essex, CT 06426

Paul Summerlin
General Delivery
Hornby Island, B.C. V0R 1Z0
Canada

Union Woodworks
7 Belknap St.
Northfield, VT 05663

John Vugrin
Star Route 2
Santa Ysabel, CA 92070

Ellis Walentine
Woodrose
RD 1
Deer Trail Rd.
Coopersburg, PA 18036

Richard Weinsteiger
RD #4
Boyertown, PA 19512

Carl Wies
529 Leetes Island Rd.
Stony Creek, CT 06405

Larry Williams
Corner Legacy
17 Hilton St.
Eureka Springs, AR 72632

Peter M. Wright
Rt. 1 Box 778
Solon Springs, WI 54873

Tim Wyndham
General Delivery
Hornby Island, B.C. V0R 1Z0
Canada

John Zoltai
John Zoltai Studio
Box 31
El Rito, NM 87530

PHOTO AND DESIGN CREDITS

These credits are listed in page sequence. The name of the craftsman or company that built the piece appears first, followed by the name of the photographer.

Front cover	Ellis Walentine, Craig Walentine, Ken Dietery, Joe Hancock, Bill McCarthy; Mitch Mandel
ii	Illka Salo; Paul Bailey
viii	Robert Brady; Michael Kanouff
ix	Alex MacLean; Michael Kanouff
x	Gary Church; Michael Kanouff
xi	Illka Salo and Tim Wyndham; Paul Bailey
xii-1	Douglas Pinney; Carl Doney
2	Larry Golden; Mitch Mandel
4, 5	Ellis Walentine; Christie Tito
6	Michael Ivan Gorchov, design by Ellis Walentine; Christie Tito
7, 8, 10, 11	Stephen Ripper; Mitch Mandel
12	Larry Golden; Mitch Mandel
13	Larry Golden; Curt Anderson
15, 16	Larry Golden; Mitch Mandel
19	Moser Bros., design by Gary Michael Jones; Sally Shenk Ullman
20, 21	Phil Gehret; Mitch Mandel
22	Dean Santner Woodworking; Michael Kanouff
24, 25	Mitch Mandel; Mitch Mandel
26	Gary Church; Michael Kanouff
27	Robert Brady; Michael Kanouff
28	Tom Larsen; Paul Bailey
29	Douglas Pinney; Carl Doney
30	Ed Colin; Paul Bailey
31	David Goldfarb, design by Barbara Boughton; David Goldfarb
32, top	Bruce McQuilkin; Michael Kanouff
32, bottom	Gary Church; Michael Kanouff
33	John Vugrin; Michael Kanouff
34, 35	Douglas Pinney; Carl Doney
36	James Connelly; Mitch Mandel
37	Steven Heckeroth; Michael Kanouff
38, left	Arthur Espenet Carpenter; Michael Kanouff
38, right	Robert Brady; Michael Kanouff
39, left	Steve Doriss; Michael Kanouff
39, right	Stony Creek Construction Corp., designed by Nelson Denny; Karen Bussolini
41	John Calella and Bruce Sexour; Michael Kanouff
44	James Connelly; Mitch Mandel
46	Larry Golden; Mitch Mandel
49	John Zoltai; John Hamel
54	Richard Weinsteiger; T. L. Gettings
56, 57	Gary Church; Michael Kanouff
58	Stan Saran; Mitch Mandel
61	Rhonda Dixon; Mitch Mandel
63, top	Peter Kerekgyarto; Sally Shenk Ullman

Page	Credit
63, bottom	John Zoltai; John Hamel
66	Alex MacLean; Michael Kanouff
67	Richard Marks; Richard Marks
69	Stony Creek Construction Corp., design by Nelson Denny; Karen Bussolini
70	Earl McFarland, glass work; Roger Gray, cabinetry; John Hamel
73	James Cottey; Mitch Mandel
74	Bruce McQuilkin; Michael Kanouff
75	John Vugrin; Michael Kanouff
76	Bruce McQuilkin; Michael Kanouff
79	Ted Scherrer, Fairhaven Woodworks Co.; David Scherrer
82	Tom Larsen; Paul Bailey
84	Paul Summerlin; Paul Bailey
91	Alan Marks; Michael Kanouff
92, top left	Stan Griskivich; Carl Doney
92, top right	Alan Marks; Michael Kanouff
92, bottom right	James Cottey; Mitch Mandel
95, top	James Cottey; Mitch Mandel
95, bottom	James Bacigalupi; Michael Kanouff
97, top	Alex MacLean; Michael Kanouff
97, bottom	craftsman unknown; Christie Tito
99	Bruce McQuilkin; Michael Kanouff
100	craftsman unknown; Carl Doney
101	Gary Church; Michael Kanouff
103	Douglas Pinney; Carl Doney
104, 105	Arthur Espenet Carpenter; Michael Kanouff
106-7	Bruce McQuilkin; Michael Kanouff
108, 109, 110	Carl Wies; Karen Bussolini
112, 114, 117	Jack Larimore, Mitch Mandel
118, 120, 121	Rick Redden; Greg Hursley
122, 124, 126, 127	Larry Williams; Mitch Mandel
128, 129, 130, 133	East Coast Wholesalers, designed by Paul Pugliese; Karen Bussolini
134, 135, 137	Larry Golden; Mitch Mandel
138, 140, 141, 143	John Vugrin; Michael Kanouff
144, 146, 147, 148	Stan Griskivich; Carl Doney
150, 151, 152, 153, 154	Roberta Katz, glass work; Robert Maris, cabinetry; Mitch Mandel
156, 159, 160, 163	Steve Doriss; Michael Kanouff
164, 166, 167, 169	Stony Creek Construction Corp., designed by Nelson Denny; Karen Bussolini
170, 171, 172, 173	Alex MacLean; Michael Kanouff
174, 176, 178, 179, 180	Tom Bender; Carl Doney
182, 183, 184, 185	Al Garvey; Michael Kanouff
186, 188, 189, 190, 191	Michael Ivan Gorchov, designed by Ellis Walentine; Christie Tito
192, 194, 195, 196	Mike and Dianne Radcliffe; Paul Bailey
198	Peter M. Wright; Peter M. Wright
Back cover, top	John Vugrin; Michael Kanouff
Back cover, bottom	Keith Pollari; Burt Levy

INDEX